Jim Henson's LABYRINTH™

CORONATION

VOLUME ONE

Published by
ARCHAIA™

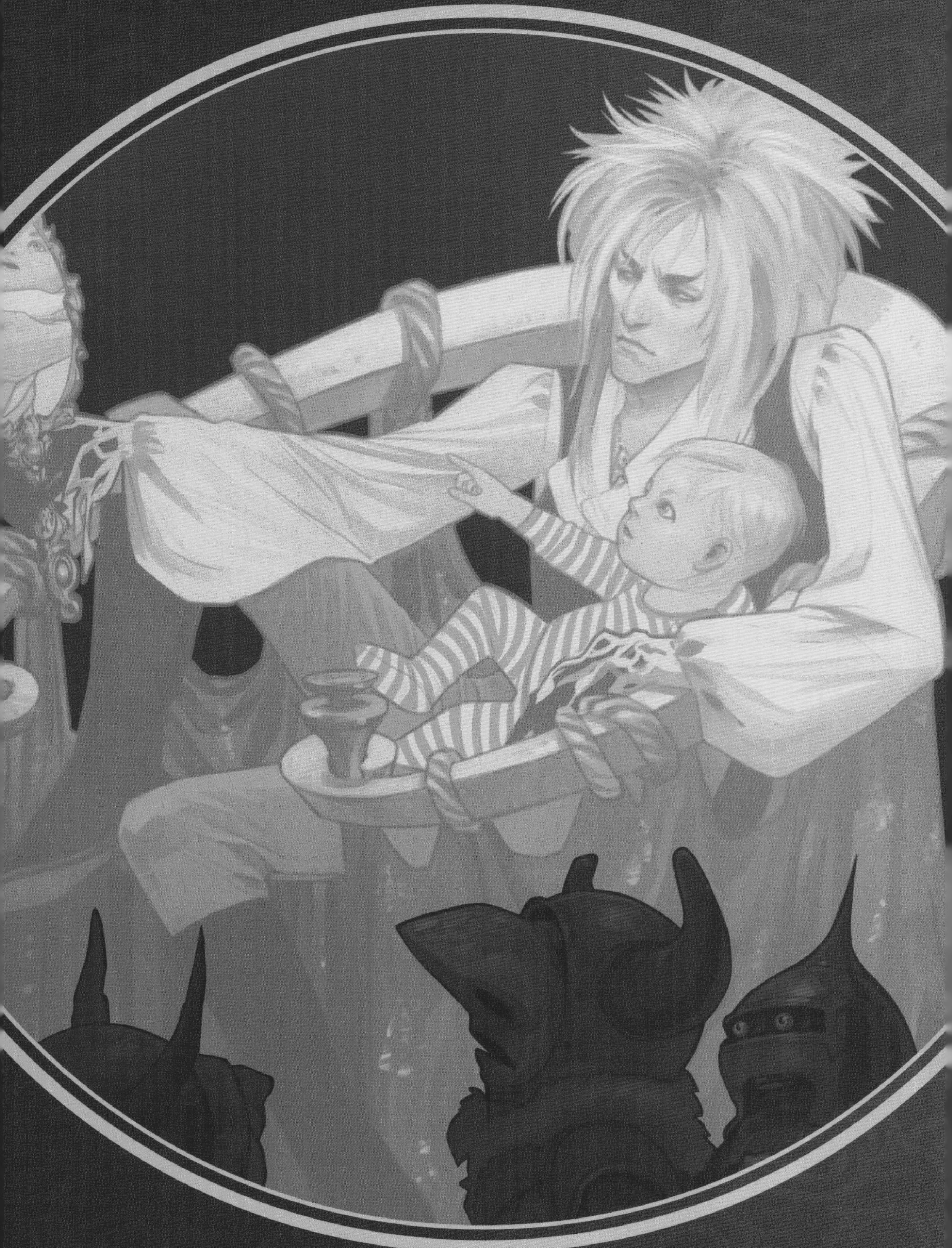

Jim Henson's
LABYRINTH™
CORONATION

Written by **Simon Spurrier**

Illustrated by **Daniel Bayliss**

with **Irene Flores**, **Mattia Di Meo**, **Matt Smith**, and **Michael Dialynas**

Colored by **Dan Jackson**

Lettered by **Jim Campbell**

Character Designs by **Kyla Vanderklugt** and **Daniel Bayliss**

Cover and Chapter Break Art by **Fiona Staples**

Forbidden Planet Exclusive Variant Cover by **Rebekah Isaacs**

Series Designer **Michelle Ankley**

Collection Designer **Scott Newman**

Assistant Editor **Gavin Gronenthal**

Editors **Cameron Chittock** and **Sierra Hahn**

Special Thanks to **Brian Henson, Lisa Henson, Jim Formanek, Nicole Goldman, Maryanne Pittman, Carla DellaVedova, Justin Hilden, Karen Falk, Blanca Lista, Fred Stresing, Laura Langston, Wendy Froud, Brian Froud,** and the entire **Jim Henson Company** team.

Ross Richie CEO & Founder
Joy Huffman CFO
Matt Gagnon Editor-in-Chief
Filip Sablik President, Publishing & Marketing
Stephen Christy President, Development
Lance Kreiter Vice President, Licensing & Merchandising
Arune Singh Vice President, Marketing
Bryce Carlson Vice President, Editorial & Creative Strategy
Scott Newman Manager, Production Design
Kate Henning Manager, Operations
Spencer Simpson Manager, Sales
Elyse Strandberg Manager, Finance
Sierra Hahn Executive Editor
Jeanine Schaefer Executive Editor
Dafna Pleban Senior Editor
Shannon Watters Senior Editor
Eric Harburn Senior Editor
Chris Rosa Editor
Matthew Levine Editor
Sophie Philips-Roberts Associate Editor
Amanda LaFranco Associate Editor
Gavin Gronenthal Assistant Editor

Gwen Waller Assistant Editor
Allyson Gronowitz Assistant Editor
Jillian Crab Design Coordinator
Michelle Ankley Design Coordinator
Kara Leopard Production Designer
Marie Krupina Production Designer
Grace Park Production Designer
Chelsea Roberts Production Design Assistant
Samantha Knapp Production Design Assistant
Paola Capalla Senior Accountant
José Meza Live Events Lead
Stephanie Hocutt Digital Marketing Lead
Esther Kim Marketing Coordinator
Cat O'Grady Digital Marketing Coordinator
Amanda Lawson Marketing Assistant
Holly Aitchison Digital Sales Coordinator
Morgan Perry Retail Sales Coordinator
Megan Christopher Operations Coordinator
Rodrigo Hernandez Mailroom Assistant
Zipporah Smith Operations Assistant
Breanna Sarpy Executive Assistant

BOOM! Studios, 5670 Wilshire Boulevard, Suite 400, Los Angeles, CA 90036-5679.
Printed in China. Second Printing.

ISBN: 978-1-68415-266-7, eISBN: 978-1-64144-128-5

Forbidden Planet Exclusive Variant Edition
ISBN: 978-1-68415-311-4

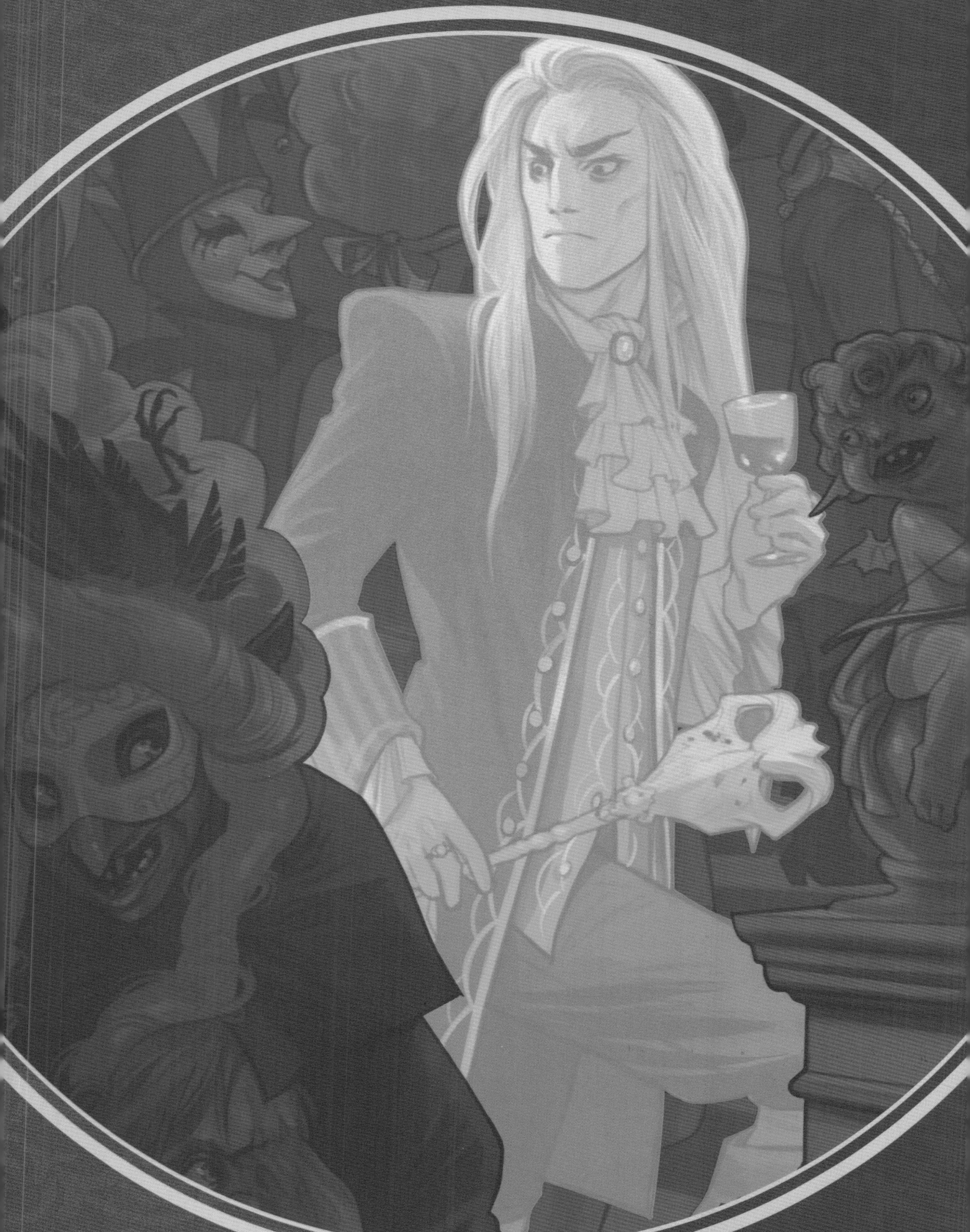

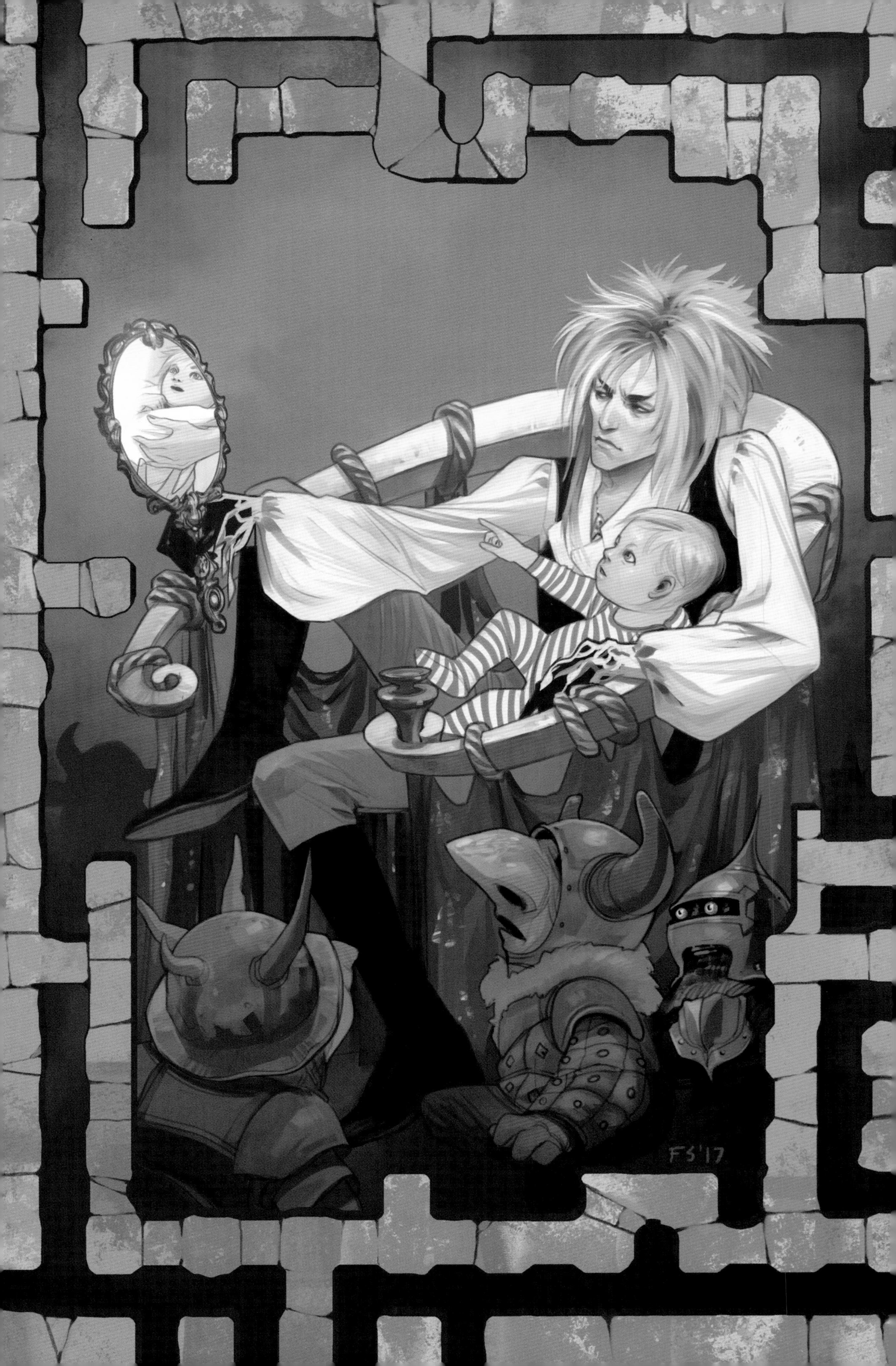
FS'17

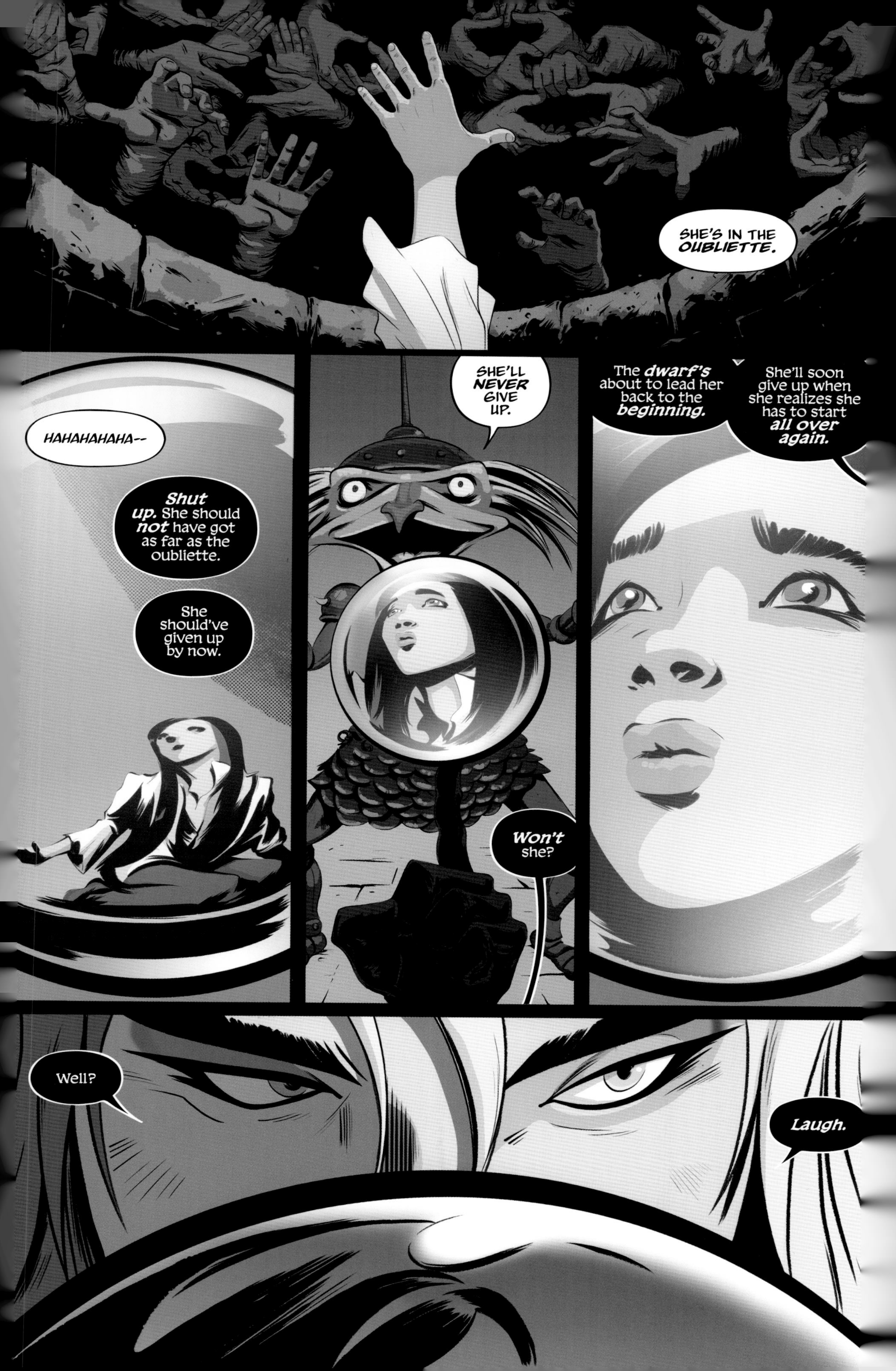
SHE'S IN THE OUBLIETTE.
HAHAHAHAHA--
Shut up. She should not have got as far as the oubliette.
She should've given up by now.
SHE'LL NEVER GIVE UP.
Won't she?
The dwarf's about to lead her back to the beginning.
She'll soon give up when she realizes she has to start all over again.
Well?
Laugh.

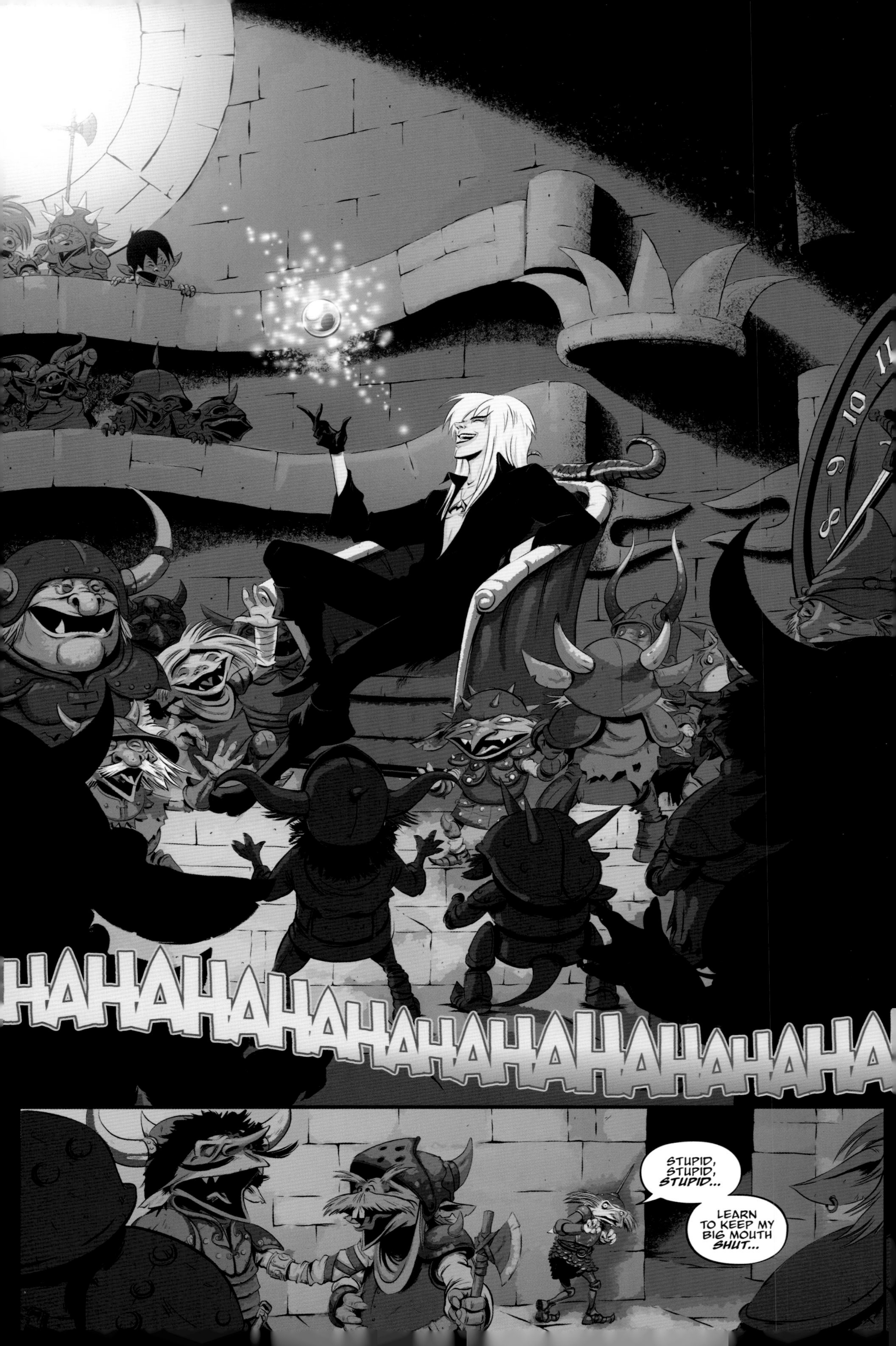
HAHAHAHAHAHAHAHAHAHAHAHAHA
STUPID, STUPID, STUPID...
LEARN TO KEEP MY BIG MOUTH SHUT...

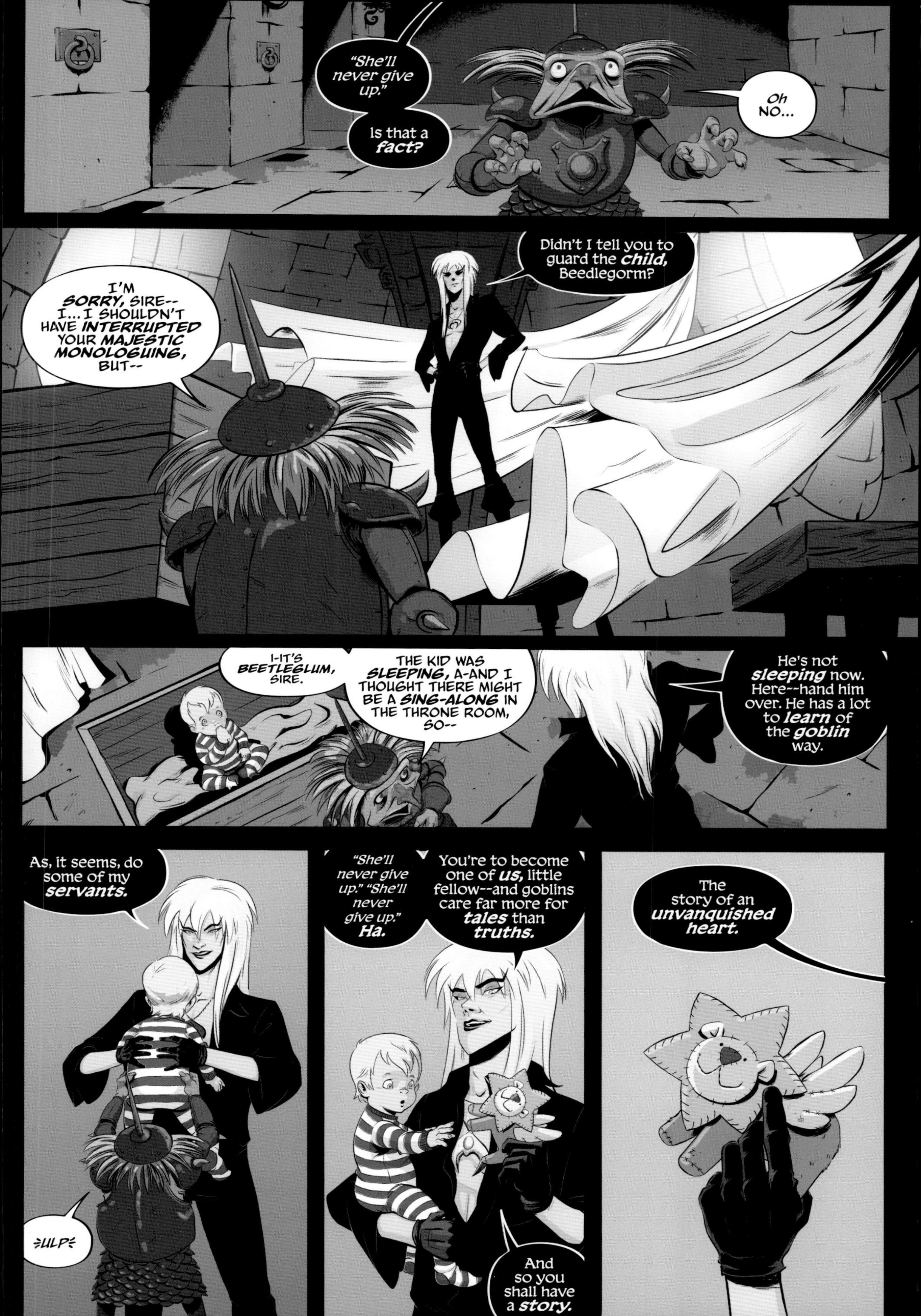

"She'll never give up."
Is that a fact?
Oh NO...
Didn't I tell you to guard the child, Beedlegorm?
I'M SORRY, SIRE-- I... I SHOULDN'T HAVE INTERRUPTED YOUR MAJESTIC MONOLOGUING, BUT--
I-IT'S BEETLEGLUM, SIRE.
THE KID WAS SLEEPING, A-AND I THOUGHT THERE MIGHT BE A SING-ALONG IN THE THRONE ROOM, SO--
He's not sleeping now. Here--hand him over. He has a lot to learn of the goblin way.
As, it seems, do some of my servants.
ULP
"She'll never give up." "She'll never give up." Ha.
You're to become one of us, little fellow--and goblins care far more for tales than truths.
And so you shall have a story.
The story of an unvanquished heart.

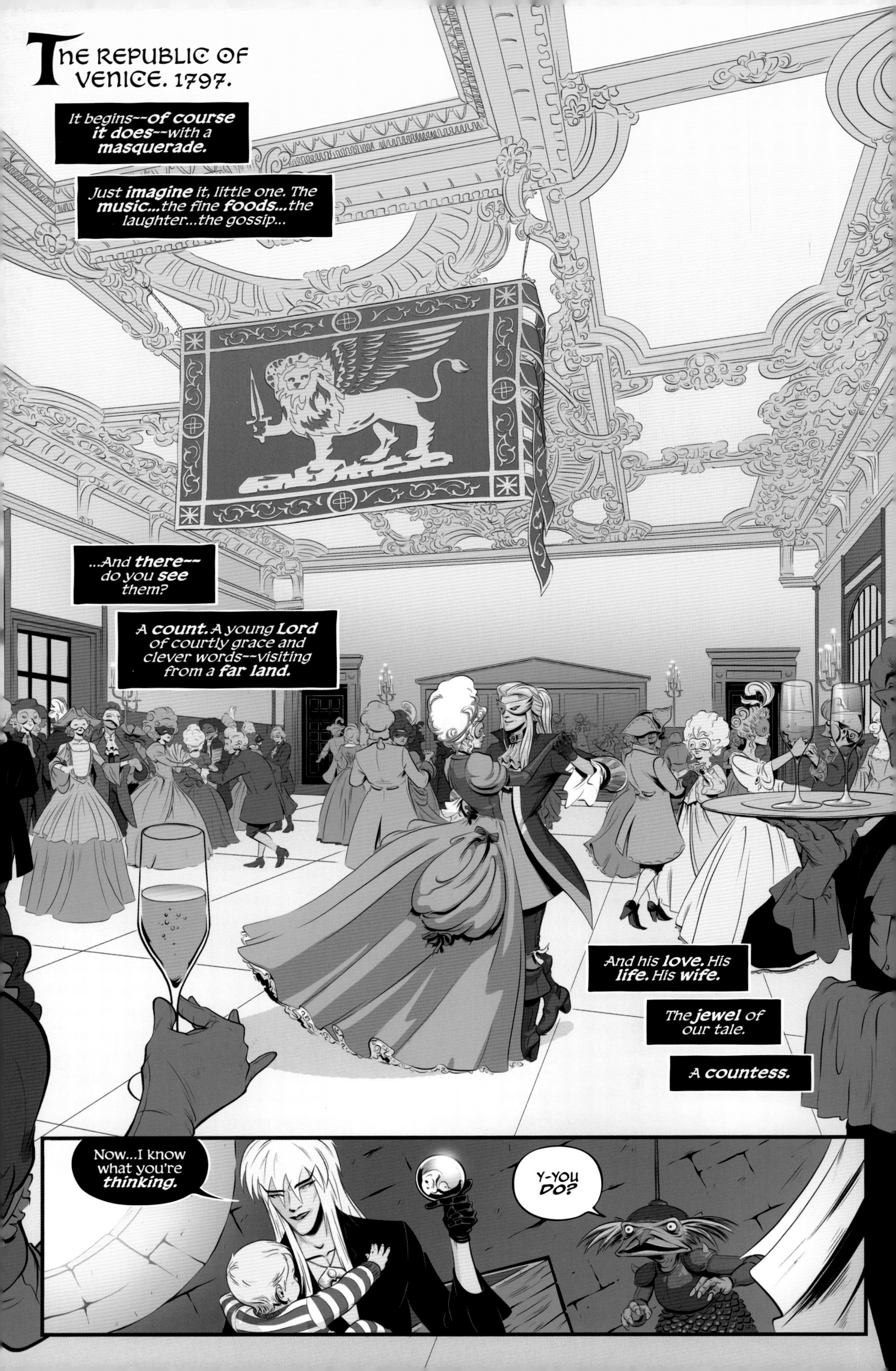
THE REPUBLIC OF VENICE. 1797.
It begins--of course it does--with a masquerade.
Just imagine it, little one. The music...the fine foods...the laughter...the gossip...
...And there--do you see them?
A count. A young Lord of courtly grace and clever words--visiting from a far land.
And his love. His life. His wife.
The jewel of our tale.
A countess.
Now...I know what you're thinking.
Y-YOU DO?

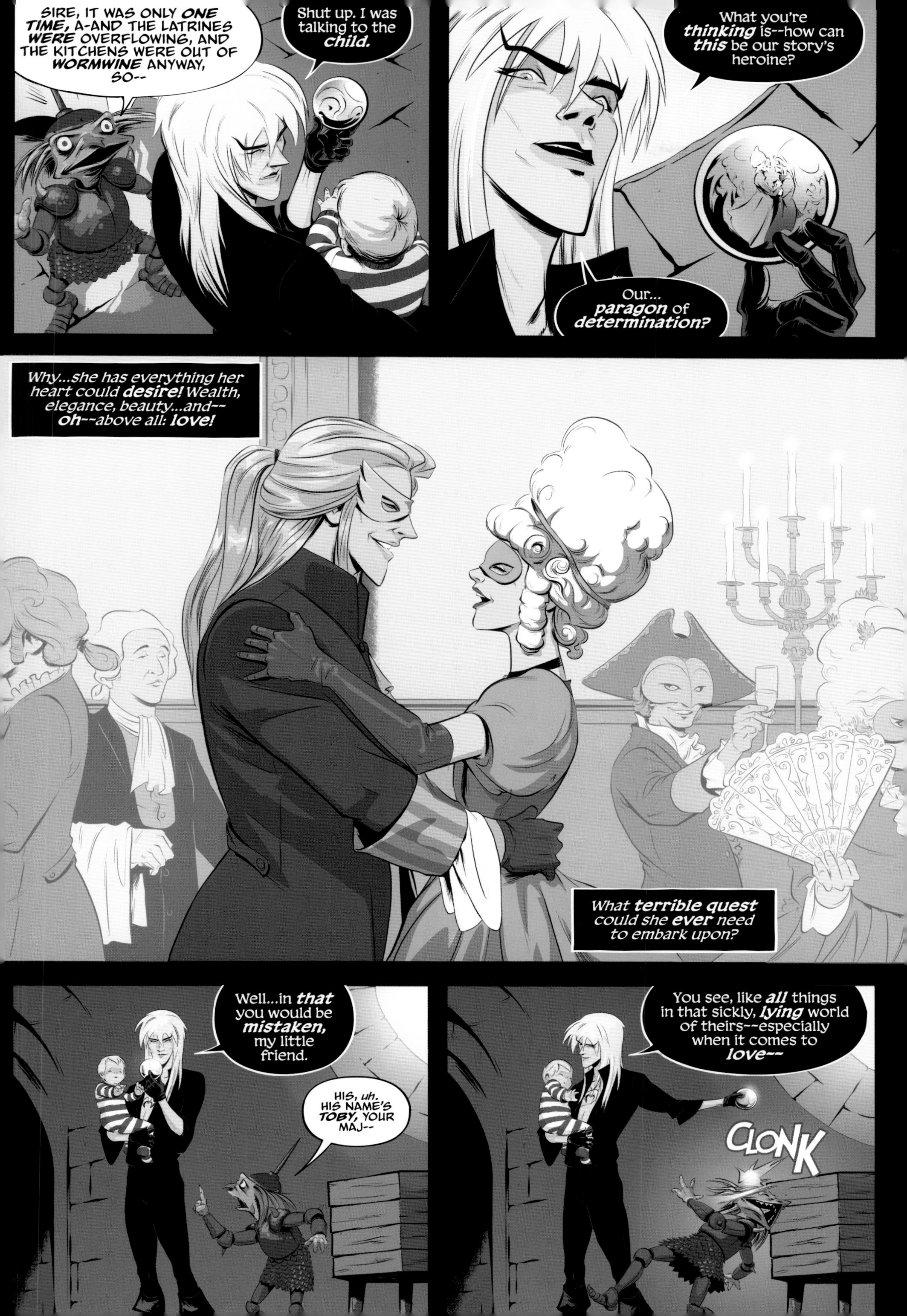

SIRE, IT WAS ONLY ONE TIME, A-AND THE LATRINES WERE OVERFLOWING, AND THE KITCHENS WERE OUT OF WORMWINE ANYWAY, SO--
Shut up. I was talking to the child.
What you're thinking is--how can this be our story's heroine?
Our... paragon of determination?
Why...she has everything her heart could desire! Wealth, elegance, beauty...and--oh--above all: love!
What terrible quest could she ever need to embark upon?
Well...in that you would be mistaken, my little friend.
HIS, uh. HIS NAME'S TOBY, YOUR MAJ--
You see, like all things in that sickly, lying world of theirs--especially when it comes to love--
CLONK

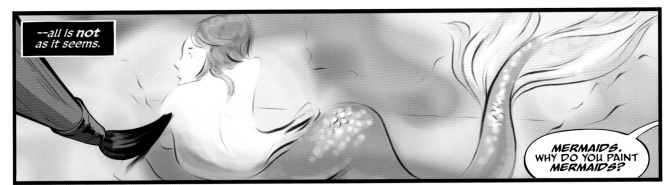

--all is **not** as it seems.

MERMAIDS. WHY DO YOU PAINT **MERMAIDS?**

LOOK-- IT'S **ROSES,** SIGNORA! **ROSES!**

THE DOGE DID NOT HIRE **MAESTRO JILANI** AS A **DIVERSION** FOR HIS GUESTS JUST SO THEY COULD PAINT **MERMAIDS!**

AND YET, MAESTRO, MY **MERMAIDS** SEEM TO BE MORE **DIVERTING** THAN YOUR **ROSES.**

BUT THEY'RE NOT **THERE!** YOU'RE SUPPOSED TO PAINT WHAT'S **THERE!**

THEN I SUGGEST YOU FETCH ME A **MERMAID,** SIGNOR.

MARIA--!

THE DOGE'S *CAMERLENGO* JUST TOLD ME...I-IT'S THE *SIGNORI DI NOTTE*. THEY'RE AT THE DOOR. THEY'RE ASKING FOR *ME*...

THE *CONSTABLES?* WHY WOULD THEY WANT *YOU?*

I...I DON'T *KNOW*. PERHAPS SOME... FOUL *ACCUSATION* HAS CAUGHT ME UP?

WHAT ACCUSATION?

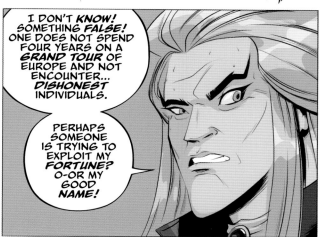

I DON'T *KNOW!* SOMETHING *FALSE!* ONE DOES NOT SPEND FOUR YEARS ON A *GRAND TOUR* OF EUROPE AND NOT ENCOUNTER... *DISHONEST* INDIVIDUALS.

PERHAPS SOMEONE IS TRYING TO EXPLOIT MY *FORTUNE?* O-OR MY GOOD *NAME!*

WELL? JUST TALK TO THE *SIGNORI--* TELL THEM IT'S A *MISTAKE.* LOOK, I'LL COME *WITH* Y--

NO!

N-NO, THERE ARE *OTHER* RUMORS. RUMORS OF *DANGER* APPROACHING THIS CITY. RUMORS OF *WAR*...

E-*EXCUSE* ME, MY LOVE.

I BELIEVE I SHALL FETCH SOME *WINE.*

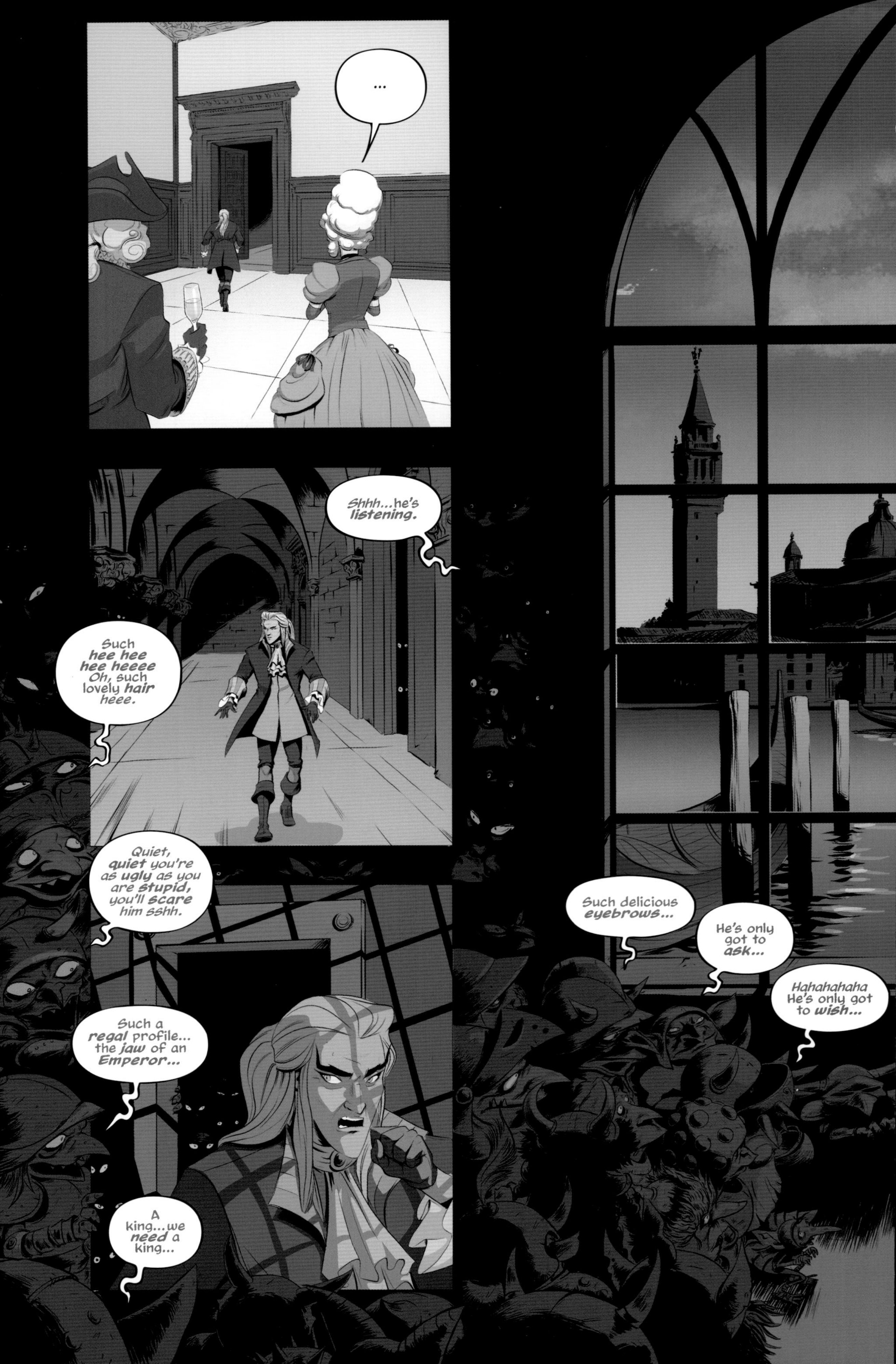
...
Shhh...he's listening.
Such hee hee hee heeee Oh, such lovely hair heee.
Quiet, quiet you're as ugly as you are stupid, you'll scare him sshh.
Such a regal profile... the jaw of an Emperor...
A king...we need a king...
Such delicious eyebrows...
He's only got to ask...
Hahahahaha He's only got to wish...

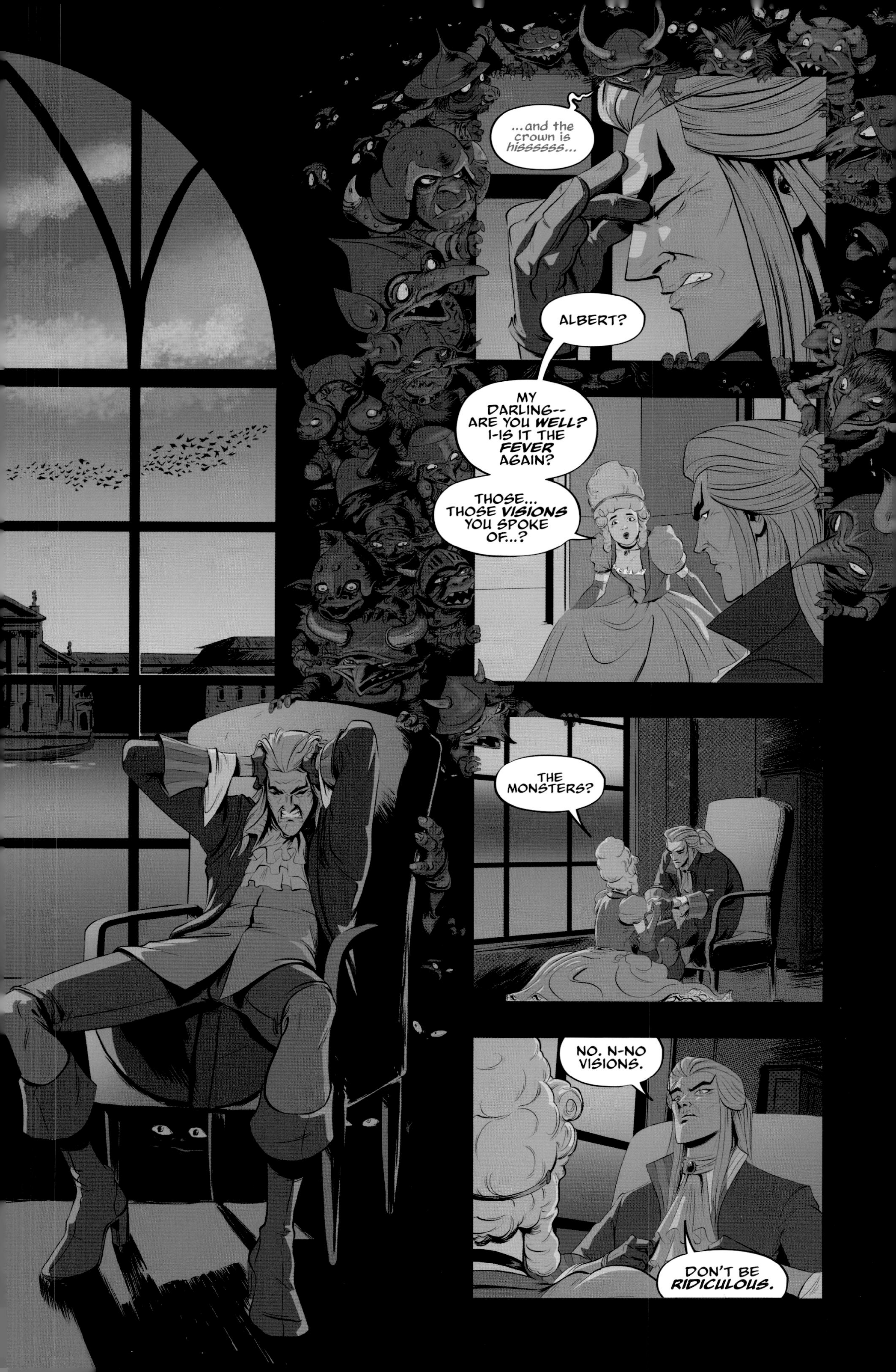
...and the crown is hissssss...
ALBERT?
MY DARLING-- ARE YOU WELL? I-IS IT THE FEVER AGAIN?
THOSE... THOSE VISIONS YOU SPOKE OF...?
THE MONSTERS?
NO. N-NO VISIONS.
DON'T BE RIDICULOUS.

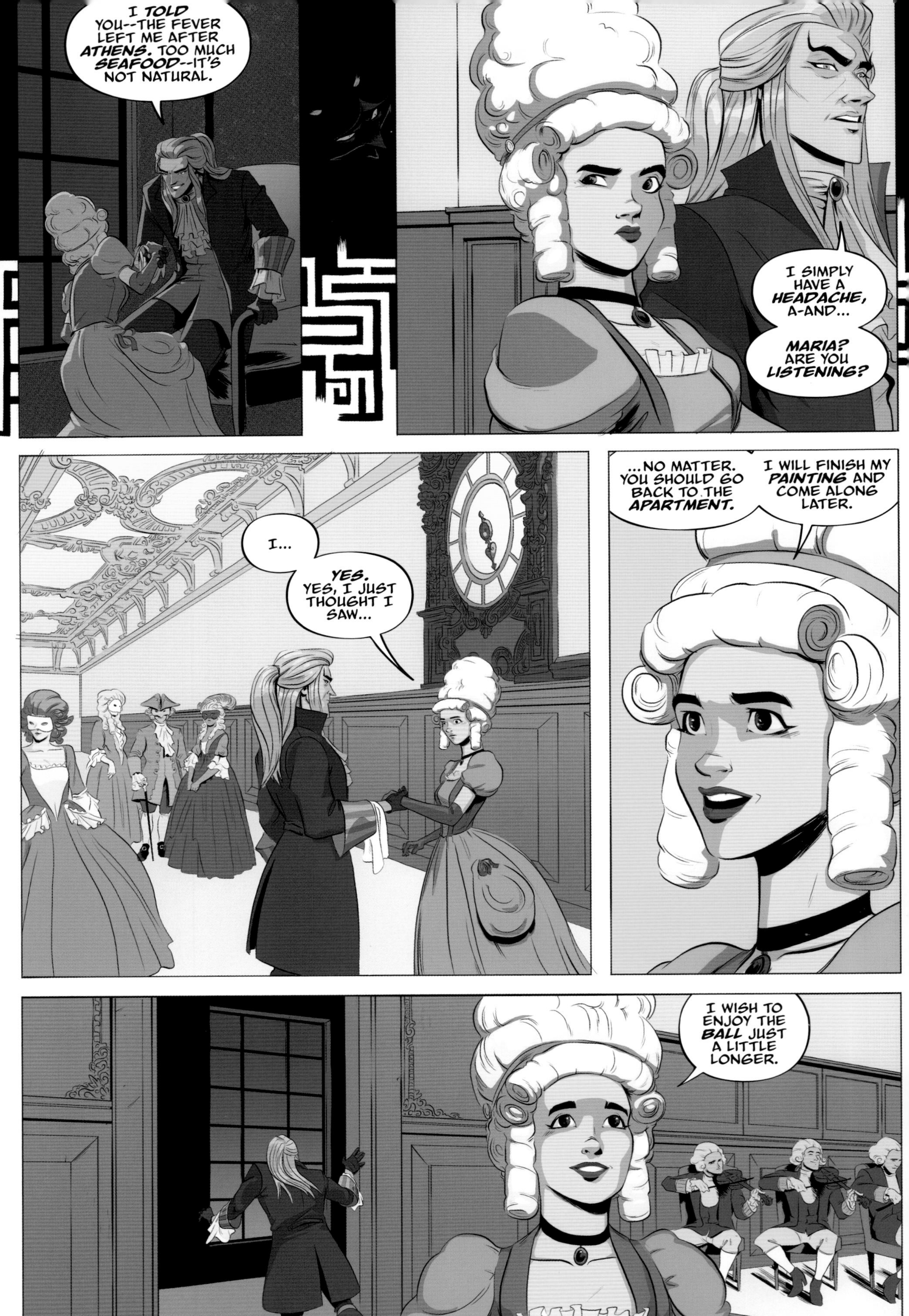
I TOLD YOU--THE FEVER LEFT ME AFTER ATHENS. TOO MUCH SEAFOOD--IT'S NOT NATURAL.
I SIMPLY HAVE A HEADACHE, A-AND...
MARIA? ARE YOU LISTENING?
I...
YES. YES, I JUST THOUGHT I SAW...
...NO MATTER. YOU SHOULD GO BACK TO THE APARTMENT.
I WILL FINISH MY PAINTING AND COME ALONG LATER.
I WISH TO ENJOY THE BALL JUST A LITTLE LONGER.

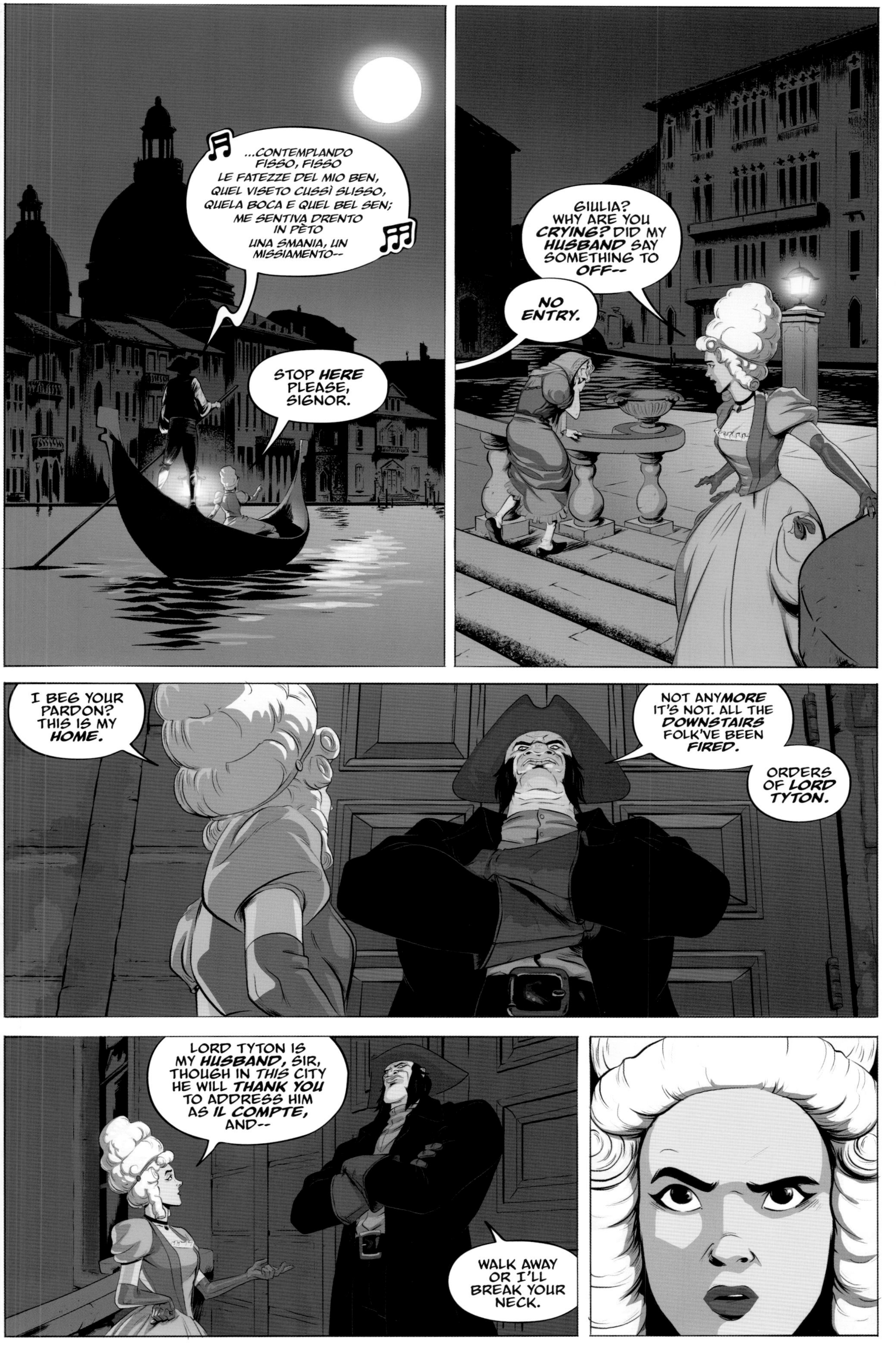
...CONTEMPLANDO FISSO, FISSO LE FATEZZE DEL MIO BEN, QUEL VISETO CUSSÌ SLISSO, QUELA BOCA E QUEL BEL SEN; ME SENTIVA DRENTO IN PÈTO UNA SMANIA, UN MISSIAMENTO--
STOP HERE PLEASE, SIGNOR.
GIULIA? WHY ARE YOU CRYING? DID MY HUSBAND SAY SOMETHING TO OFF--
NO ENTRY.
I BEG YOUR PARDON? THIS IS MY HOME.
NOT ANYMORE IT'S NOT. ALL THE DOWNSTAIRS FOLK'VE BEEN FIRED.
ORDERS OF LORD TYTON.
LORD TYTON IS MY HUSBAND, SIR, THOUGH IN THIS CITY HE WILL THANK YOU TO ADDRESS HIM AS IL COMPTE, AND--
WALK AWAY OR I'LL BREAK YOUR NECK.

ALBERT.

EXPLAIN.

NOW.

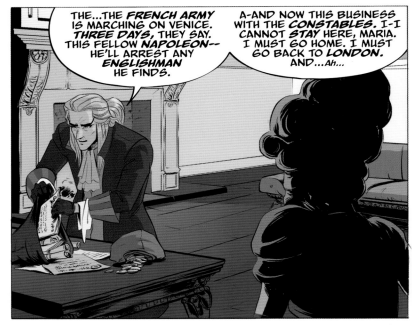

THE...THE *FRENCH ARMY* IS MARCHING ON VENICE. *THREE DAYS*, THEY SAY. THIS FELLOW *NAPOLEON--* HE'LL ARREST ANY *ENGLISHMAN* HE FINDS.

A-AND NOW THIS BUSINESS WITH THE *CONSTABLES.* I-I CANNOT *STAY* HERE, MARIA. I MUST GO HOME. I MUST GO BACK TO *LONDON.* AND... *Ah...*

YOU CANNOT COME WITH ME.

ALBERT-- YOU'RE *SCARING* ME. WHAT DO YOU *M--*

YOU KNOW *VERY WELL* WHAT I MEAN, YOU *SILLY* GIRL!

W-WE *BOTH* KNOW YOU'RE NO *COUNTESS!*

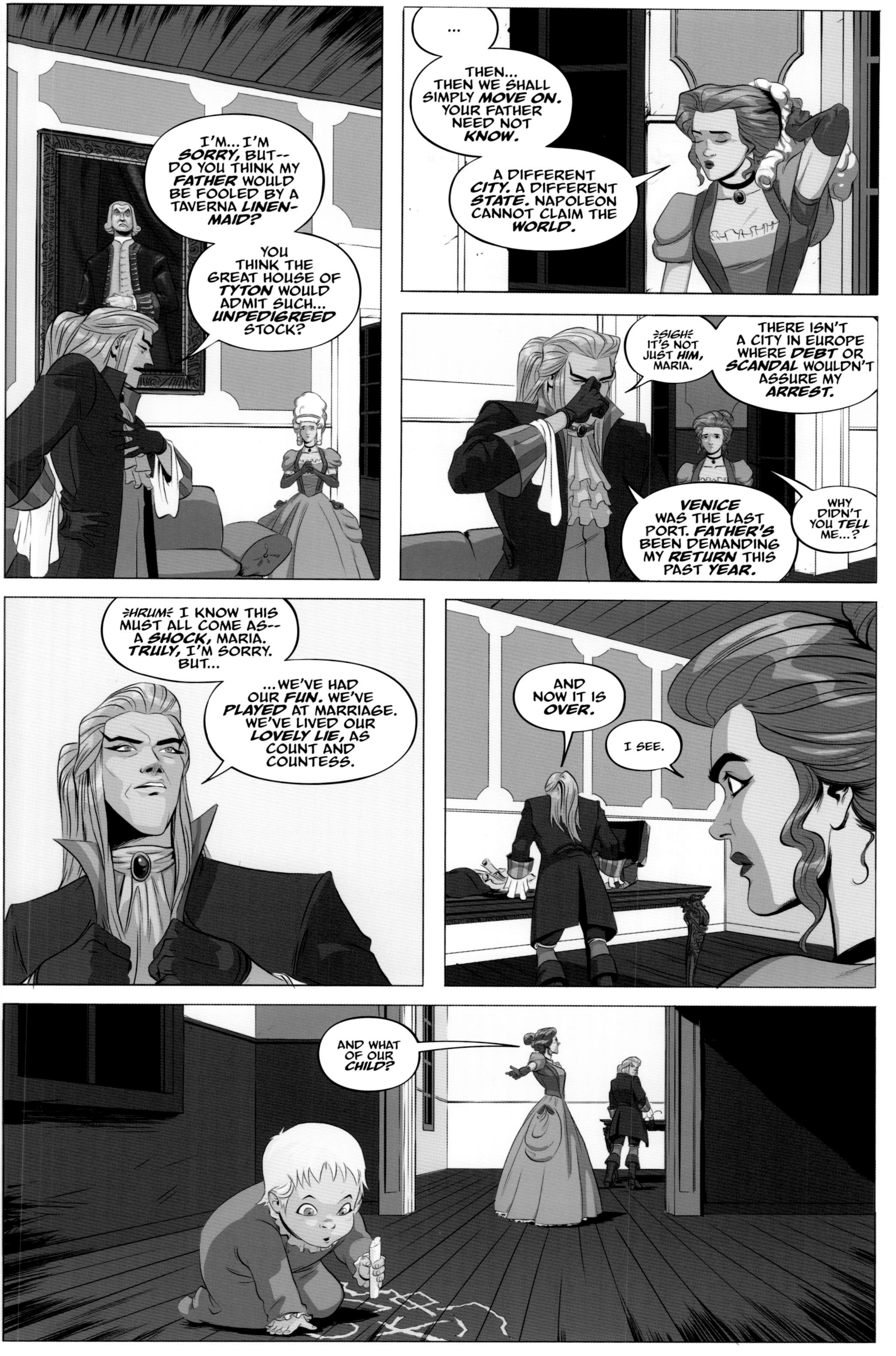
I'M... I'M SORRY, BUT-- DO YOU THINK MY FATHER WOULD BE FOOLED BY A TAVERNA LINEN-MAID?
YOU THINK THE GREAT HOUSE OF TYTON WOULD ADMIT SUCH... UNPEDIGREED STOCK?
...
THEN... THEN WE SHALL SIMPLY MOVE ON. YOUR FATHER NEED NOT KNOW.
A DIFFERENT CITY. A DIFFERENT STATE. NAPOLEON CANNOT CLAIM THE WORLD.
SIGH IT'S NOT JUST HIM, MARIA.
THERE ISN'T A CITY IN EUROPE WHERE DEBT OR SCANDAL WOULDN'T ASSURE MY ARREST.
VENICE WAS THE LAST PORT. FATHER'S BEEN DEMANDING MY RETURN THIS PAST YEAR.
WHY DIDN'T YOU TELL ME...?
HRUM I KNOW THIS MUST ALL COME AS--A SHOCK, MARIA. TRULY, I'M SORRY. BUT...
...WE'VE HAD OUR FUN. WE'VE PLAYED AT MARRIAGE. WE'VE LIVED OUR LOVELY LIE, AS COUNT AND COUNTESS.
AND NOW IT IS OVER.
I SEE.
AND WHAT OF OUR CHILD?

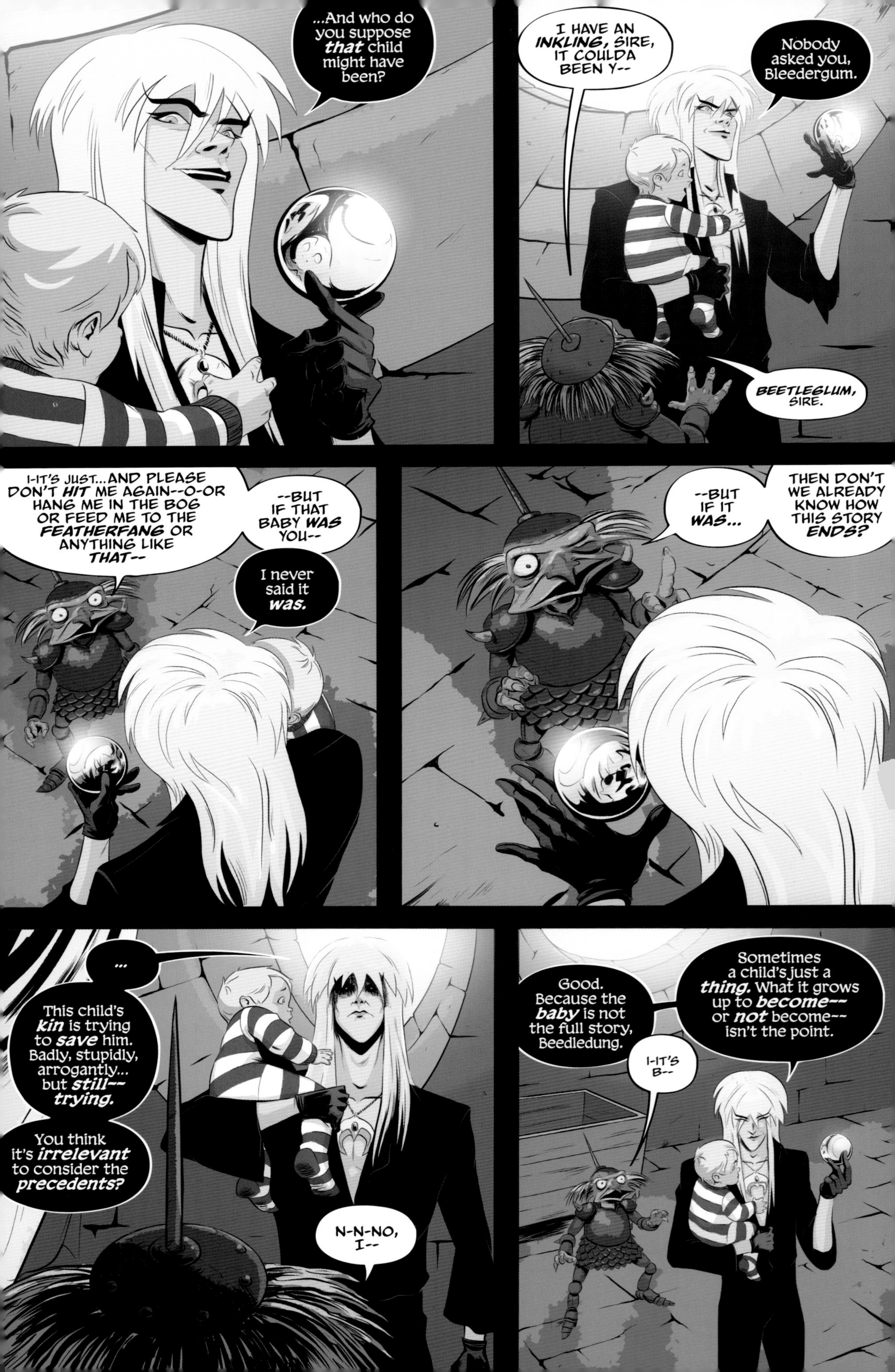
...And who do you suppose that child might have been?
I HAVE AN INKLING, SIRE, IT COULDA BEEN Y--
Nobody asked you, Bleedergum.
BEETLEGLUM, SIRE.
I-IT'S JUST...AND PLEASE DON'T HIT ME AGAIN--O-OR HANG ME IN THE BOG OR FEED ME TO THE FEATHERFANG OR ANYTHING LIKE THAT--
--BUT IF THAT BABY WAS YOU--
I never said it was.
--BUT IF IT WAS...
THEN DON'T WE ALREADY KNOW HOW THIS STORY ENDS?
...
This child's kin is trying to save him. Badly, stupidly, arrogantly... but still--trying.
You think it's irrelevant to consider the precedents?
N-N-NO, I--
Good. Because the baby is not the full story, Beedledung.
I-IT'S B--
Sometimes a child's just a thing. What it grows up to become--or not become--isn't the point.

The **real** story belongs to those who **love** it.

...THE BOY WILL...HE WILL GO INTO AN **ORPHANAGE**. OBVIOUSLY HE CANNOT REMAIN WITH **YOU**. THE RISK OF **BLACKMAIL**, YOU UNDERSTAND?

MY MAN **LORENZO**-- OUTSIDE. HE'LL SEE TO IT.

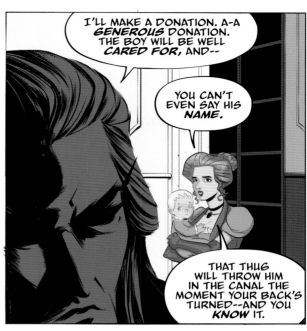

I'LL MAKE A DONATION. A-A **GENEROUS** DONATION. THE BOY WILL BE WELL **CARED FOR**, AND--

YOU CAN'T EVEN SAY HIS **NAME**.

THAT THUG WILL THROW HIM IN THE CANAL THE MOMENT YOUR BACK'S TURNED--AND YOU **KNOW** IT.

ARE YOU SO SCARED OF **HIM**...SO SCARED OF LOSING YOUR **NAME** AND **PRIVILEGE**-- THAT YOU'D **FORSAKE** YOUR OWN **BOY**?

Oh, ALBERT. YOU TRULY **ARE** SICK, AREN'T YOU?

≥SOB≤

T-THIS IS **YOUR** FAULT! YOURS FOR...FOR **ENTRAPPING** ME!

FOR BEING **NAIVE** ENOUGH TO **BELIEVE** ALL THIS! YOU SHOULD'VE **KNOWN** IT COULDN'T LAST! **YOU** BORE THE CHILD-- NOT **ME**!

IT WAS JUST A **DREAM**, MARIA! A STUPID **DREAM**!

Hm.

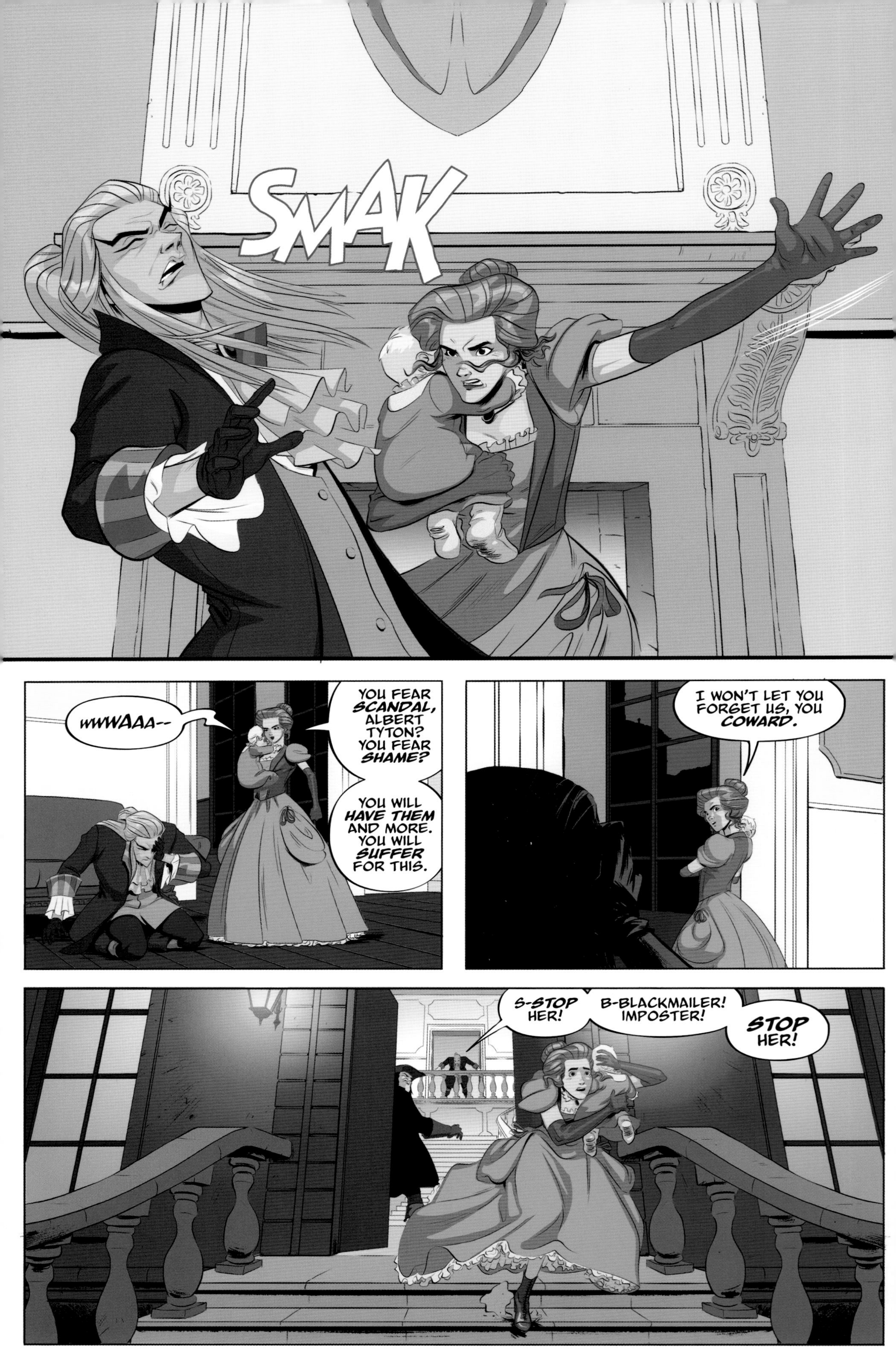
SMAK
WWWAAA--
YOU FEAR SCANDAL, ALBERT TYTON? YOU FEAR SHAME?
YOU WILL HAVE THEM AND MORE. YOU WILL SUFFER FOR THIS.
I WON'T LET YOU FORGET US, YOU COWARD.
S-STOP HER!
B-BLACKMAILER! IMPOSTER!
STOP HER!

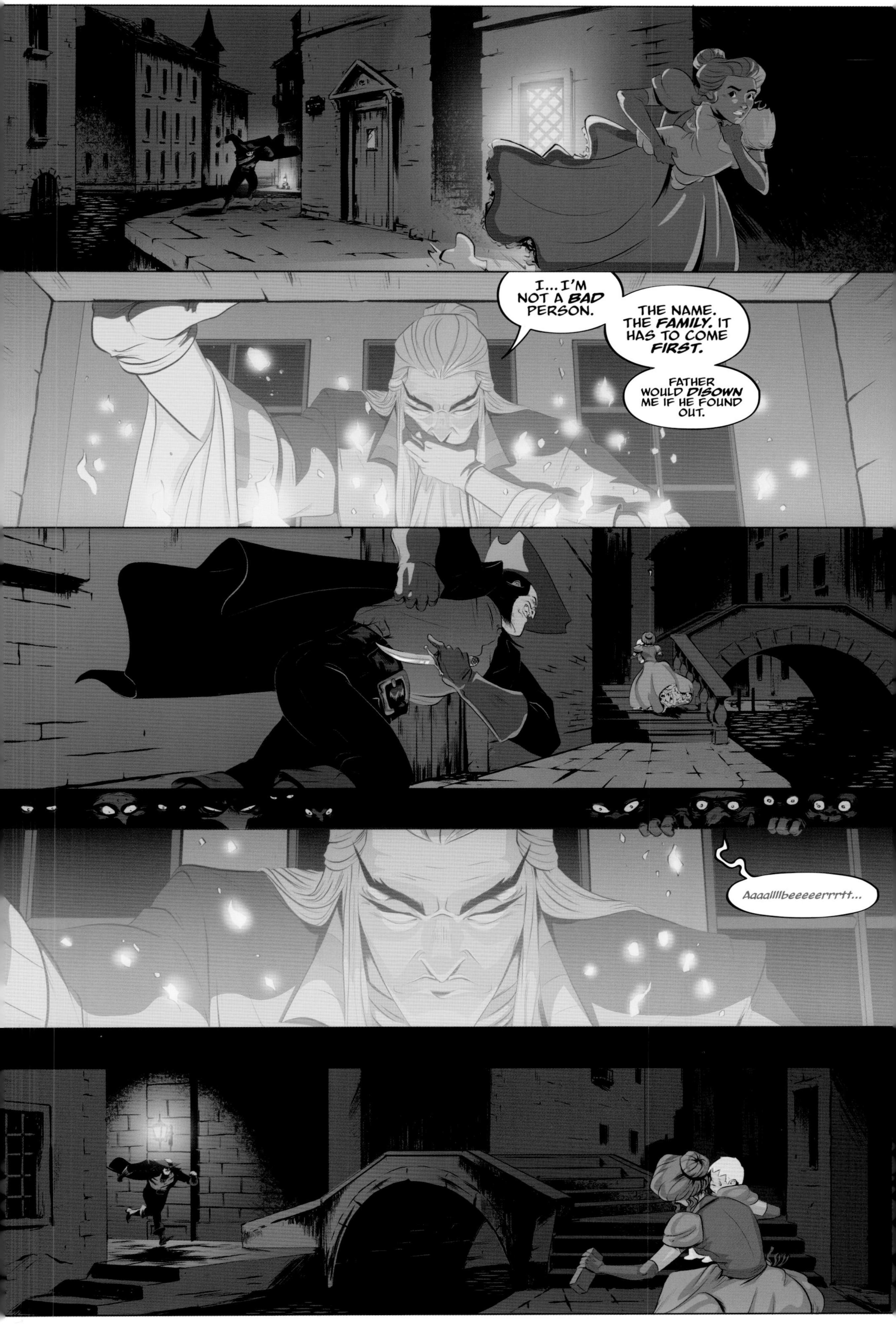
I... I'M NOT A BAD PERSON.
THE NAME. THE FAMILY. IT HAS TO COME FIRST.
FATHER WOULD DISOWN ME IF HE FOUND OUT.
Aaaalllbeeeeerrrtt...

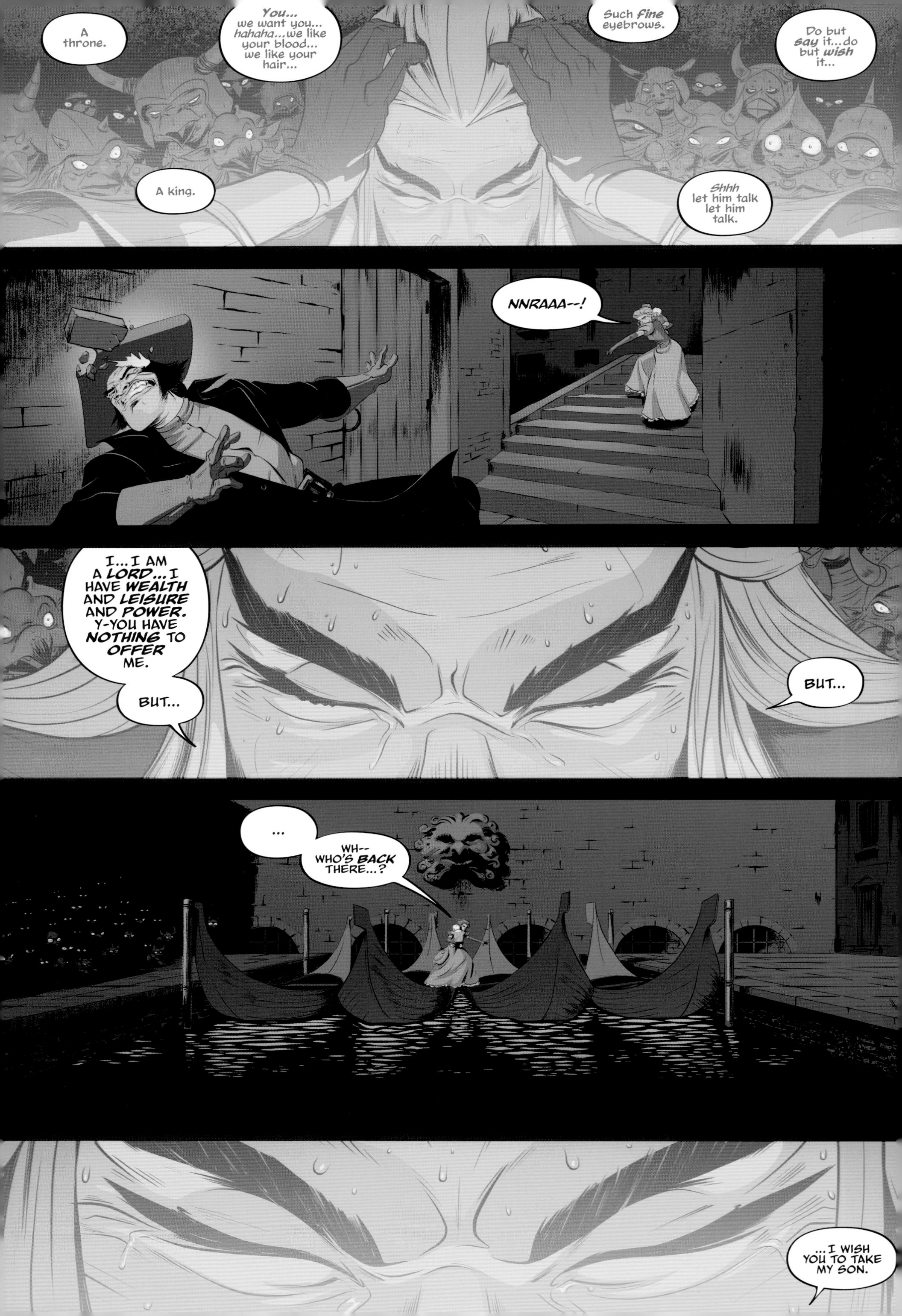

A throne.
You... we want you... *hahaha*...we like your blood... we like your hair...
A king.
Such *fine* eyebrows.
Do but *say* it...do but *wish* it...
Shhh let him talk let him talk.
NNRAAA--!
I...I AM A **LORD**...I HAVE **WEALTH** AND **LEISURE** AND **POWER.** Y-YOU HAVE **NOTHING** TO **OFFER** ME.
BUT...
BUT...
...
WH-- WHO'S **BACK** THERE...?
...I WISH YOU TO TAKE MY SON.

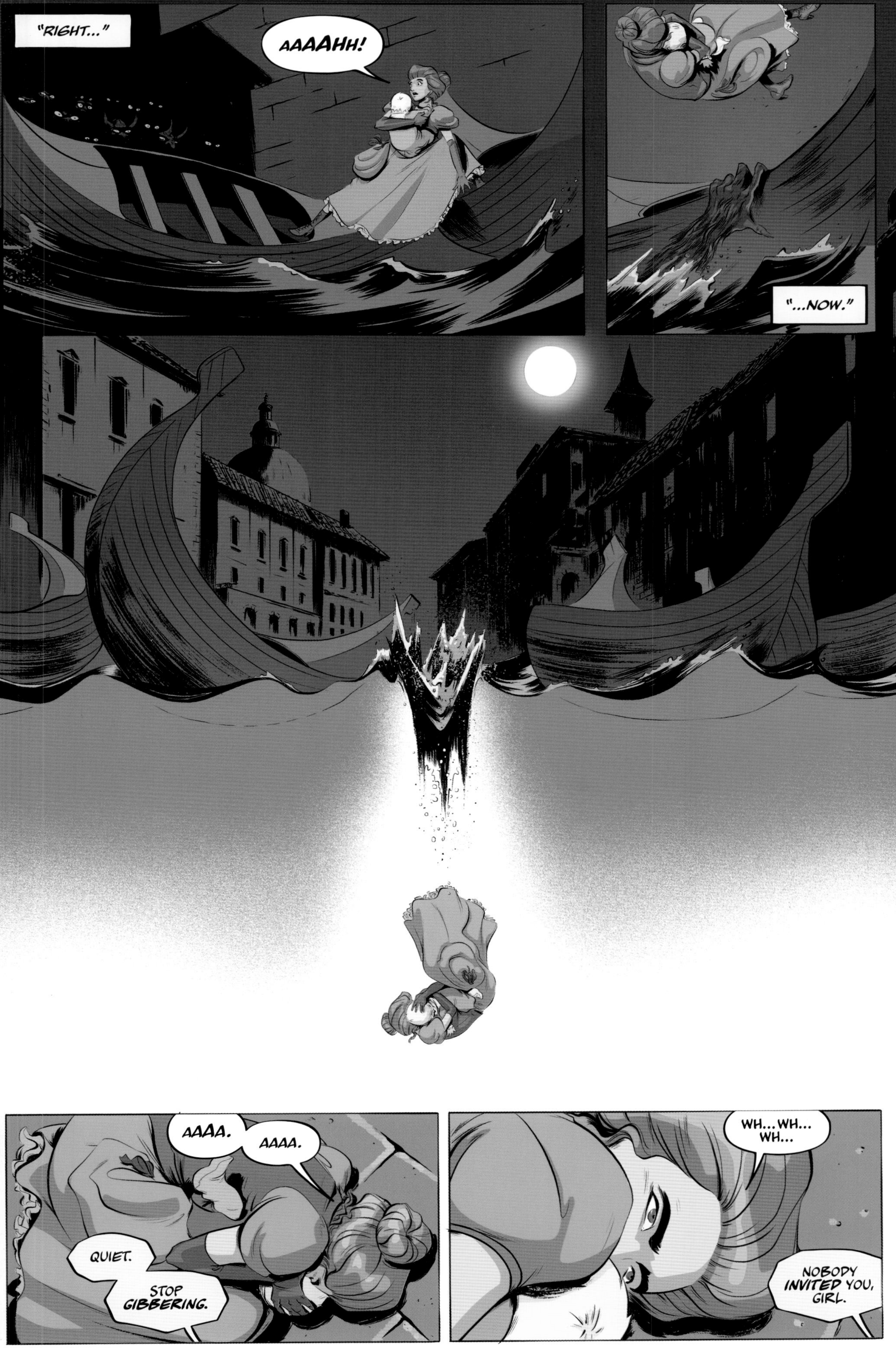
"RIGHT..."
AAAAHH!
"...NOW."
AAAA.
AAAA.
QUIET.
STOP GIBBERING.
WH... WH... WH...
NOBODY INVITED YOU, GIRL.

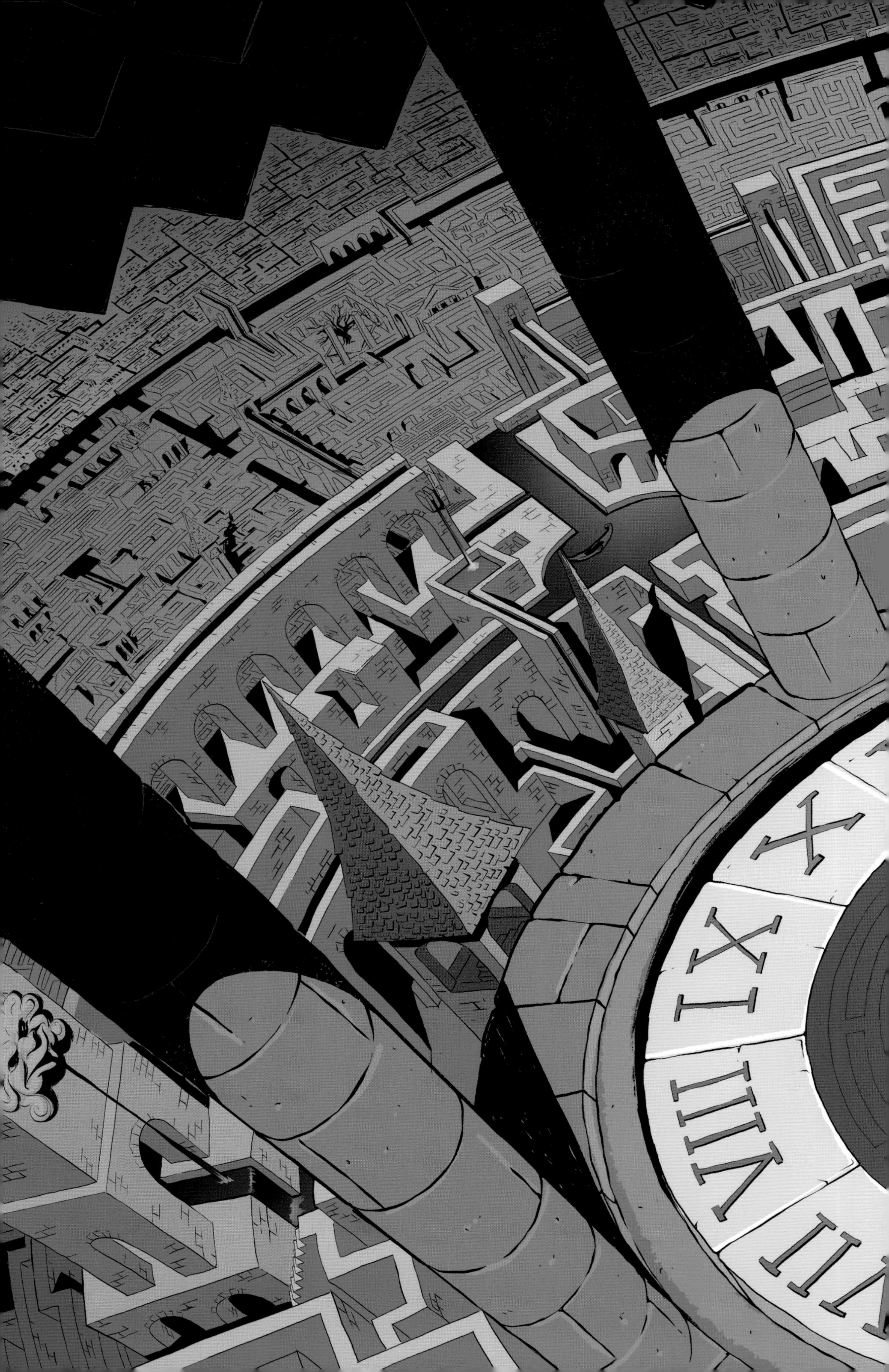

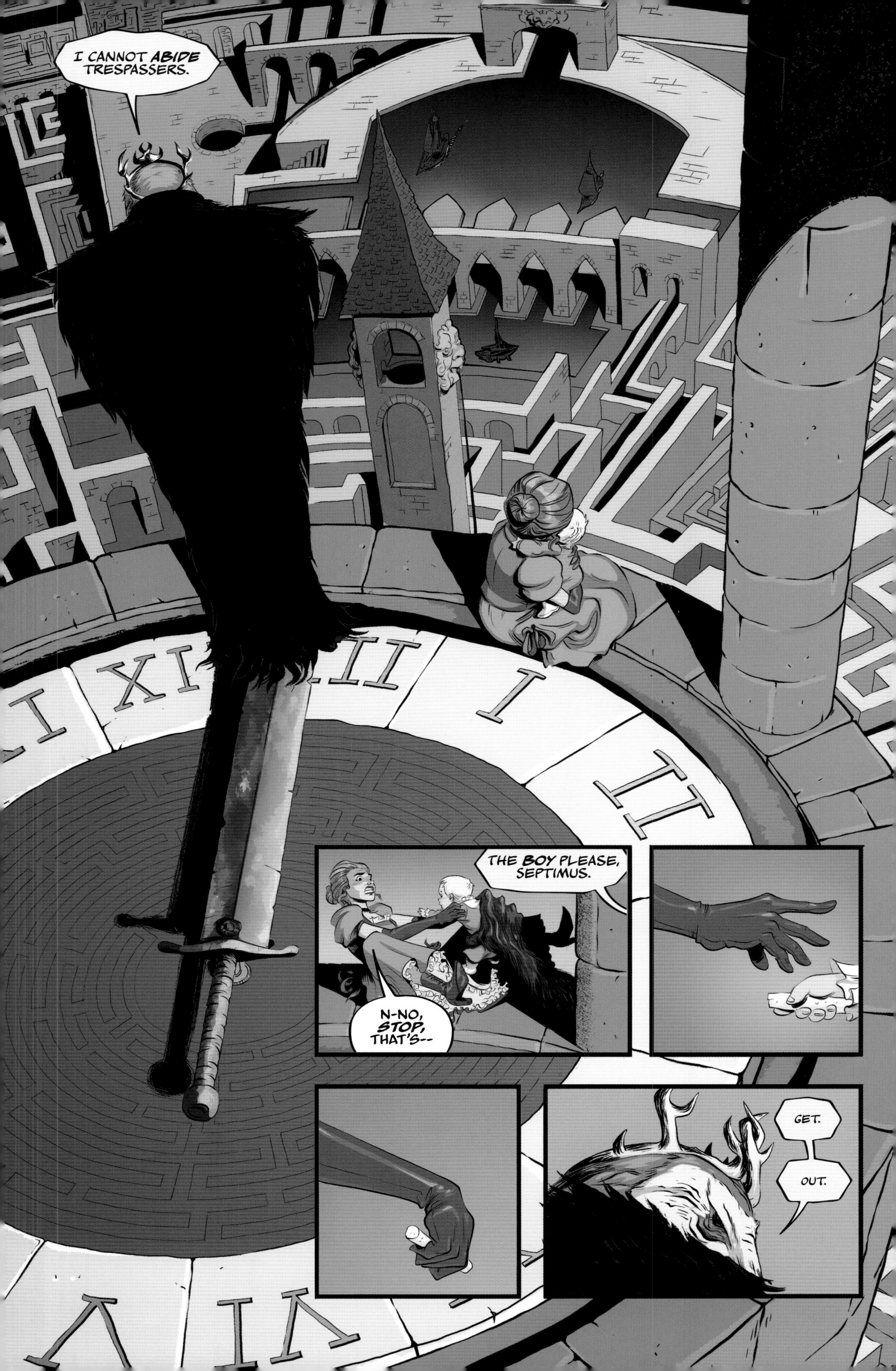
I CANNOT ABIDE TRESPASSERS.
THE BOY PLEASE, SEPTIMUS.
N-NO, STOP, THAT'S--
GET.
OUT.

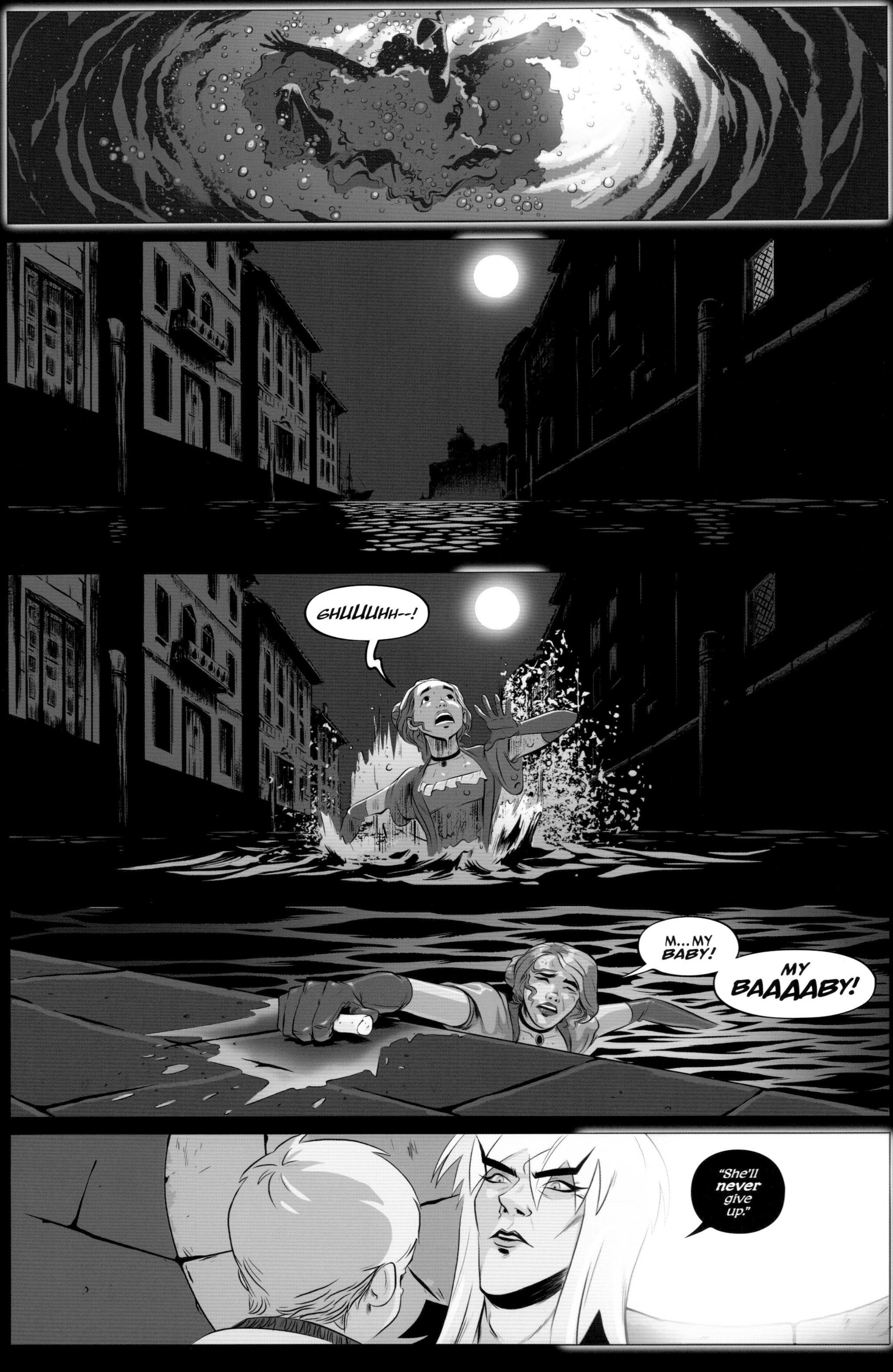
GHUUUHH--!
M...MY BABY!
MY BAAAABY!
"She'll never give up."

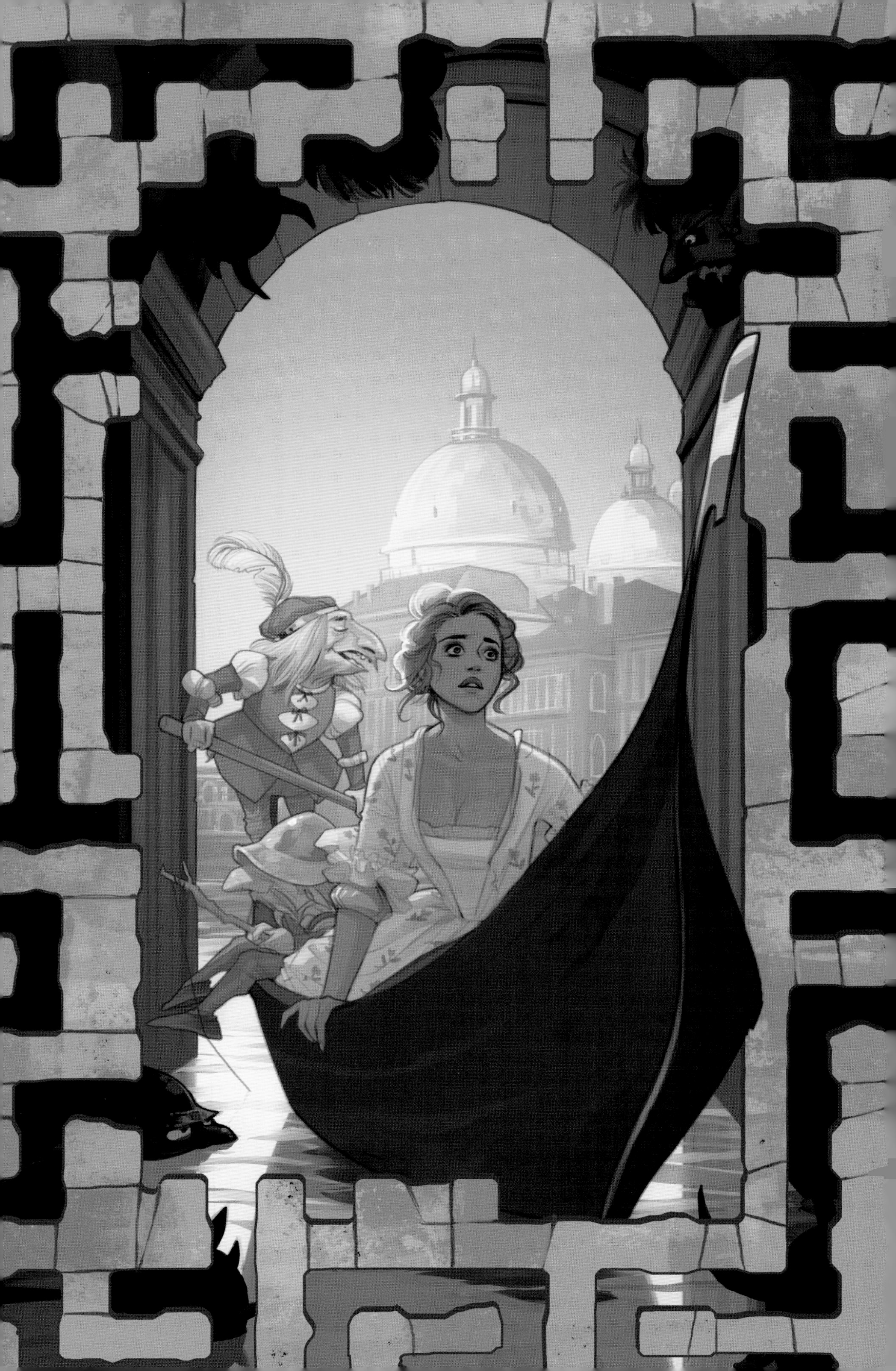

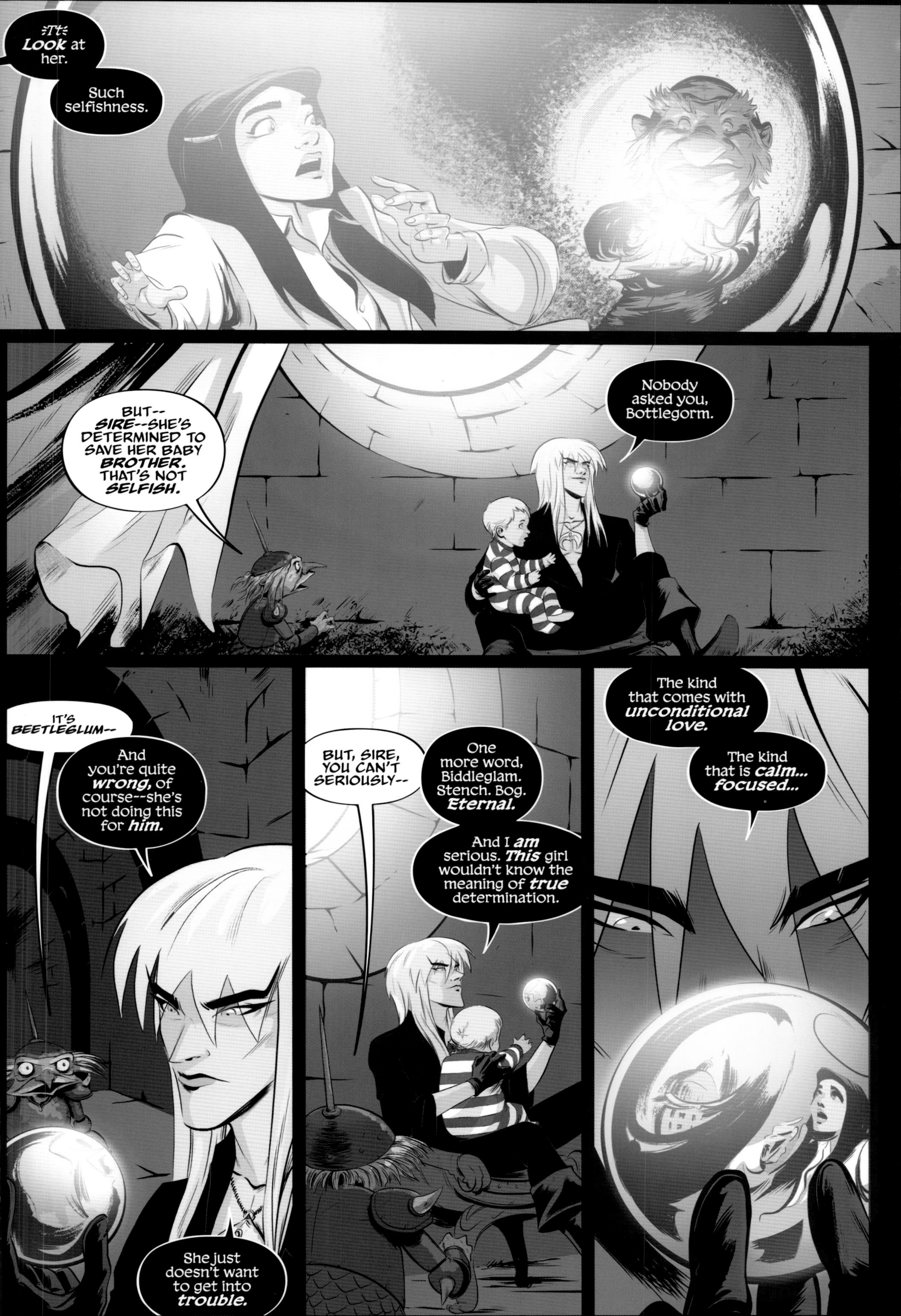

Tt *Look* at her.
Such selfishness.
BUT-- *SIRE*--SHE'S DETERMINED TO SAVE HER BABY *BROTHER*. THAT'S NOT *SELFISH*.
Nobody asked you, Bottlegorm.
IT'S *BEETLEGLUM*--
And you're quite *wrong*, of course--she's not doing this for *him*.
She just doesn't want to get into *trouble*.
BUT, SIRE, YOU CAN'T SERIOUSLY--
One more word, Biddleglam. Stench. Bog. *Eternal*.
And I *am* serious. *This* girl wouldn't know the meaning of *true* determination.
The kind that comes with *unconditional love*.
The kind that is *calm... focused...*

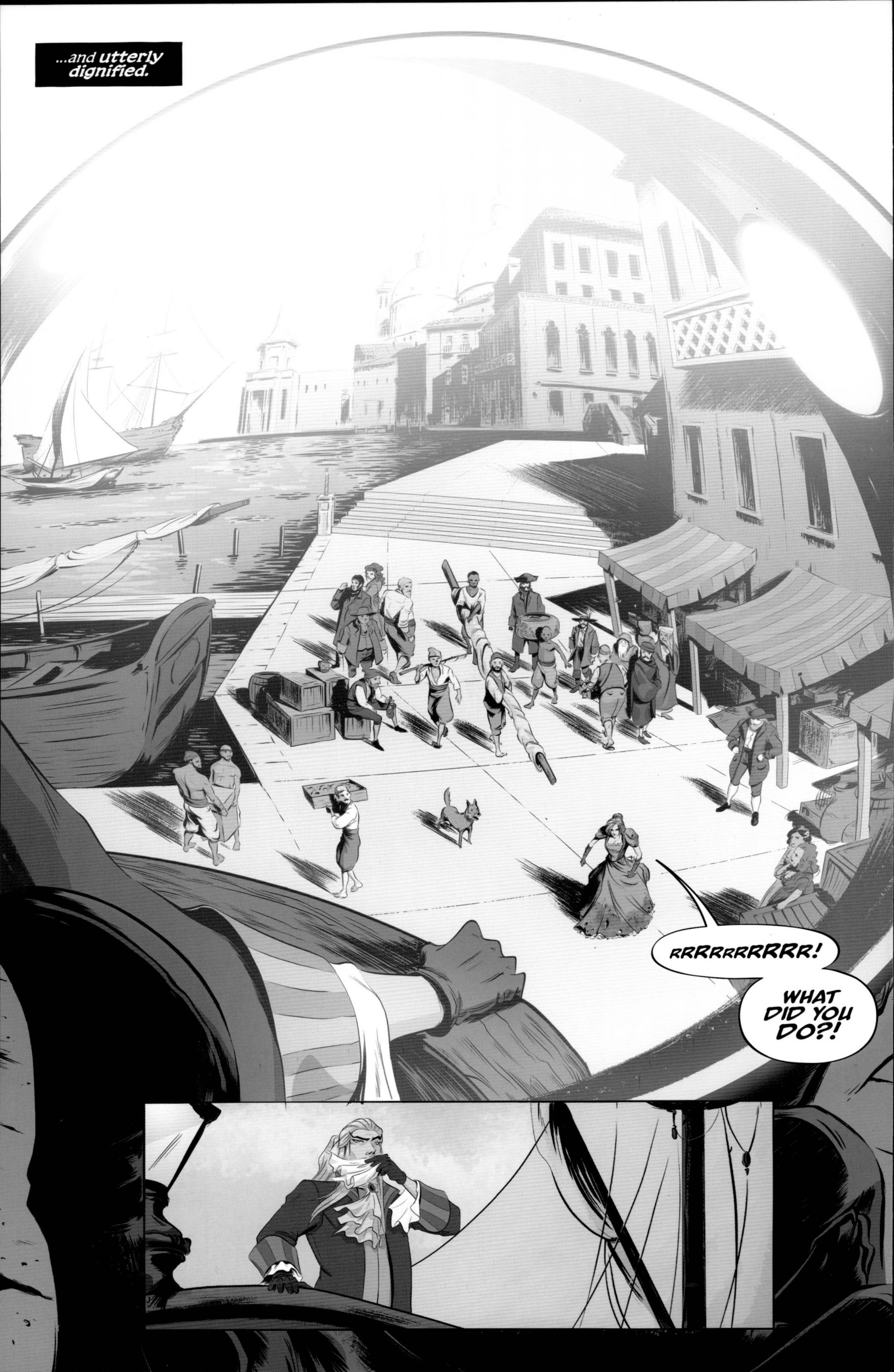
...and utterly dignified.
RRRRRRRRRR!
WHAT DID YOU DO?!

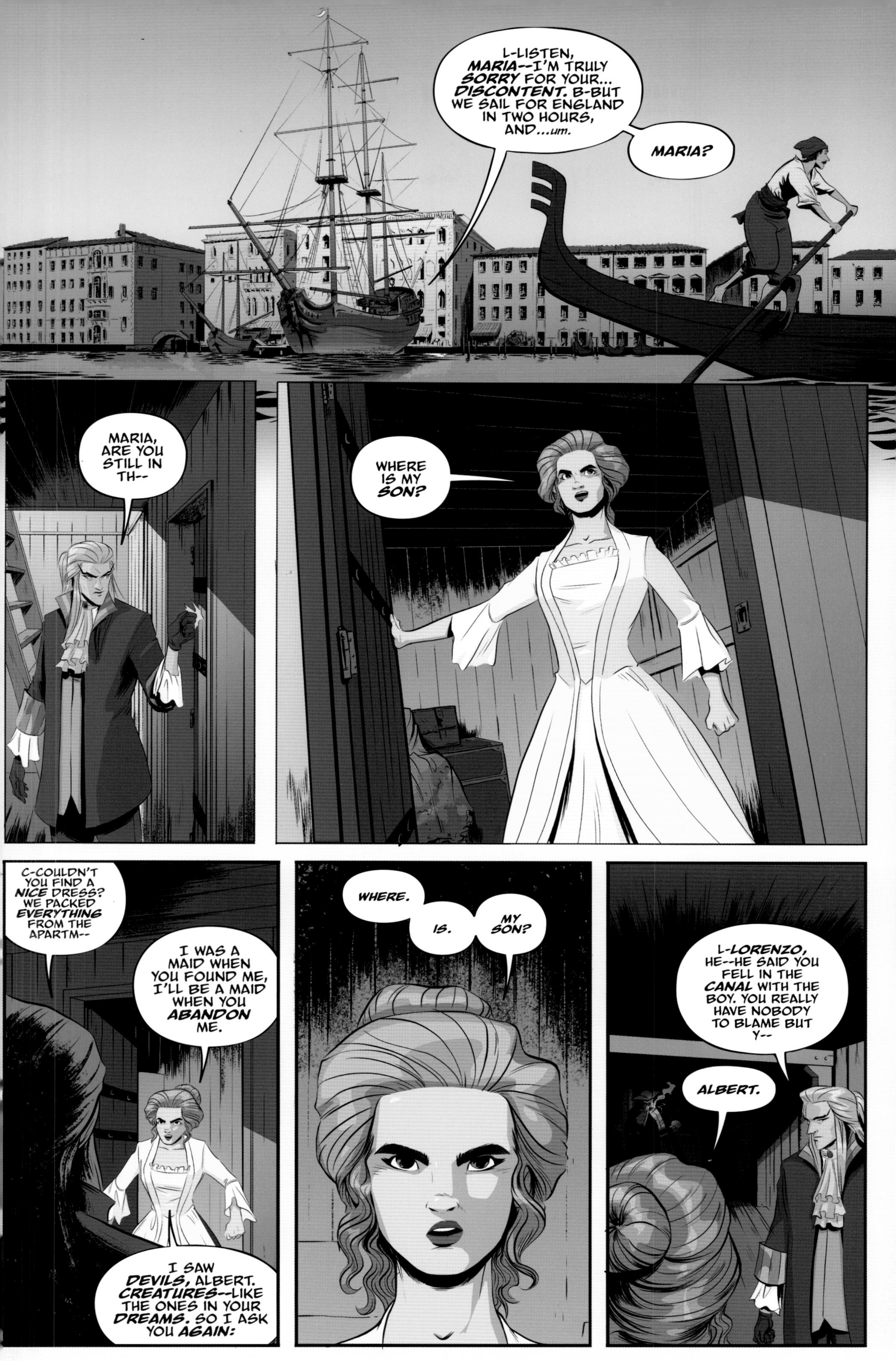
L-LISTEN, MARIA--I'M TRULY SORRY FOR YOUR... DISCONTENT. B-BUT WE SAIL FOR ENGLAND IN TWO HOURS, AND...um.
MARIA?
MARIA, ARE YOU STILL IN TH--
WHERE IS MY SON?
C-COULDN'T YOU FIND A NICE DRESS? WE PACKED EVERYTHING FROM THE APARTM--
I WAS A MAID WHEN YOU FOUND ME, I'LL BE A MAID WHEN YOU ABANDON ME.
I SAW DEVILS, ALBERT. CREATURES--LIKE THE ONES IN YOUR DREAMS. SO I ASK YOU AGAIN:
WHERE.
IS.
MY SON?
L-LORENZO, HE--HE SAID YOU FELL IN THE CANAL WITH THE BOY. YOU REALLY HAVE NOBODY TO BLAME BUT Y--
ALBERT.

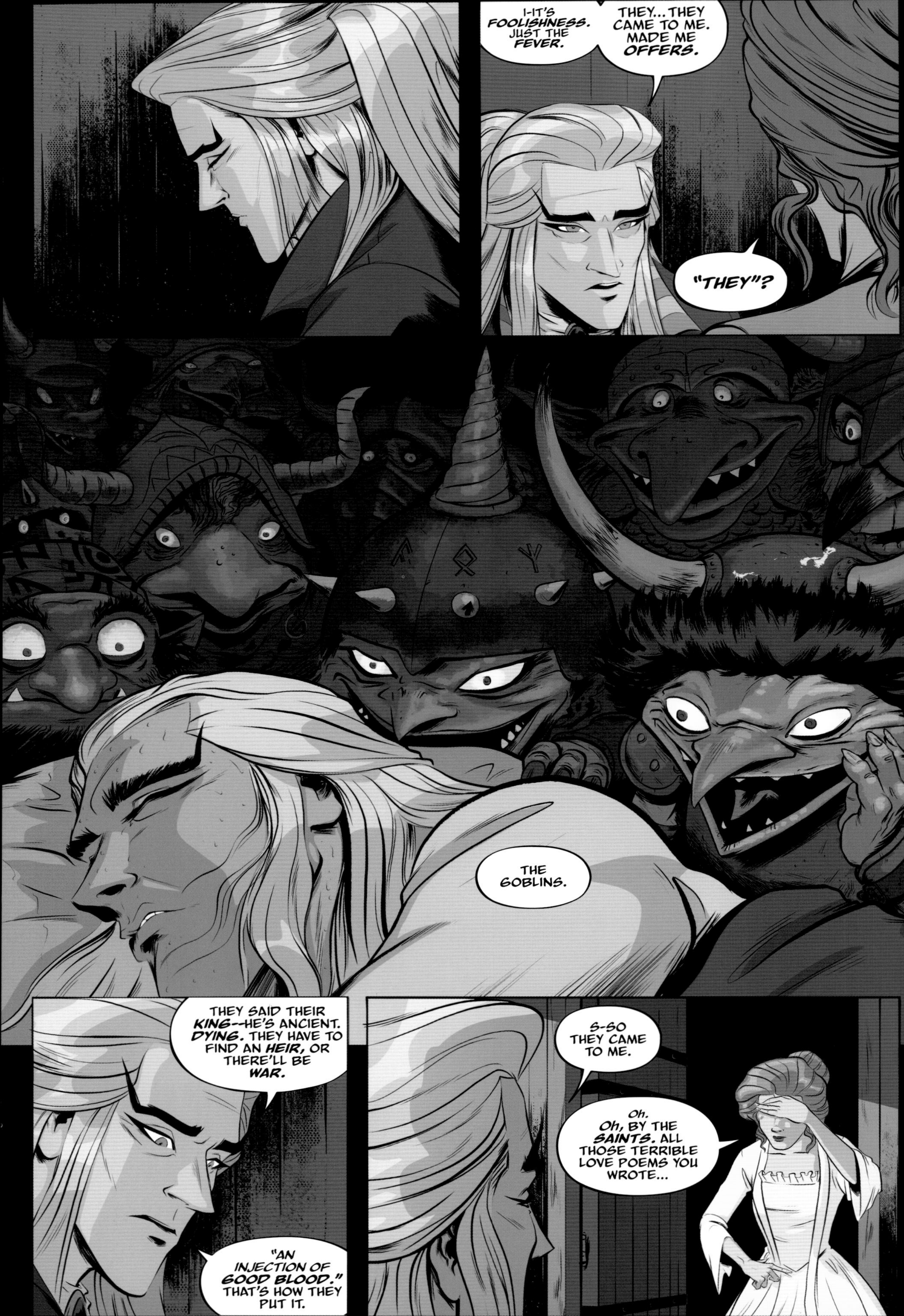
I-IT'S FOOLISHNESS. JUST THE FEVER.
THEY... THEY CAME TO ME. MADE ME OFFERS.
"THEY"?
THE GOBLINS.
THEY SAID THEIR KING--HE'S ANCIENT. DYING. THEY HAVE TO FIND AN HEIR, OR THERE'LL BE WAR.
"AN INJECTION OF GOOD BLOOD." THAT'S HOW THEY PUT IT.
S-SO THEY CAME TO ME.
Oh. Oh, BY THE SAINTS. ALL THOSE TERRIBLE LOVE POEMS YOU WROTE...

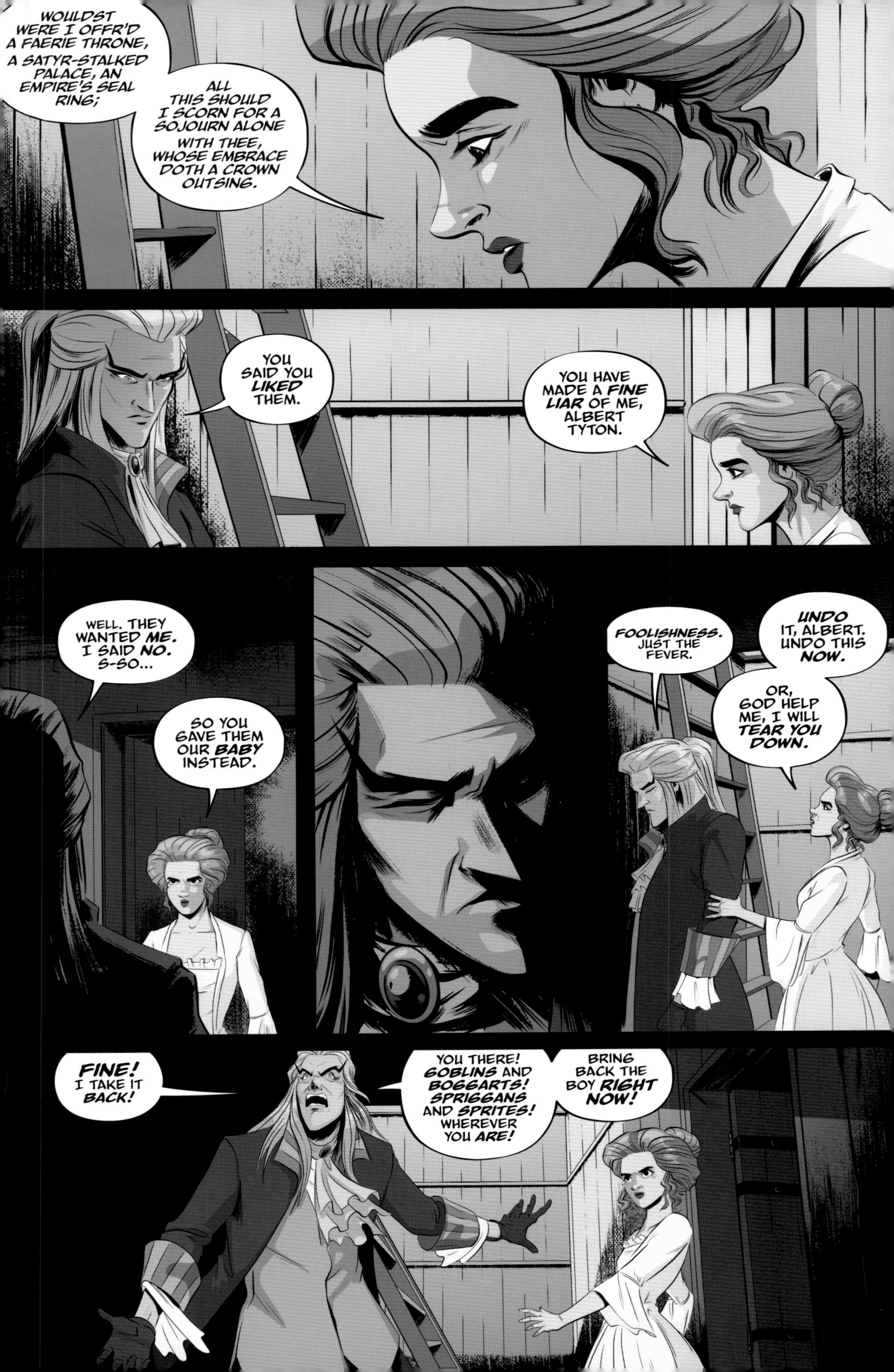
WOULDST WERE I OFFR'D A FAERIE THRONE, A SATYR-STALKED PALACE, AN EMPIRE'S SEAL RING;
ALL THIS SHOULD I SCORN FOR A SOJOURN ALONE WITH THEE, WHOSE EMBRACE DOTH A CROWN OUTSING.
YOU SAID YOU *LIKED* THEM.
YOU HAVE MADE A *FINE LIAR* OF ME, ALBERT TYTON.
WELL. THEY WANTED *ME*. I SAID *NO*. S-SO...
SO YOU GAVE THEM OUR *BABY* INSTEAD.
FOOLISHNESS. JUST THE FEVER.
UNDO IT, ALBERT. UNDO THIS *NOW*.
OR, GOD HELP ME, I WILL *TEAR YOU DOWN*.
FINE! I TAKE IT *BACK!*
YOU THERE! *GOBLINS* AND *BOGGARTS! SPRIGGANS* AND *SPRITES!* WHEREVER YOU *ARE!*
BRING BACK THE BOY *RIGHT NOW!*

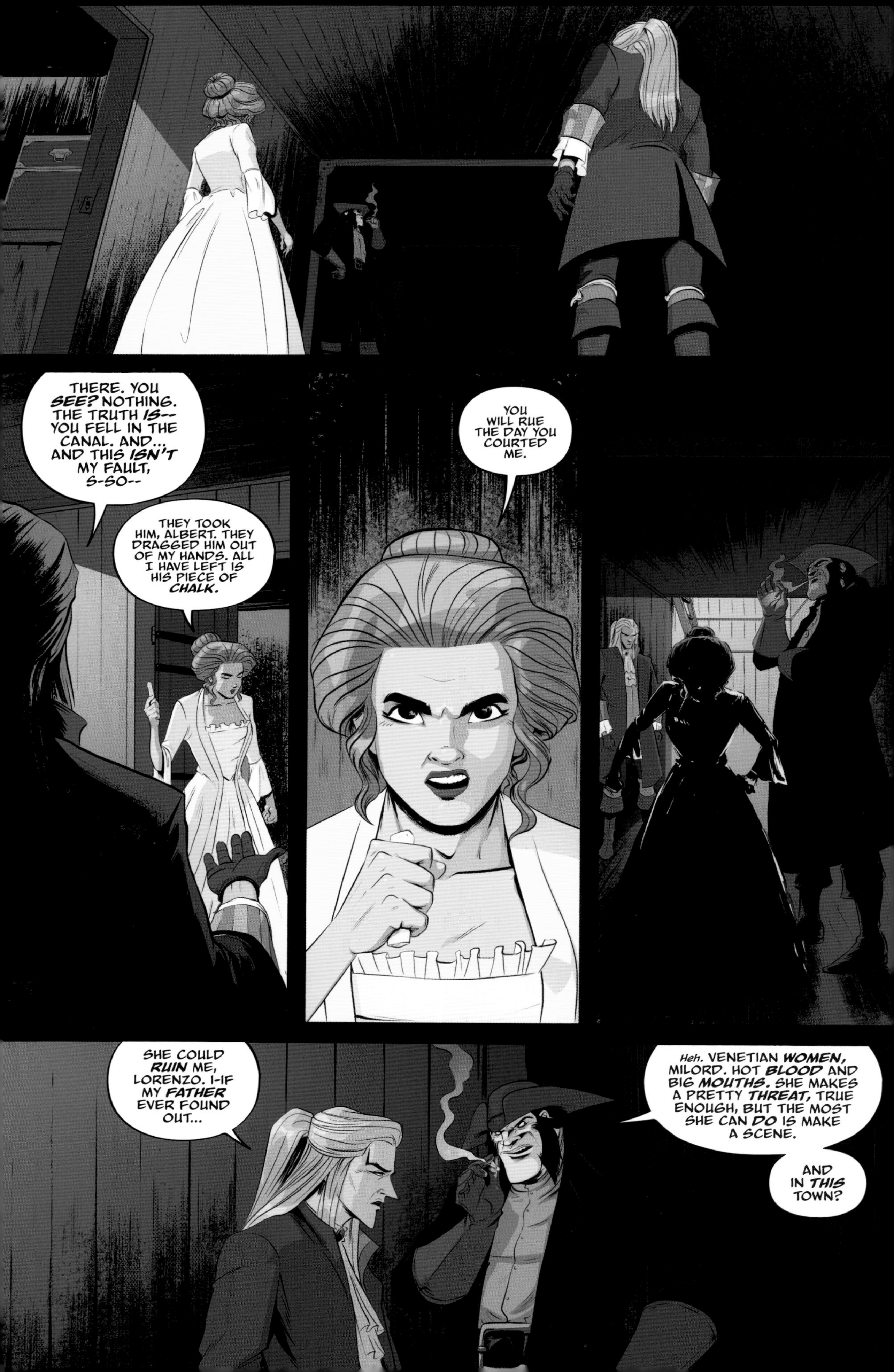
THERE. YOU SEE? NOTHING. THE TRUTH IS-- YOU FELL IN THE CANAL. AND... AND THIS ISN'T MY FAULT, S-SO--
THEY TOOK HIM, ALBERT. THEY DRAGGED HIM OUT OF MY HANDS. ALL I HAVE LEFT IS HIS PIECE OF CHALK.
YOU WILL RUE THE DAY YOU COURTED ME.
SHE COULD RUIN ME, LORENZO. I-IF MY FATHER EVER FOUND OUT...
Heh. VENETIAN WOMEN, MILORD. HOT BLOOD AND BIG MOUTHS. SHE MAKES A PRETTY THREAT, TRUE ENOUGH, BUT THE MOST SHE CAN DO IS MAKE A SCENE.
AND IN THIS TOWN?

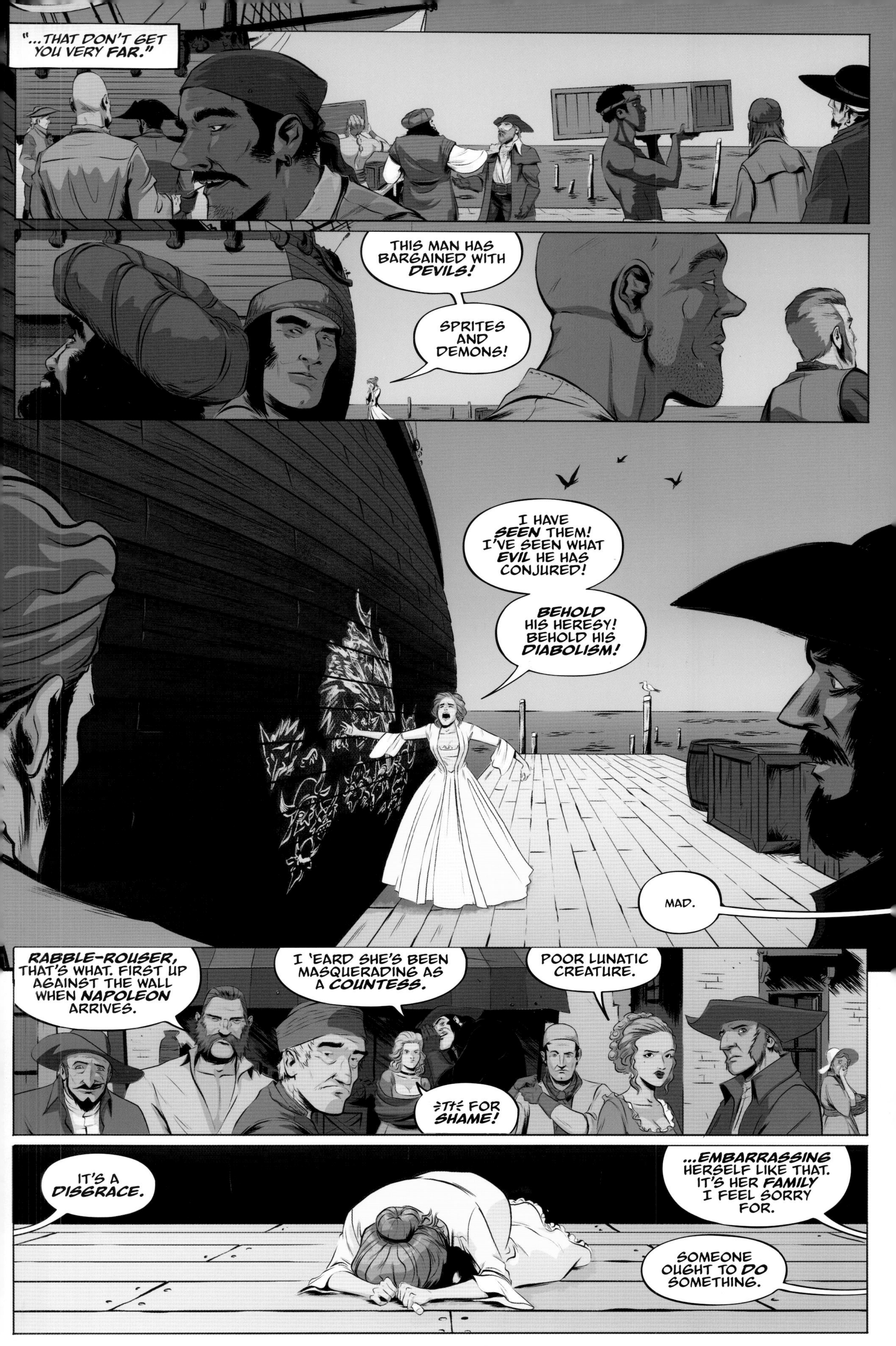
"...THAT DON'T GET YOU VERY FAR."
THIS MAN HAS BARGAINED WITH DEVILS!
SPRITES AND DEMONS!
I HAVE SEEN THEM! I'VE SEEN WHAT EVIL HE HAS CONJURED!
BEHOLD HIS HERESY! BEHOLD HIS DIABOLISM!
MAD.
RABBLE-ROUSER, THAT'S WHAT. FIRST UP AGAINST THE WALL WHEN NAPOLEON ARRIVES.
I 'EARD SHE'S BEEN MASQUERADING AS A COUNTESS.
POOR LUNATIC CREATURE.
TT FOR SHAME!
IT'S A DISGRACE.
...EMBARRASSING HERSELF LIKE THAT. IT'S HER FAMILY I FEEL SORRY FOR.
SOMEONE OUGHT TO DO SOMETHING.

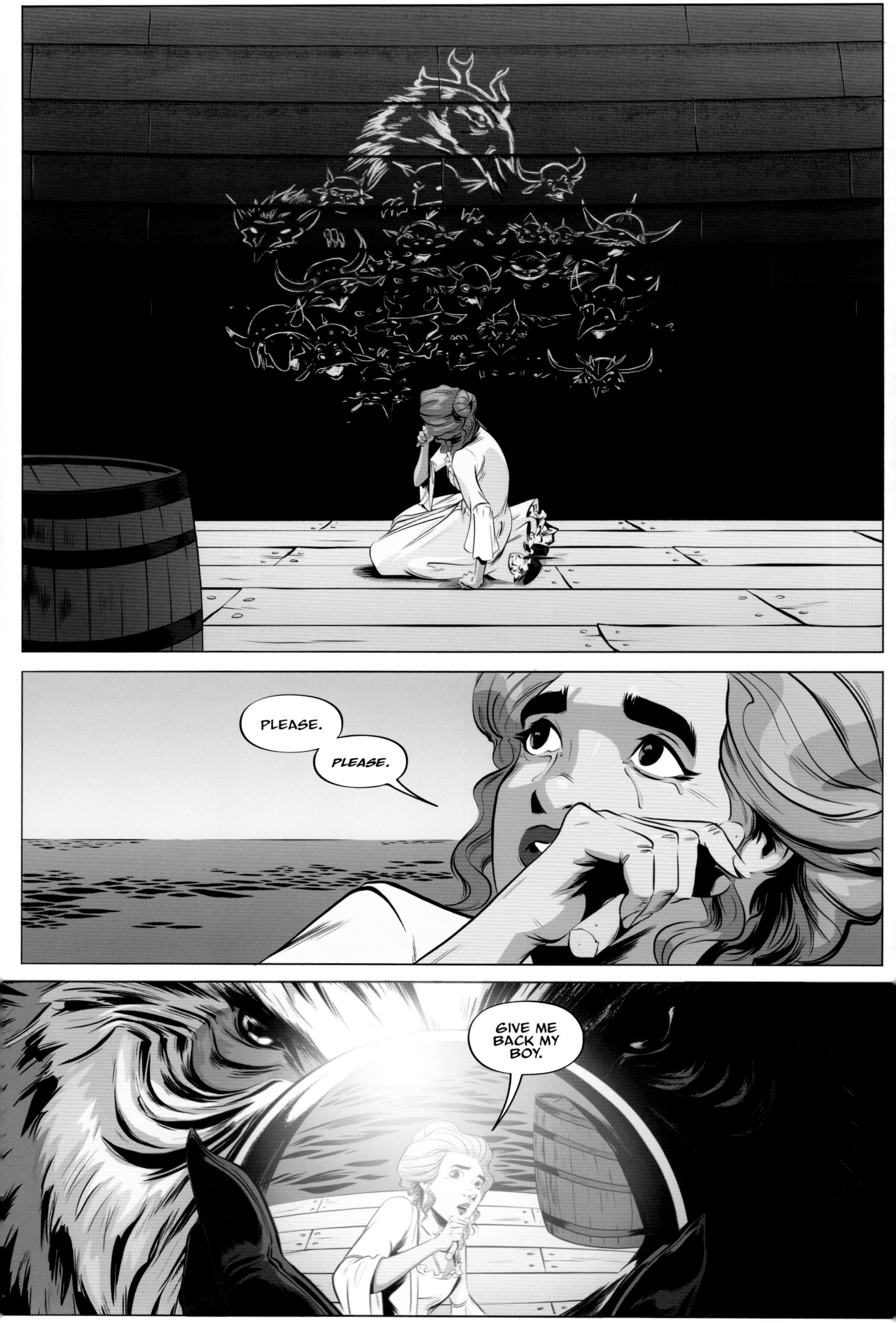
PLEASE.
PLEASE.
GIVE ME BACK MY BOY.

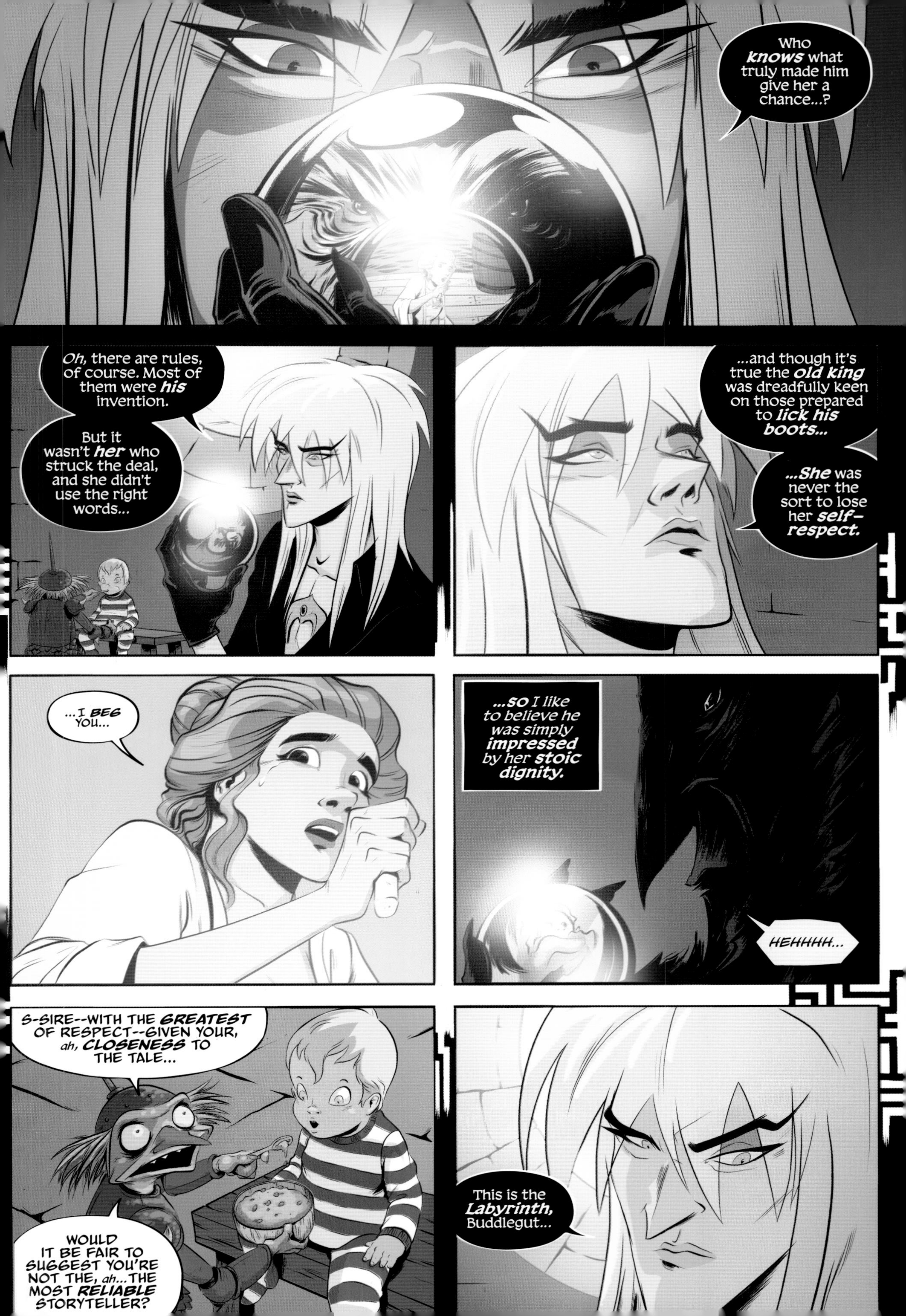
Who **knows** what truly made him give her a chance...?
Oh, there are rules, of course. Most of them were ***his*** invention.
But it wasn't ***her*** who struck the deal, and she didn't use the right words...
...and though it's true the ***old king*** was dreadfully keen on those prepared to ***lick his boots...***
...She was never the sort to lose her ***self-respect.***
...I ***BEG*** YOU...
...so *I like to believe he was simply* ***impressed*** *by her* ***stoic dignity.***
HEHHHH...
S-SIRE--WITH THE ***GREATEST*** OF RESPECT--GIVEN YOUR, *ah,* ***CLOSENESS*** TO THE TALE...
WOULD IT BE FAIR TO SUGGEST YOU'RE NOT THE, *ah*...THE MOST ***RELIABLE*** STORYTELLER?
This is the ***Labyrinth,*** Buddlegut...

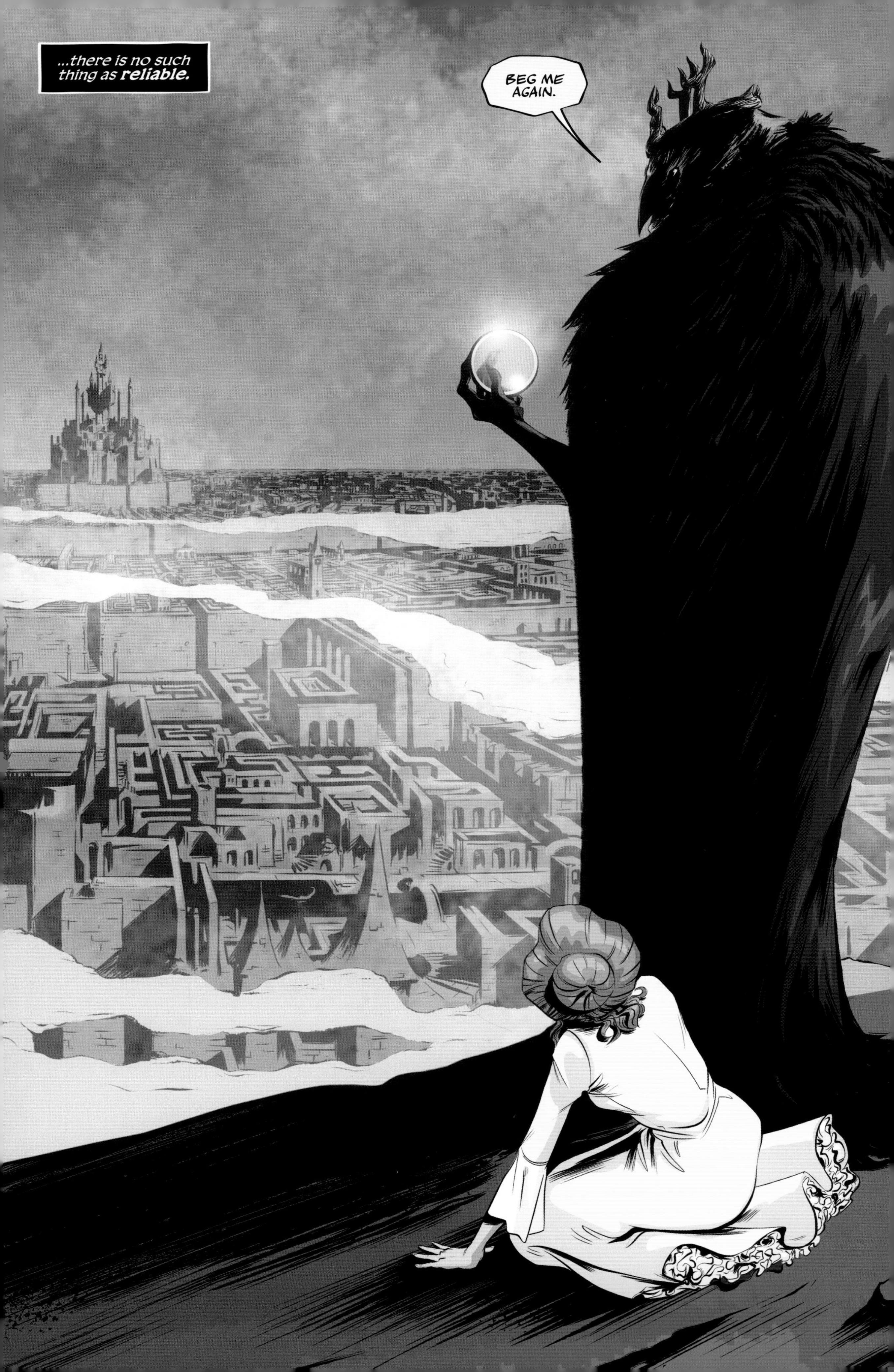
...there is no such thing as **reliable.**
BEG ME AGAIN.

I WILL *NOT.*

HM. YOU *WILL.*

ALL TRAVELERS BOW TO THE *OWL KING,* BEFORE THE END.

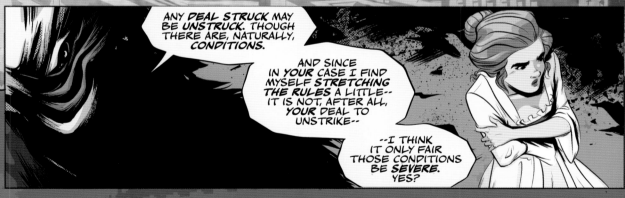

IN THE *MEANTIME,* KNOW THAT THERE ARE RULES.

THE GOBLIN MASSES RARELY *APPRECIATE* THAT, BUT EVEN THEY-- IN *TIME*--WILL RESPECT THE GIFT OF *ORDER.*

ANY *DEAL STRUCK* MAY BE *UNSTRUCK.* THOUGH THERE ARE, NATURALLY, *CONDITIONS.*

AND SINCE IN *YOUR* CASE I FIND MYSELF *STRETCHING THE RULES* A LITTLE-- IT IS NOT, AFTER ALL, *YOUR* DEAL TO UNSTRIKE--

--I THINK IT ONLY FAIR THOSE CONDITIONS BE *SEVERE.* YES?

YOU TALK A *LOT.*

WHERE IS MY *SON?*

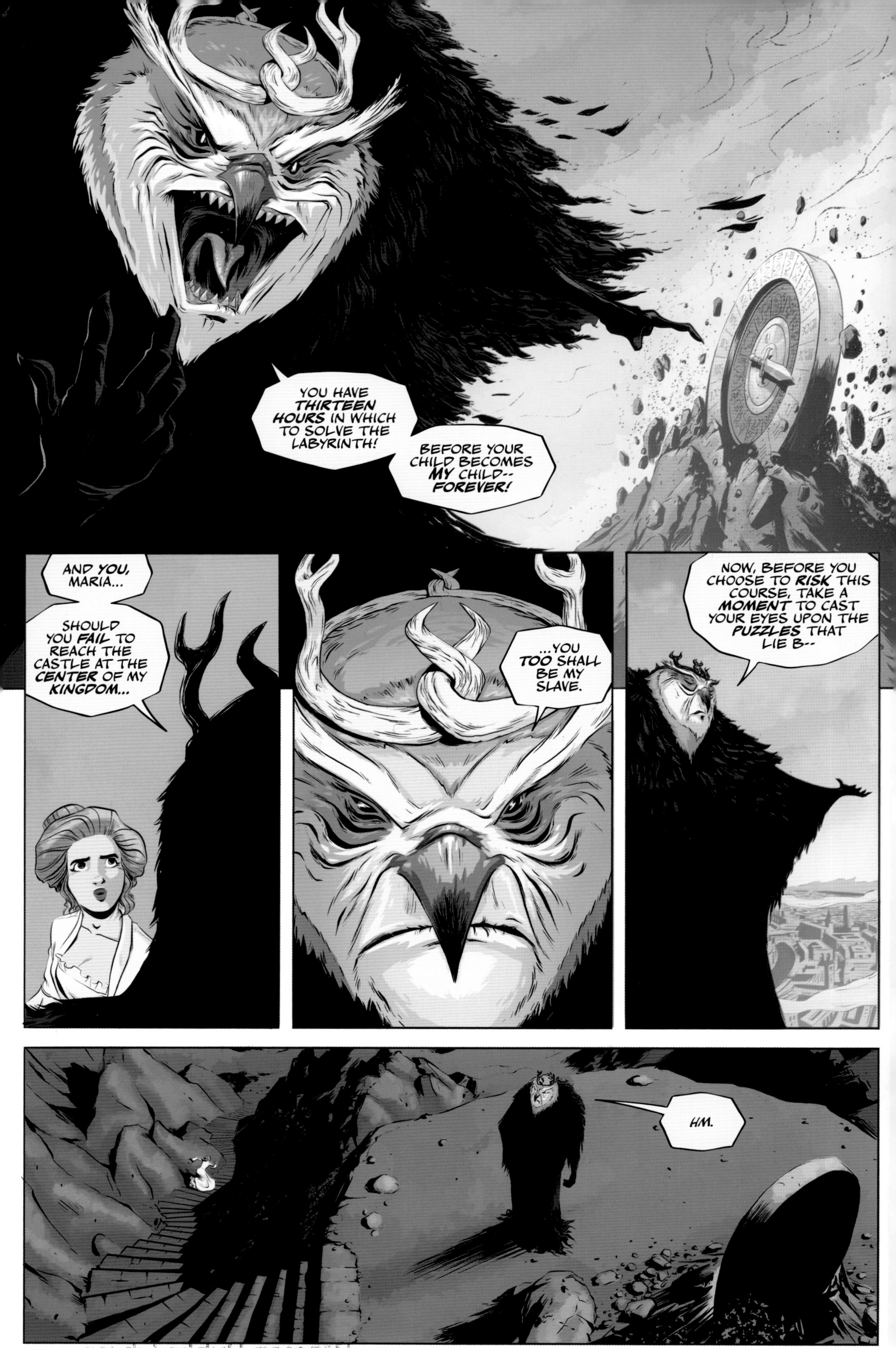
YOU HAVE THIRTEEN HOURS IN WHICH TO SOLVE THE LABYRINTH!
BEFORE YOUR CHILD BECOMES MY CHILD-- FOREVER!
AND YOU, MARIA...
SHOULD YOU FAIL TO REACH THE CASTLE AT THE CENTER OF MY KINGDOM...
...YOU TOO SHALL BE MY SLAVE.
NOW, BEFORE YOU CHOOSE TO RISK THIS COURSE, TAKE A MOMENT TO CAST YOUR EYES UPON THE PUZZLES THAT LIE B--
HM.

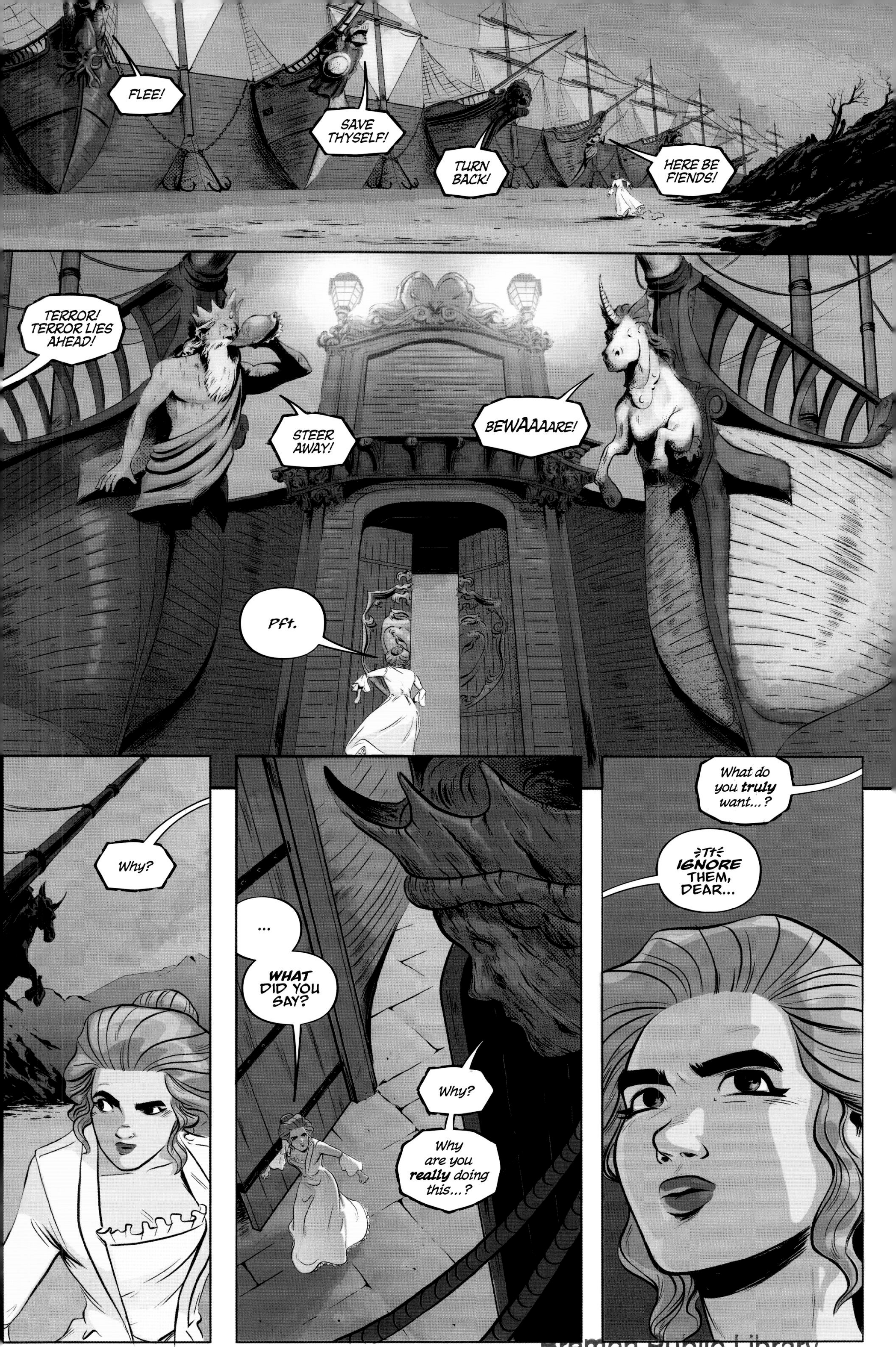
FLEE!
SAVE THYSELF!
TURN BACK!
HERE BE FIENDS!
TERROR! TERROR LIES AHEAD!
STEER AWAY!
BEWAAAARE!
Pft.
Why?
...
WHAT DID YOU SAY?
Why?
Why are you **really** doing this...?
What do you **truly** want...?
Tt IGNORE THEM, DEAR...

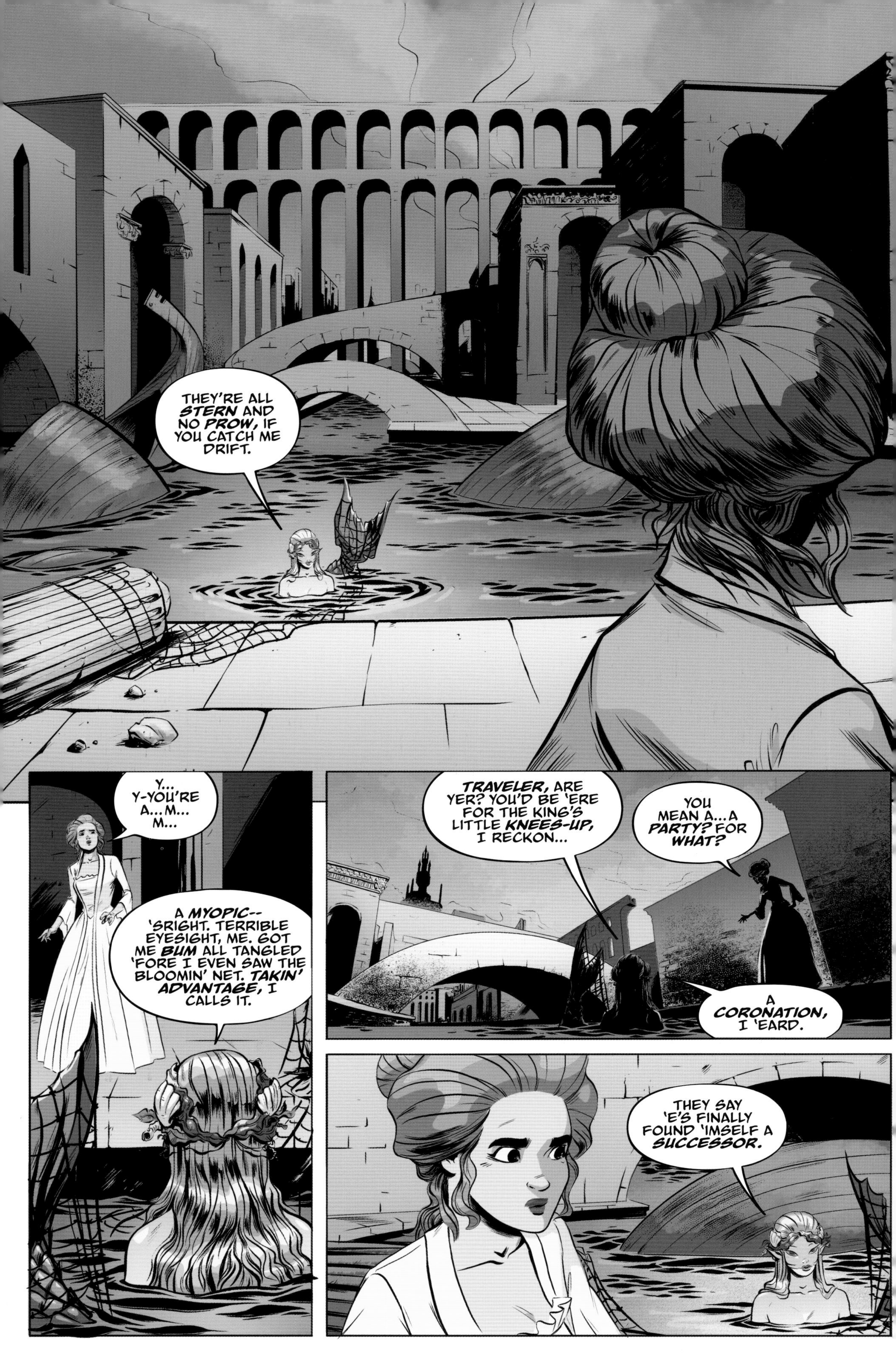
THEY'RE ALL STERN AND NO PROW, IF YOU CATCH ME DRIFT.
Y... Y-YOU'RE A...M... M...
A MYOPIC-- 'SRIGHT. TERRIBLE EYESIGHT, ME. GOT ME BUM ALL TANGLED 'FORE I EVEN SAW THE BLOOMIN' NET. TAKIN' ADVANTAGE, I CALLS IT.
TRAVELER, ARE YER? YOU'D BE 'ERE FOR THE KING'S LITTLE KNEES-UP, I RECKON...
YOU MEAN A...A PARTY? FOR WHAT?
A CORONATION, I 'EARD.
THEY SAY 'E'S FINALLY FOUND 'IMSELF A SUCCESSOR.

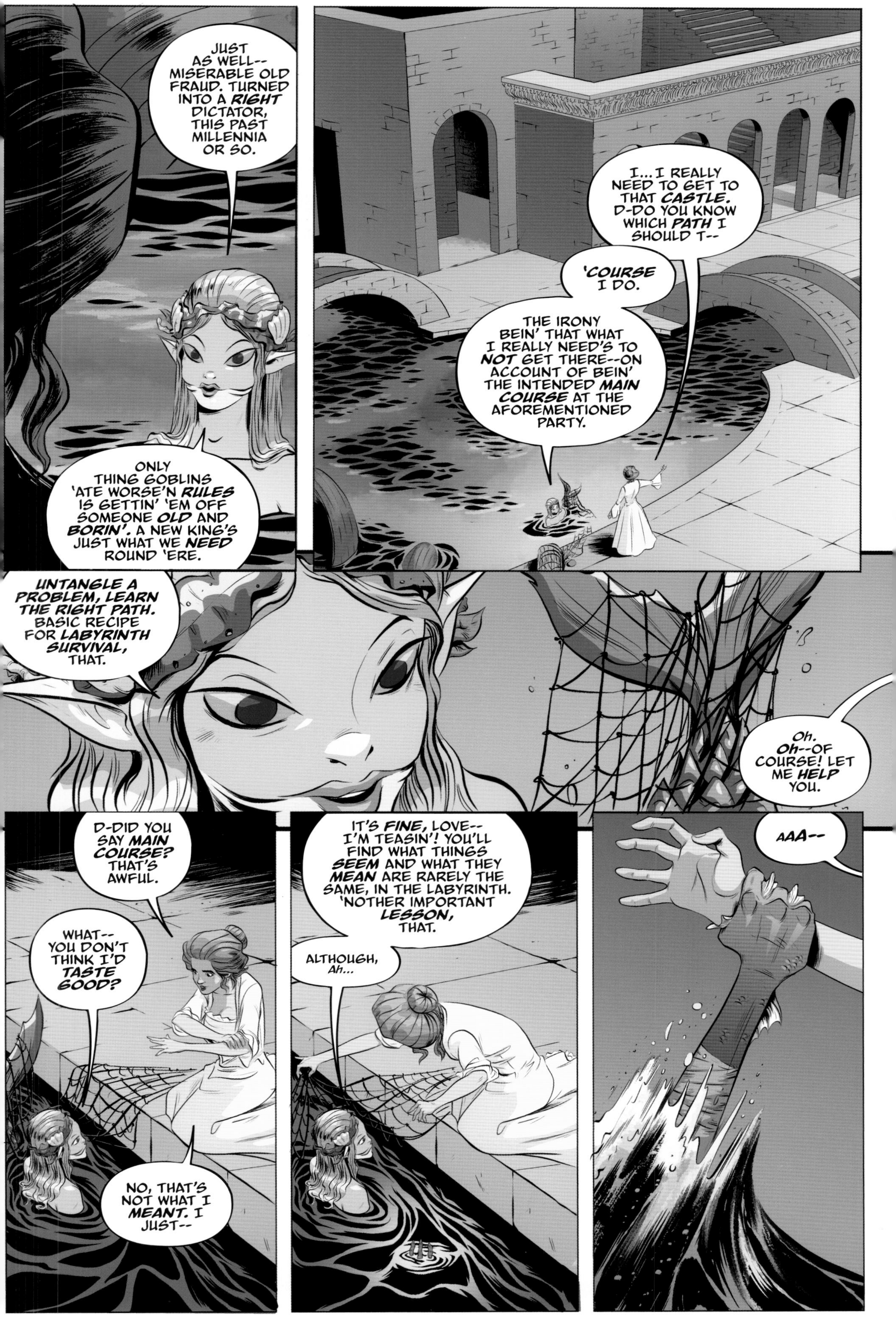
JUST AS WELL-- MISERABLE OLD FRAUD. TURNED INTO A RIGHT DICTATOR, THIS PAST MILLENNIA OR SO.
ONLY THING GOBLINS 'ATE WORSE'N RULES IS GETTIN' 'EM OFF SOMEONE OLD AND BORIN'. A NEW KING'S JUST WHAT WE NEED ROUND 'ERE.
I... I REALLY NEED TO GET TO THAT CASTLE. D-DO YOU KNOW WHICH PATH I SHOULD T--
'COURSE I DO.
THE IRONY BEIN' THAT WHAT I REALLY NEED'S TO NOT GET THERE--ON ACCOUNT OF BEIN' THE INTENDED MAIN COURSE AT THE AFOREMENTIONED PARTY.
UNTANGLE A PROBLEM, LEARN THE RIGHT PATH. BASIC RECIPE FOR LABYRINTH SURVIVAL, THAT.
Oh. Oh--OF COURSE! LET ME HELP YOU.
D-DID YOU SAY MAIN COURSE? THAT'S AWFUL.
WHAT-- YOU DON'T THINK I'D TASTE GOOD?
NO, THAT'S NOT WHAT I MEANT. I JUST--
IT'S FINE, LOVE-- I'M TEASIN'! YOU'LL FIND WHAT THINGS SEEM AND WHAT THEY MEAN ARE RARELY THE SAME, IN THE LABYRINTH. 'NOTHER IMPORTANT LESSON, THAT.
ALTHOUGH, Ah...
AAA--

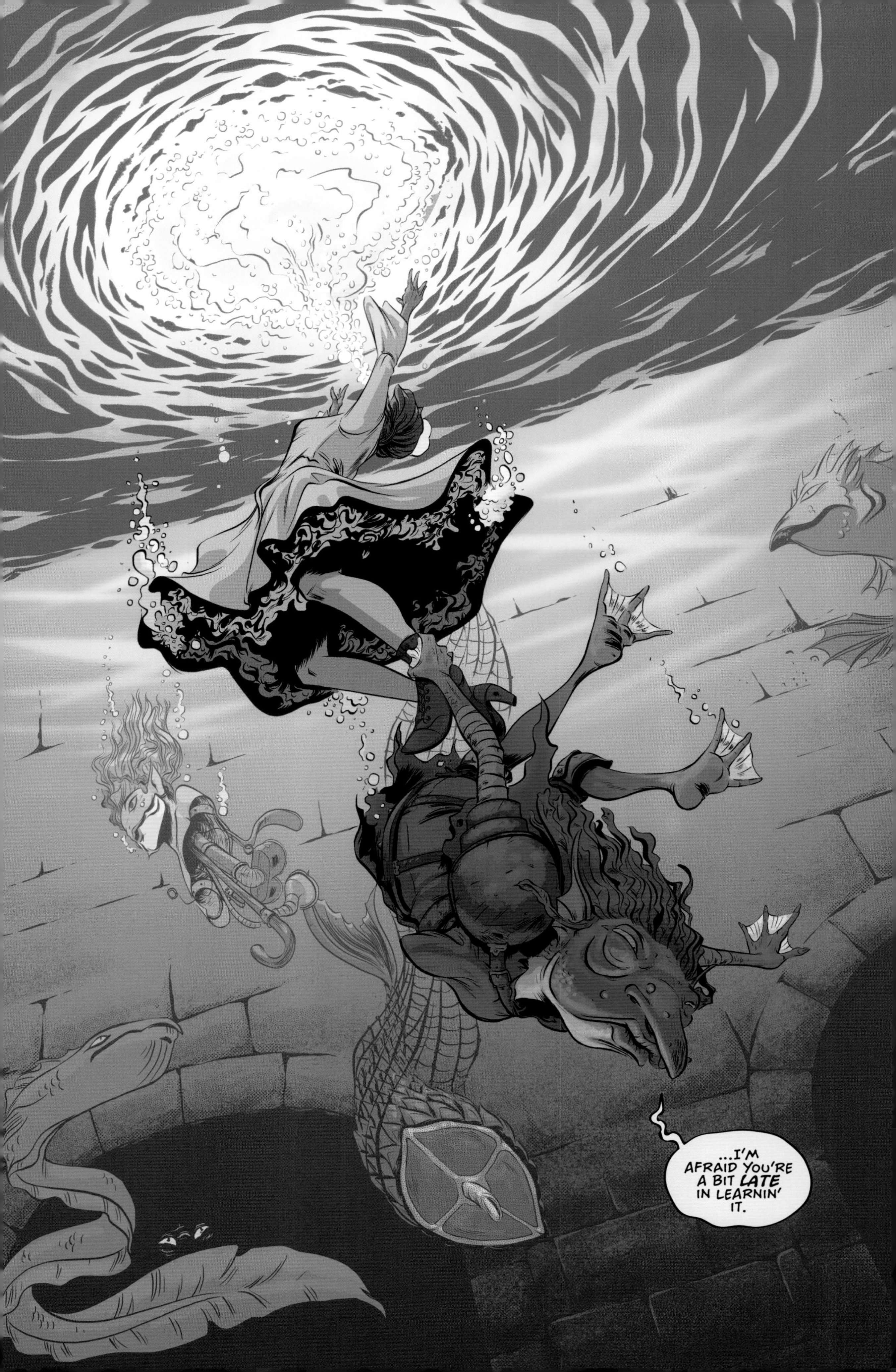
...I'M AFRAID YOU'RE A BIT LATE IN LEARNIN' IT.

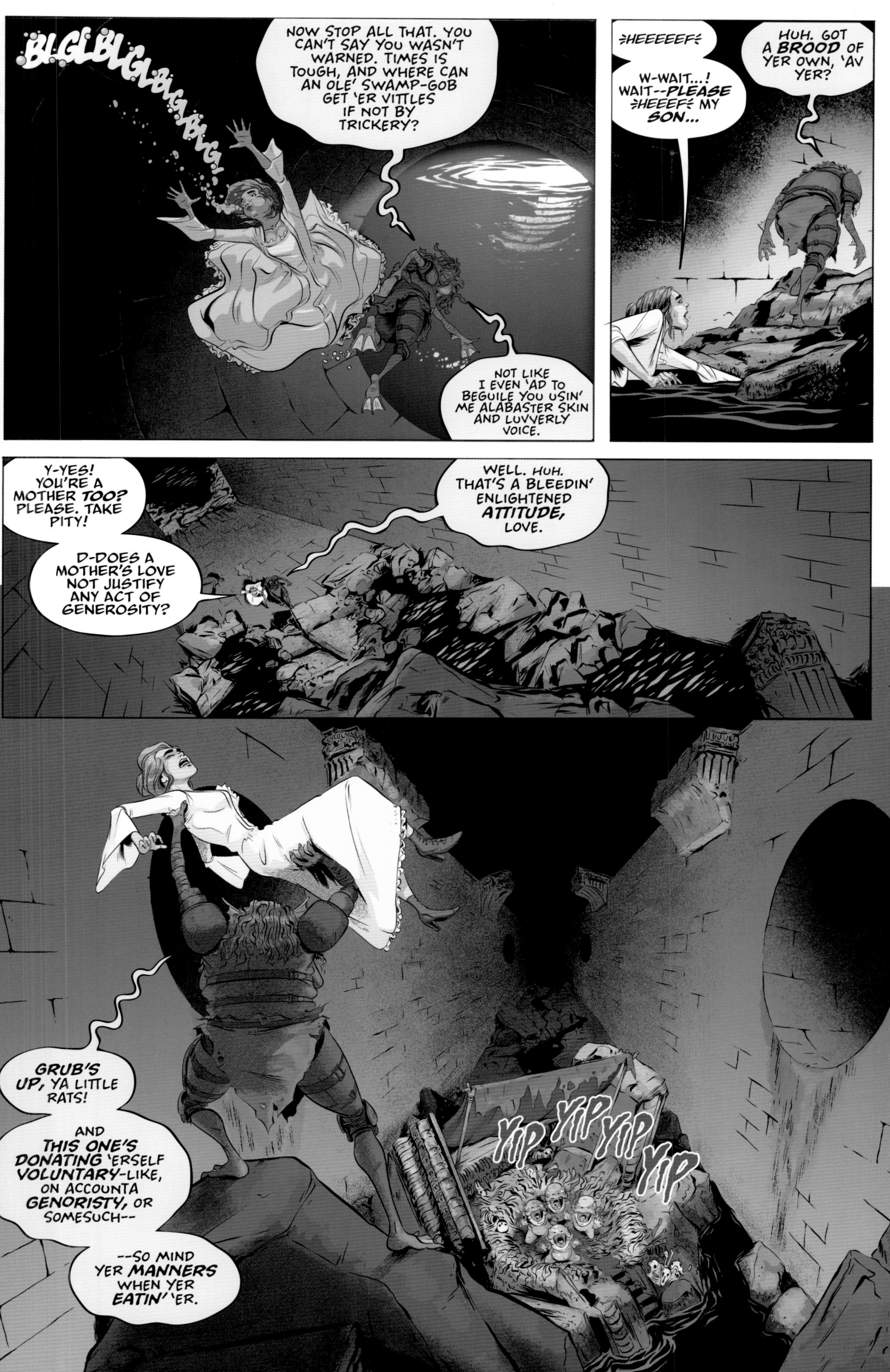
BLGLBLGLBLGBLG!
NOW STOP ALL THAT. YOU CAN'T SAY YOU WASN'T WARNED. TIMES IS TOUGH, AND WHERE CAN AN OLE' SWAMP-GOB GET 'ER VITTLES IF NOT BY TRICKERY?
NOT LIKE I EVEN 'AD TO BEGUILE YOU USIN' ME ALABASTER SKIN AND LUVVERLY VOICE.
HEEEEEF
W-WAIT...! WAIT--PLEASE HEEEF MY SON...
HUH. GOT A BROOD OF YER OWN, 'AV YER?
Y-YES! YOU'RE A MOTHER TOO? PLEASE. TAKE PITY!
D-DOES A MOTHER'S LOVE NOT JUSTIFY ANY ACT OF GENEROSITY?
WELL. HUH. THAT'S A BLEEDIN' ENLIGHTENED ATTITUDE, LOVE.
GRUB'S UP, YA LITTLE RATS!
AND THIS ONE'S DONATING 'ERSELF VOLUNTARY-LIKE, ON ACCOUNTA GENORISTY, OR SOMESUCH--
--SO MIND YER MANNERS WHEN YER EATIN' 'ER.
YIP YIP YIP YIP

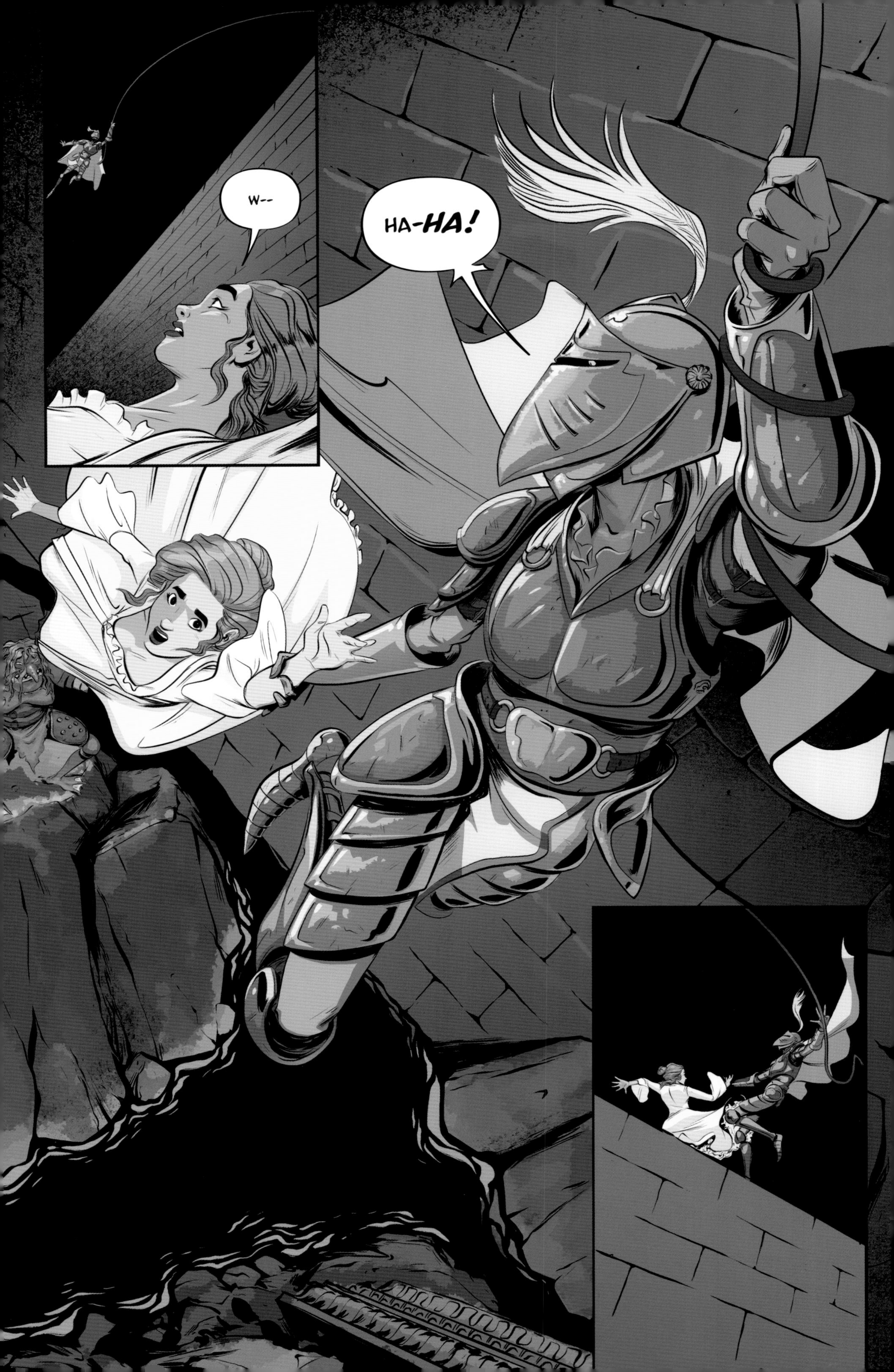
W--
HA-HA!

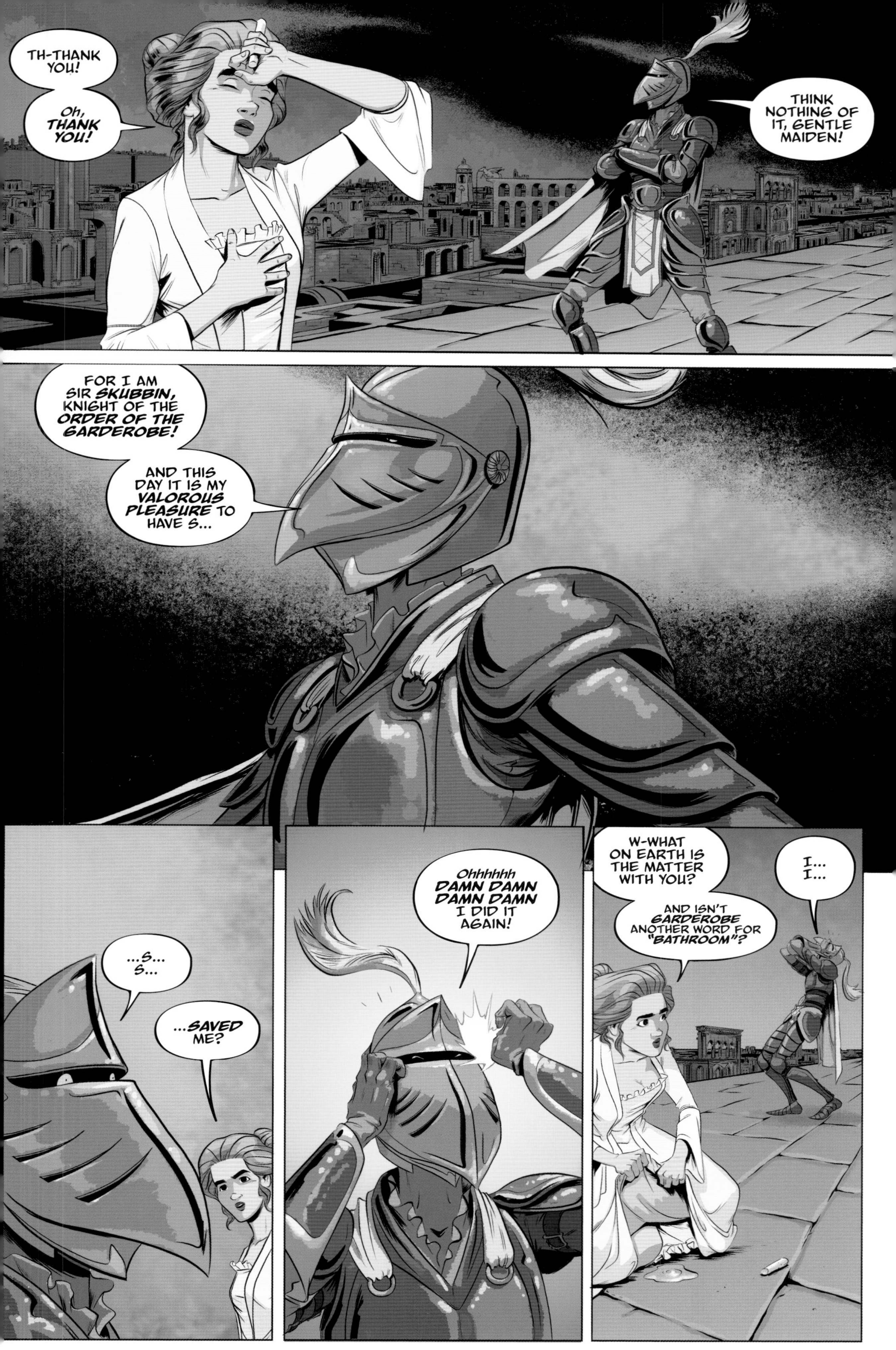
TH-THANK YOU!
Oh, THANK YOU!
THINK NOTHING OF IT, GENTLE MAIDEN!
FOR I AM SIR SKUBBIN, KNIGHT OF THE ORDER OF THE GARDEROBE!
AND THIS DAY IT IS MY VALOROUS PLEASURE TO HAVE S...
...S... S...
...SAVED ME?
Ohhhhhh DAMN DAMN DAMN DAMN I DID IT AGAIN!
W-WHAT ON EARTH IS THE MATTER WITH YOU?
AND ISN'T GARDEROBE ANOTHER WORD FOR "BATHROOM"?
I... I...

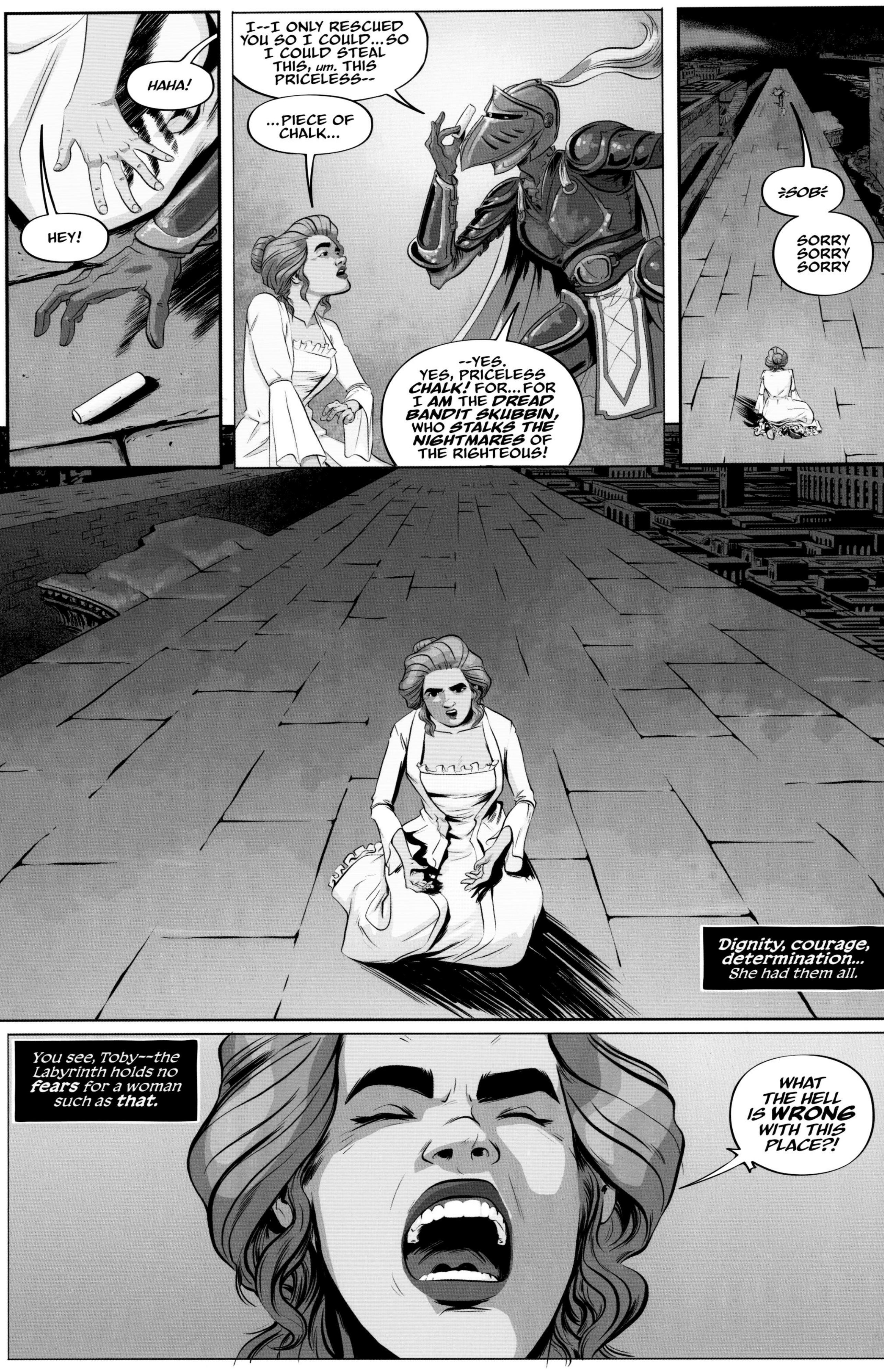
HAHA!
HEY!
I--I ONLY RESCUED YOU SO I COULD...SO I COULD STEAL THIS, um. THIS PRICELESS--
...PIECE OF CHALK...
--YES. YES, PRICELESS CHALK! FOR...FOR I AM THE DREAD BANDIT SKUBBIN, WHO STALKS THE NIGHTMARES OF THE RIGHTEOUS!
SOB
SORRY SORRY SORRY
Dignity, courage, determination... She had them all.
You see, Toby--the Labyrinth holds no fears for a woman such as that.
WHAT THE HELL IS WRONG WITH THIS PLACE?!

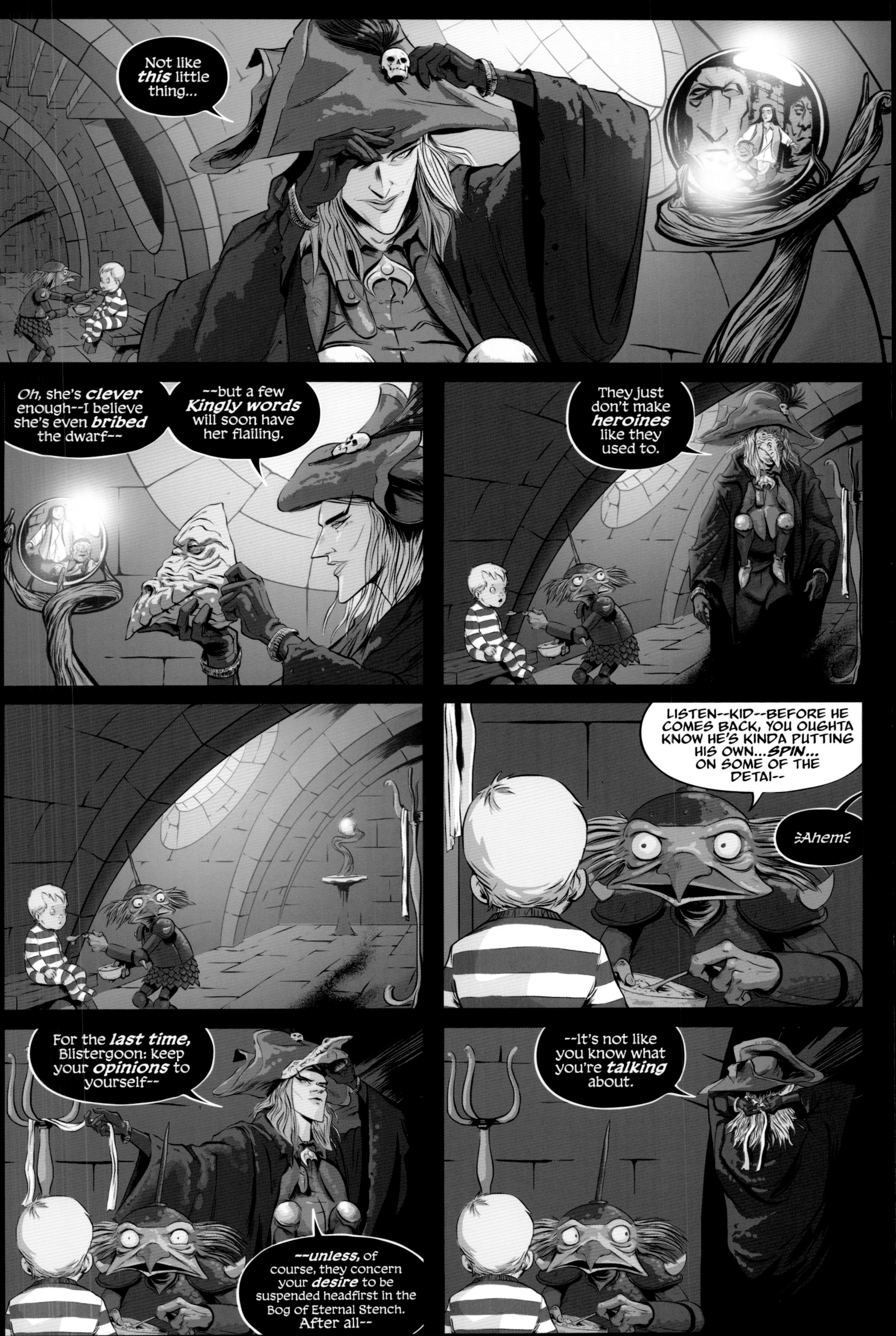

Not like *this* little thing...
Oh, she's *clever* enough--I believe she's even *bribed* the dwarf--
--but a few *Kingly words* will soon have her flailing.
They just don't make *heroines* like they used to.
LISTEN--KID--BEFORE HE COMES BACK, YOU OUGHTA KNOW HE'S KINDA PUTTING HIS OWN...*SPIN...* ON SOME OF THE DETAI--
Ahem
For the *last time,* Blistergoon: keep your *opinions* to yourself--
--unless, of course, they concern your *desire* to be suspended headfirst in the Bog of Eternal Stench. After all--
--It's not like you know what you're *talking* about.

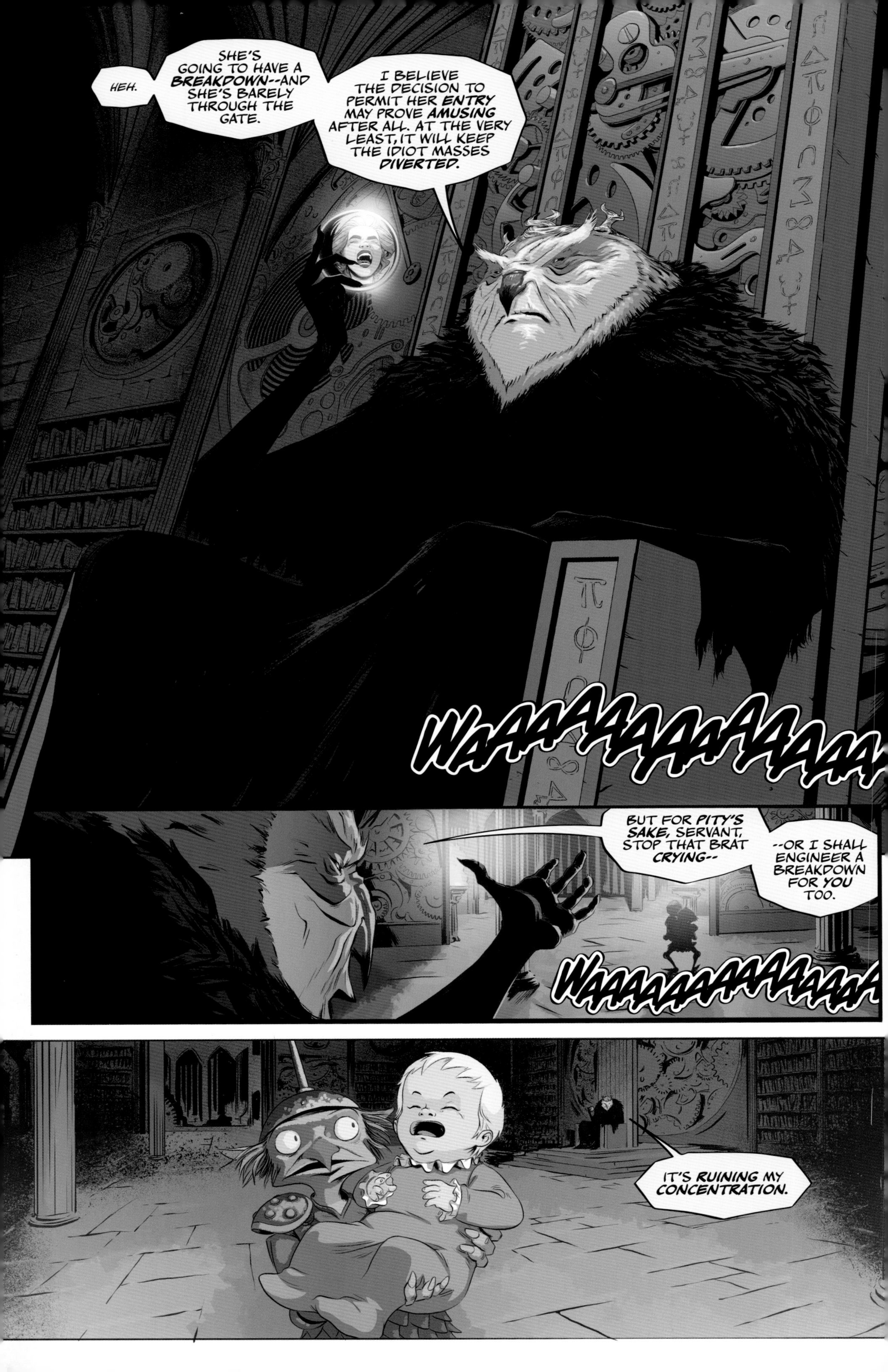

HEH.
SHE'S GOING TO HAVE A BREAKDOWN--AND SHE'S BARELY THROUGH THE GATE.
I BELIEVE THE DECISION TO PERMIT HER ENTRY MAY PROVE AMUSING AFTER ALL. AT THE VERY LEAST, IT WILL KEEP THE IDIOT MASSES DIVERTED.
WAAAAAAAAAAAAAA
BUT FOR PITY'S SAKE, SERVANT, STOP THAT BRAT CRYING--
--OR I SHALL ENGINEER A BREAKDOWN FOR YOU TOO.
WAAAAAAAAAAAAAAA
IT'S RUINING MY CONCENTRATION.

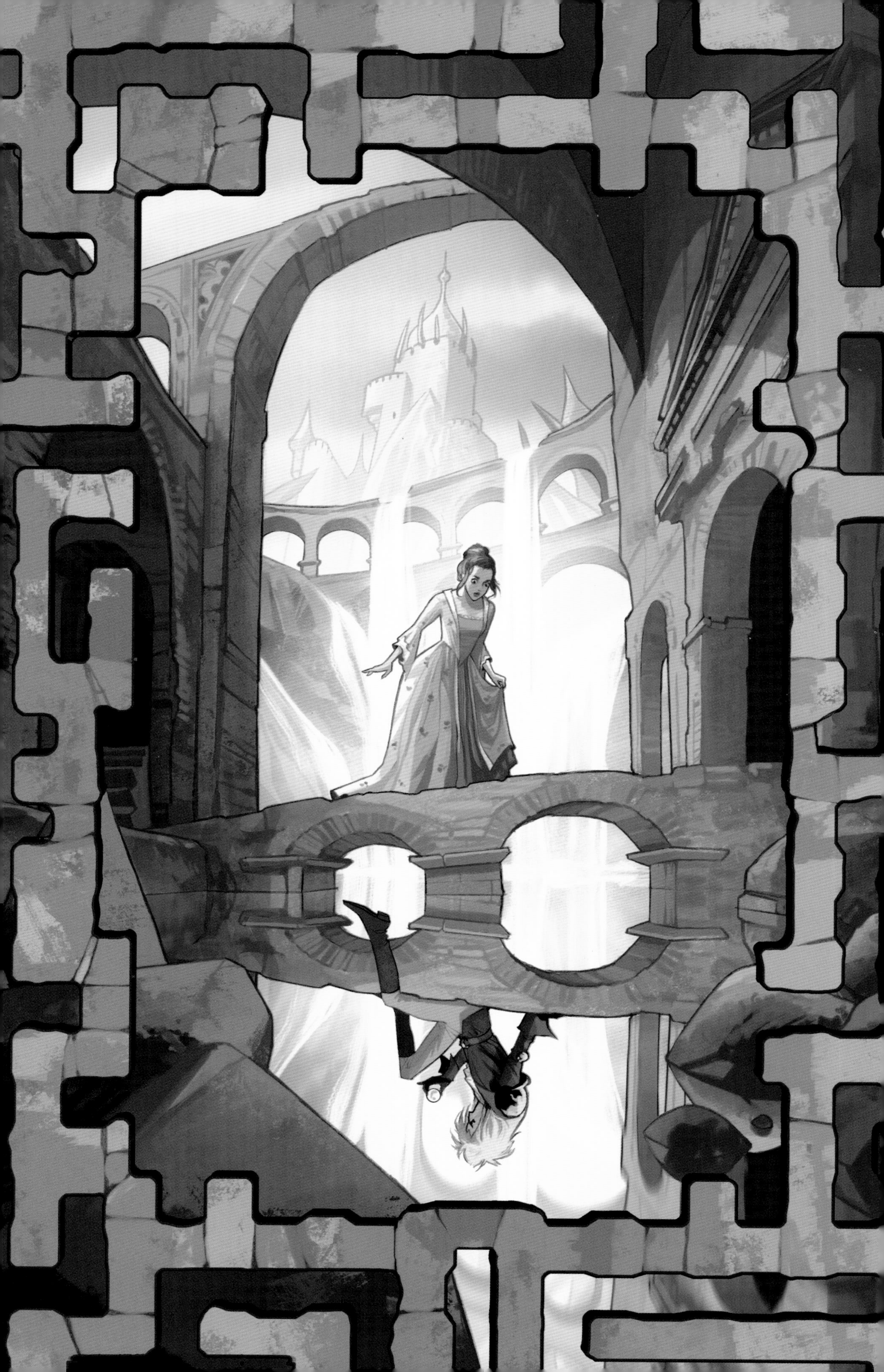

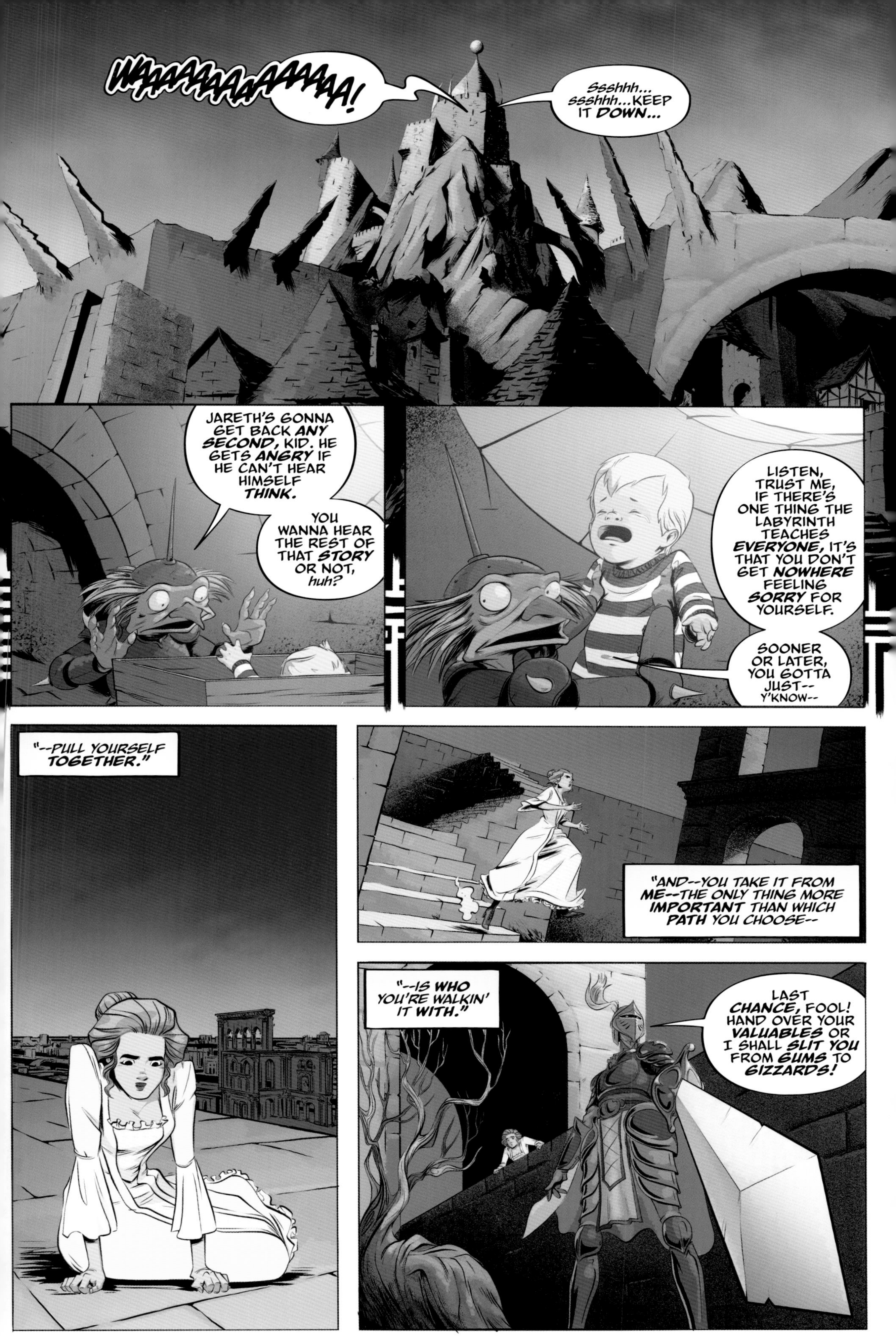
WAAAAAAAAAAAAAA!
Ssshhh... ssshhh...KEEP IT DOWN...
JARETH'S GONNA GET BACK ANY SECOND, KID. HE GETS ANGRY IF HE CAN'T HEAR HIMSELF THINK.
YOU WANNA HEAR THE REST OF THAT STORY OR NOT, huh?
LISTEN, TRUST ME, IF THERE'S ONE THING THE LABYRINTH TEACHES EVERYONE, IT'S THAT YOU DON'T GET NOWHERE FEELING SORRY FOR YOURSELF.
SOONER OR LATER, YOU GOTTA JUST-- Y'KNOW--
"--PULL YOURSELF TOGETHER."
"AND--YOU TAKE IT FROM ME--THE ONLY THING MORE IMPORTANT THAN WHICH PATH YOU CHOOSE--
"--IS WHO YOU'RE WALKIN' IT WITH."
LAST CHANCE, FOOL! HAND OVER YOUR VALUABLES OR I SHALL SLIT YOU FROM GUMS TO GIZZARDS!

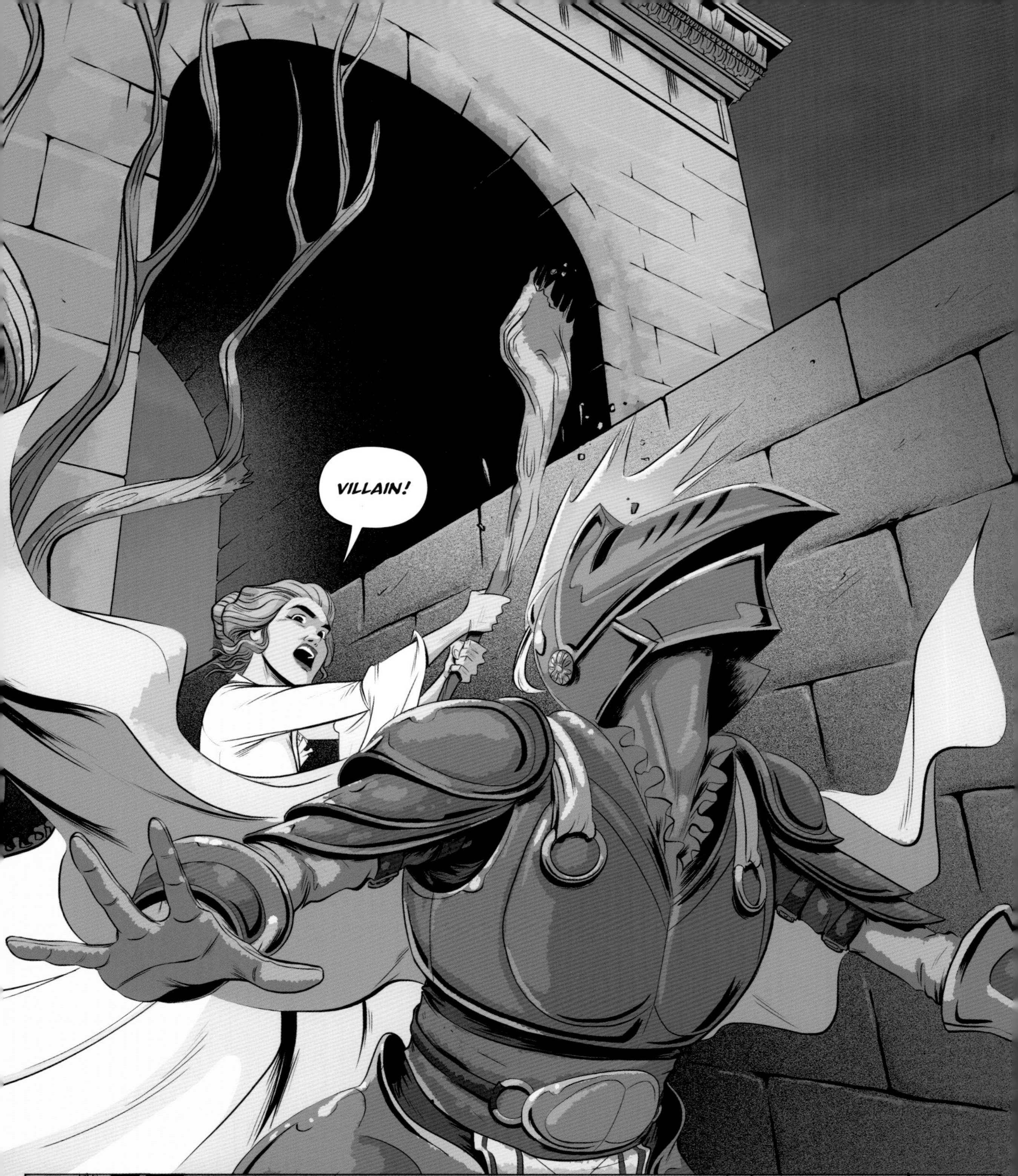
VILLAIN!

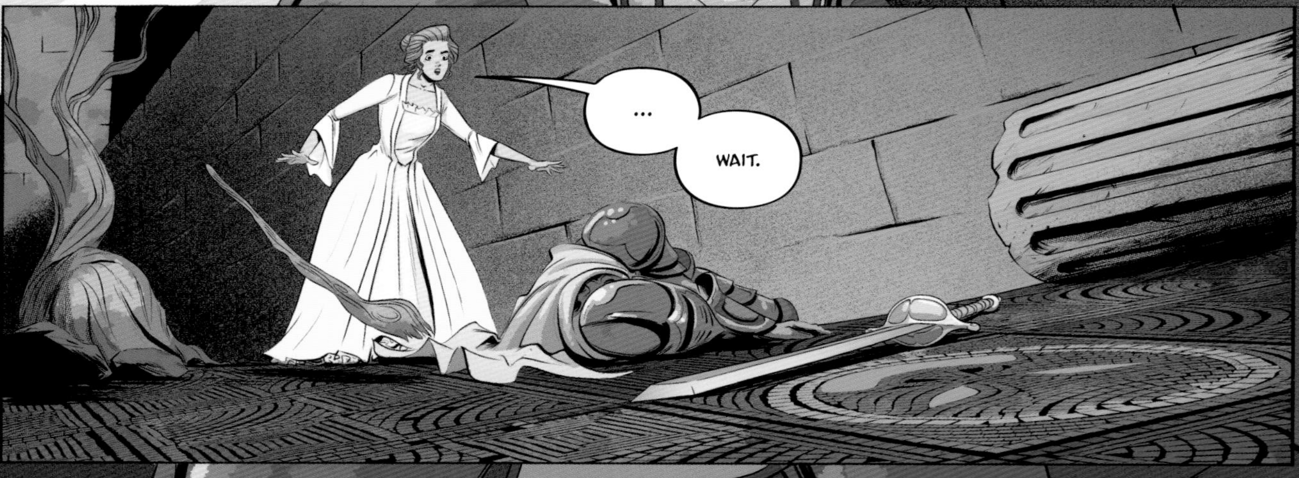
...
WAIT.

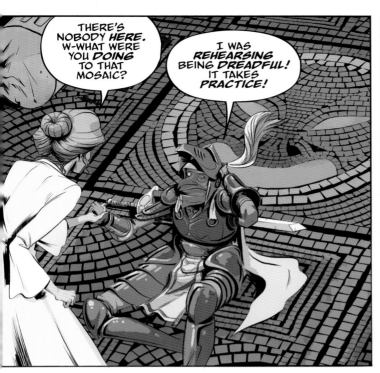

THERE'S NOBODY *HERE.* W-WHAT WERE YOU *DOING* TO THAT MOSAIC?

I WAS *REHEARSING* BEING *DREADFUL!* IT TAKES *PRACTICE!*

THAT *REALLY* HURT!

I'M *SORRY!* I CAN GET A BIT-- *CARRIED AWAY--* BUT--

--THEN, MADAM, *I TOO* SHALL GET *CARRIED AWAY*--WITH MY *SWORD* OF *TERROR,* AND, AND, uhm...

"OH, FOR PITY'S SAKE--*COME ON!* YOU THINK YOU'RE THE *FIRST* TO BE OVERWHELMED?"

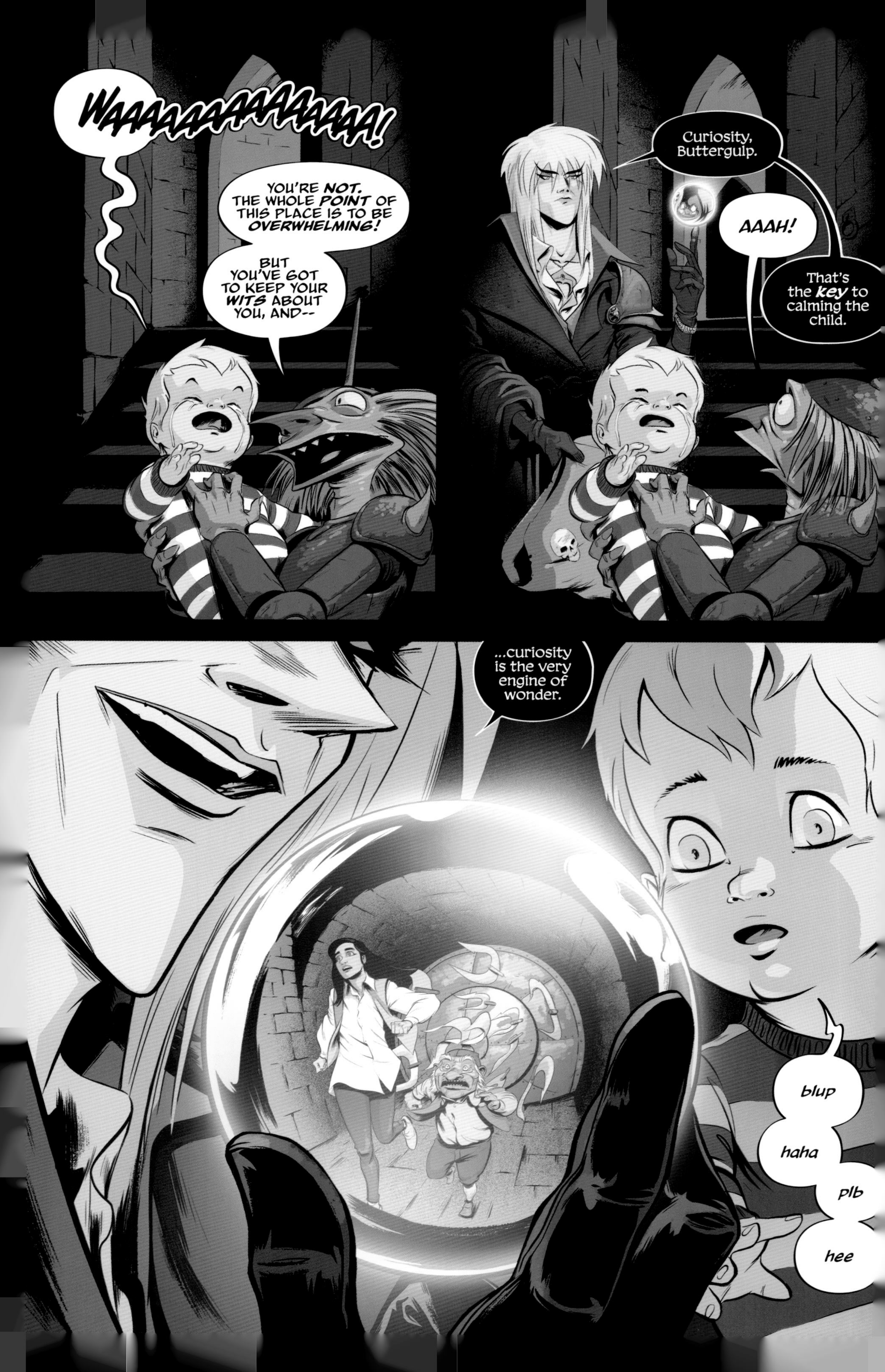
WAAAAAAAAAAAAAA!
YOU'RE NOT. THE WHOLE POINT OF THIS PLACE IS TO BE OVERWHELMING!
BUT YOU'VE GOT TO KEEP YOUR WITS ABOUT YOU, AND--
Curiosity, Buttergulp.
AAAH!
That's the key to calming the child.
...curiosity is the very engine of wonder.
blup
haha
plb
hee

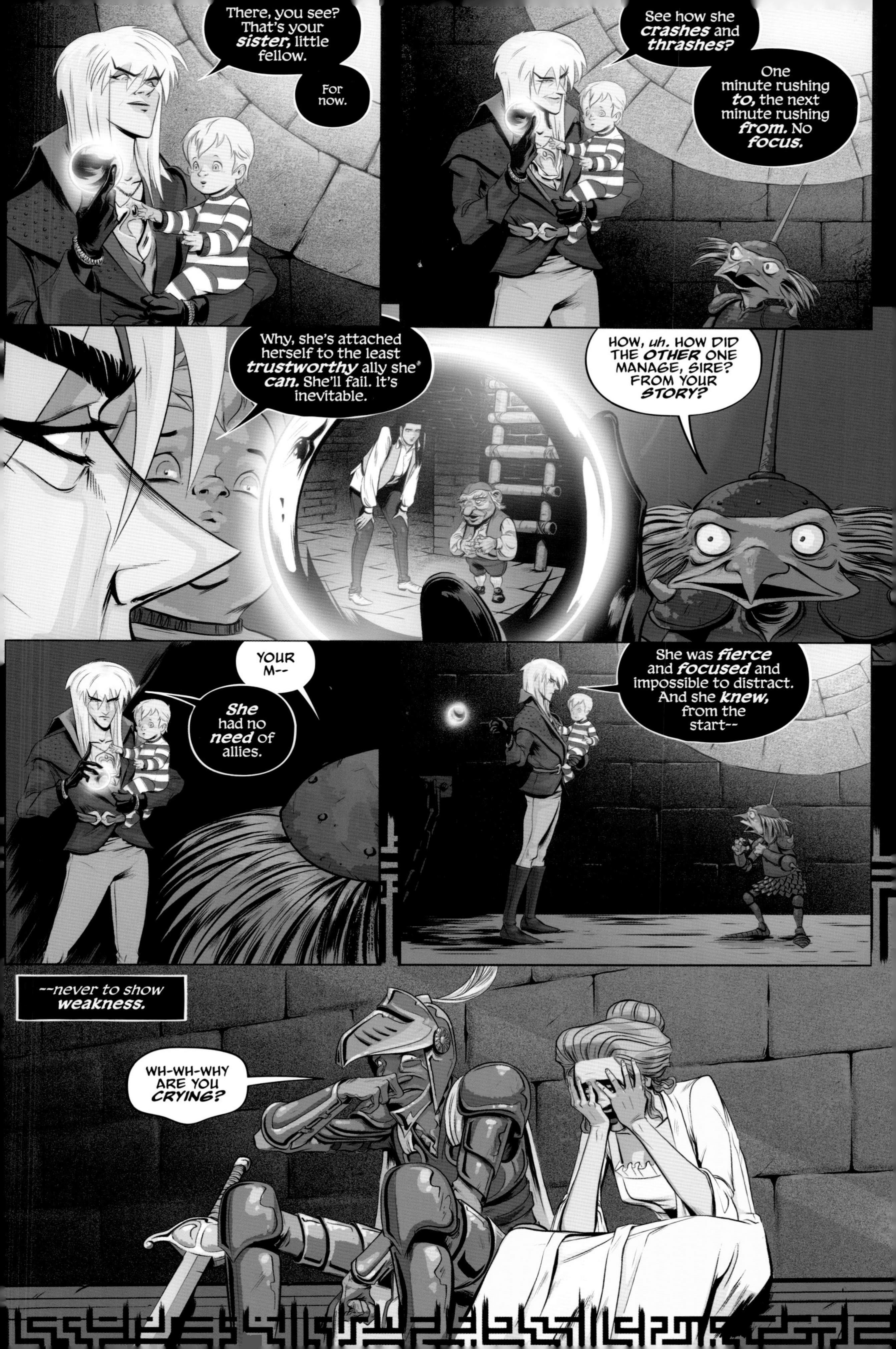
There, you see? That's your sister, little fellow.
For now.
See how she crashes and thrashes?
One minute rushing to, the next minute rushing from. No focus.
Why, she's attached herself to the least trustworthy ally she can. She'll fail. It's inevitable.
HOW, uh. HOW DID THE OTHER ONE MANAGE, SIRE? FROM YOUR STORY?
YOUR M--
She had no need of allies.
She was fierce and focused and impossible to distract. And she knew, from the start--
--never to show weakness.
WH-WH-WHY ARE YOU CRYING?

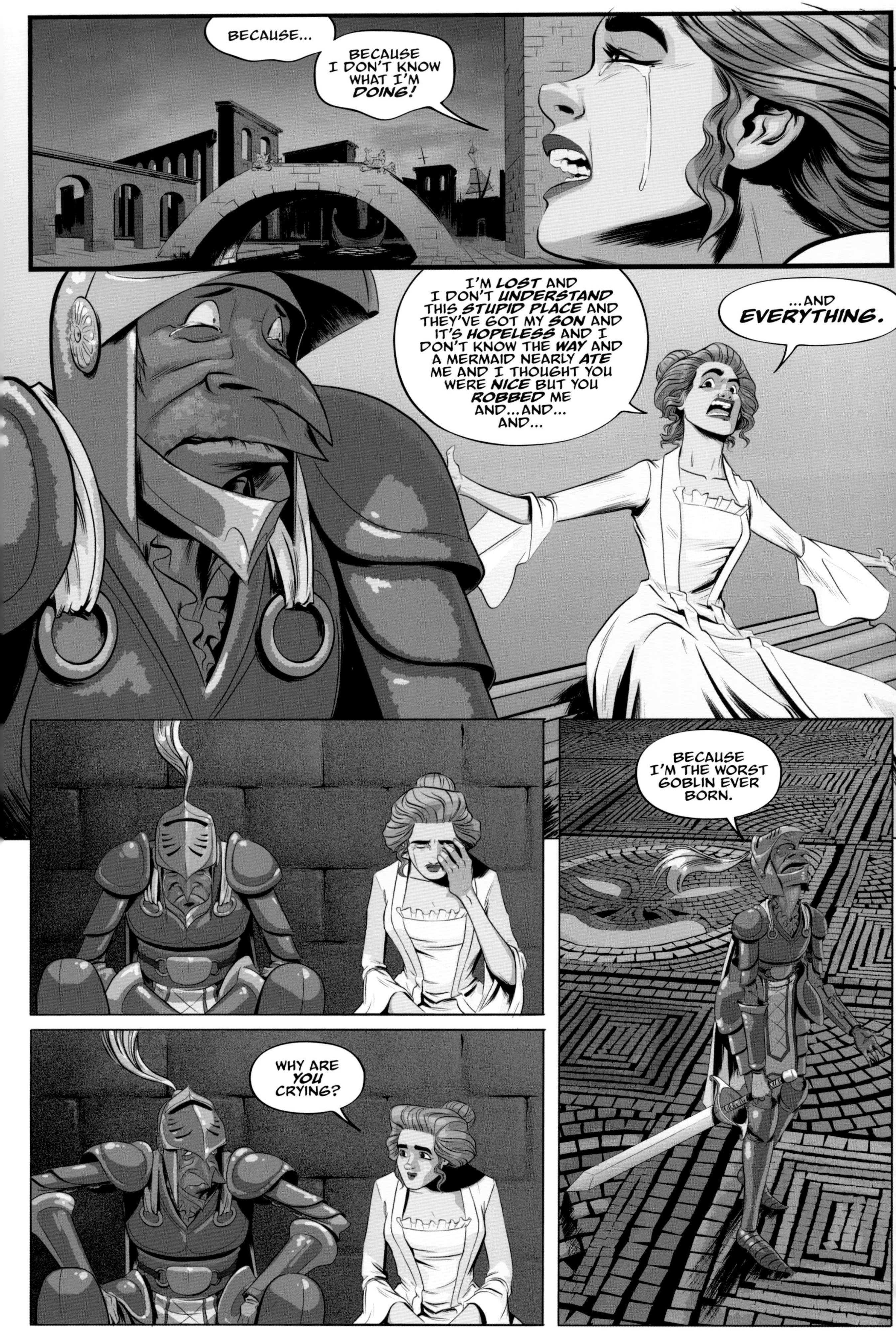
BECAUSE...
BECAUSE I DON'T KNOW WHAT I'M DOING!
I'M LOST AND I DON'T UNDERSTAND THIS STUPID PLACE AND THEY'VE GOT MY SON AND IT'S HOPELESS AND I DON'T KNOW THE WAY AND A MERMAID NEARLY ATE ME AND I THOUGHT YOU WERE NICE BUT YOU ROBBED ME AND...AND... AND...
...AND EVERYTHING.
BECAUSE I'M THE WORST GOBLIN EVER BORN.
WHY ARE YOU CRYING?

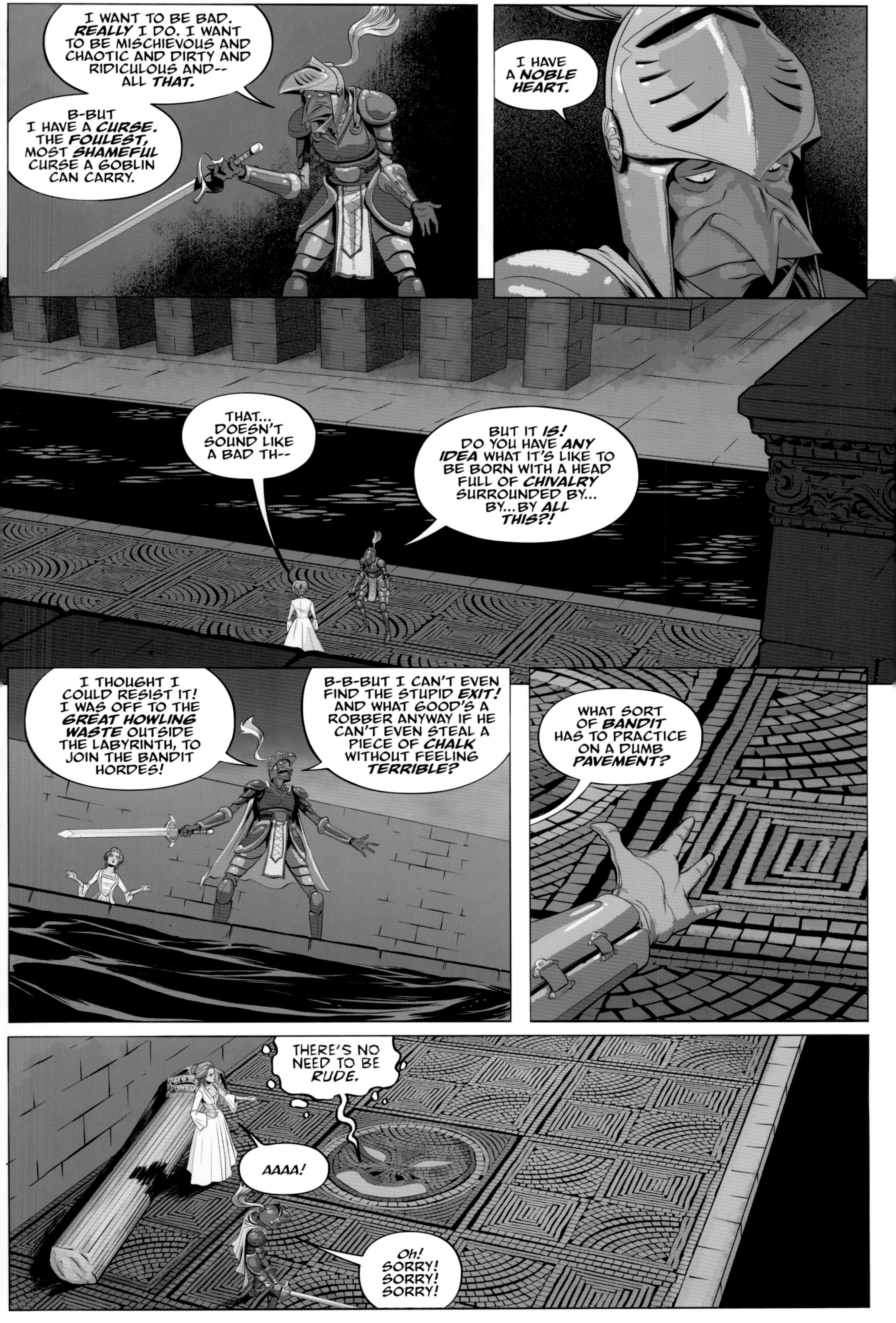
I WANT TO BE BAD. REALLY I DO. I WANT TO BE MISCHIEVOUS AND CHAOTIC AND DIRTY AND RIDICULOUS AND-- ALL THAT.
B-BUT I HAVE A CURSE. THE FOULEST, MOST SHAMEFUL CURSE A GOBLIN CAN CARRY.
I HAVE A NOBLE HEART.
THAT... DOESN'T SOUND LIKE A BAD TH--
BUT IT IS! DO YOU HAVE ANY IDEA WHAT IT'S LIKE TO BE BORN WITH A HEAD FULL OF CHIVALRY SURROUNDED BY... BY...BY ALL THIS?!
I THOUGHT I COULD RESIST IT! I WAS OFF TO THE GREAT HOWLING WASTE OUTSIDE THE LABYRINTH, TO JOIN THE BANDIT HORDES!
B-B-BUT I CAN'T EVEN FIND THE STUPID EXIT! AND WHAT GOOD'S A ROBBER ANYWAY IF HE CAN'T EVEN STEAL A PIECE OF CHALK WITHOUT FEELING TERRIBLE?
WHAT SORT OF BANDIT HAS TO PRACTICE ON A DUMB PAVEMENT?
THERE'S NO NEED TO BE RUDE.
AAAA!
Oh! SORRY! SORRY! SORRY!

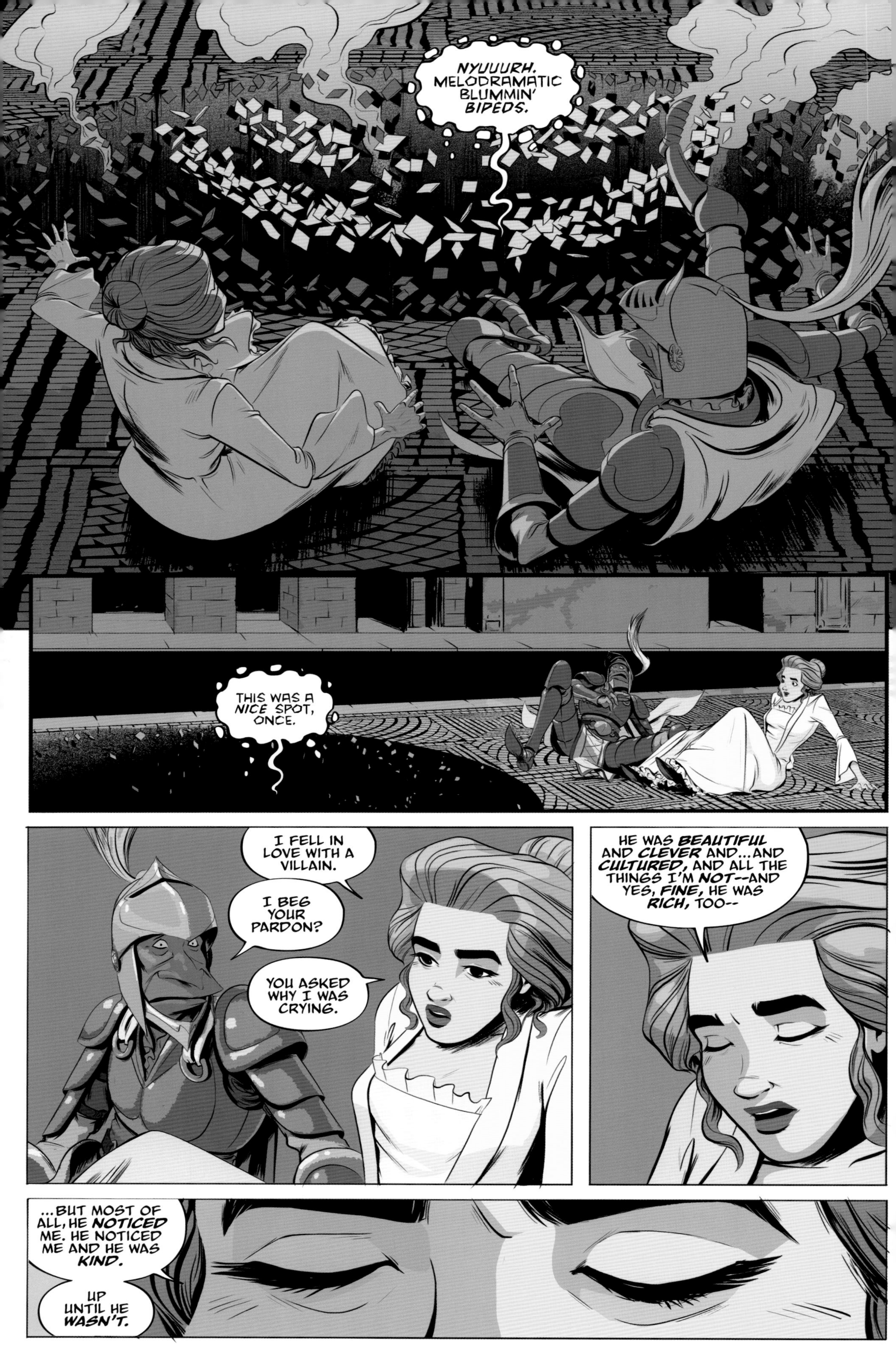
NYUUURH. MELODRAMATIC BLUMMIN' BIPEDS.
THIS WAS A NICE SPOT, ONCE.
I FELL IN LOVE WITH A VILLAIN.
I BEG YOUR PARDON?
YOU ASKED WHY I WAS CRYING.
HE WAS BEAUTIFUL AND CLEVER AND...AND CULTURED, AND ALL THE THINGS I'M NOT--AND YES, FINE, HE WAS RICH, TOO--
...BUT MOST OF ALL, HE NOTICED ME. HE NOTICED ME AND HE WAS KIND.
UP UNTIL HE WASN'T.

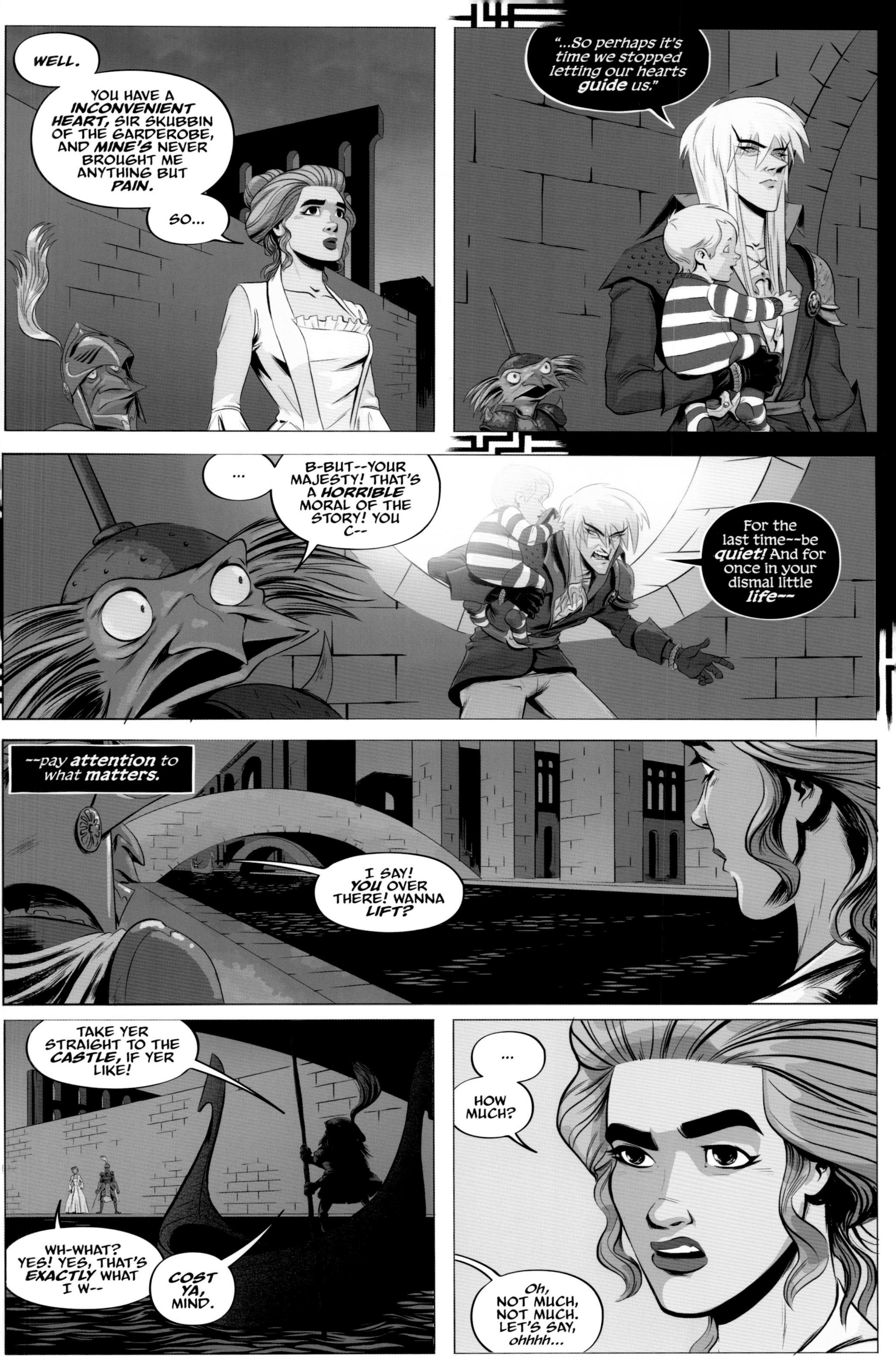
WELL.
YOU HAVE A INCONVENIENT HEART, SIR SKUBBIN OF THE GARDEROBE, AND MINE'S NEVER BROUGHT ME ANYTHING BUT PAIN.
SO...
"...So perhaps it's time we stopped letting our hearts guide us."
...
B-BUT--YOUR MAJESTY! THAT'S A HORRIBLE MORAL OF THE STORY! YOU C--
For the last time--be quiet! And for once in your dismal little life--
--pay attention to what matters.
I SAY! YOU OVER THERE! WANNA LIFT?
TAKE YER STRAIGHT TO THE CASTLE, IF YER LIKE!
WH-WHAT? YES! YES, THAT'S EXACTLY WHAT I W--
COST YA, MIND.
...
HOW MUCH?
Oh, NOT MUCH, NOT MUCH. LET'S SAY, ohhhh...

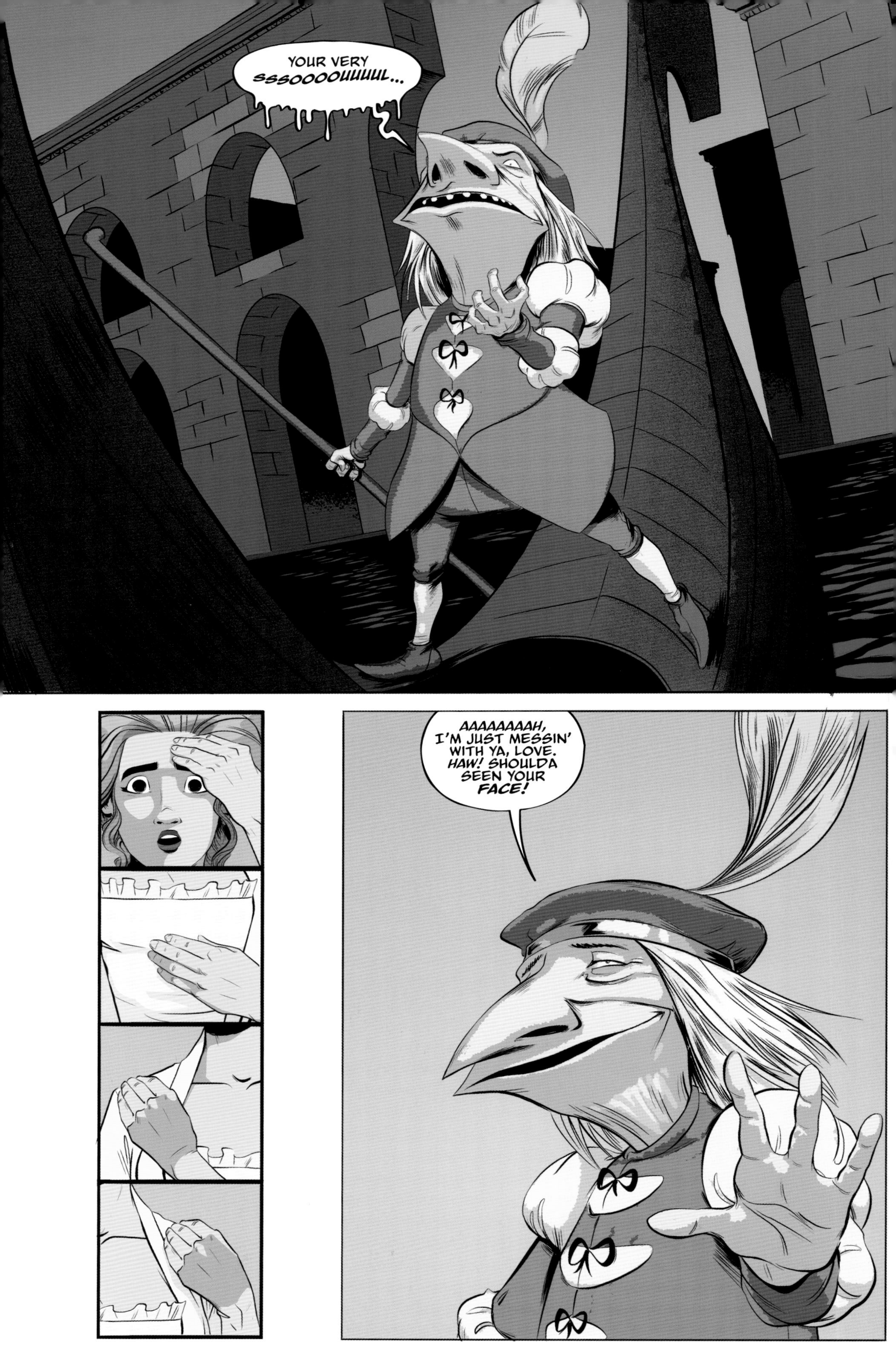
YOUR VERY SSSOOOOUUUUL...
AAAAAAAAH, I'M JUST MESSIN' WITH YA, LOVE. HAW! SHOULDA SEEN YOUR FACE!

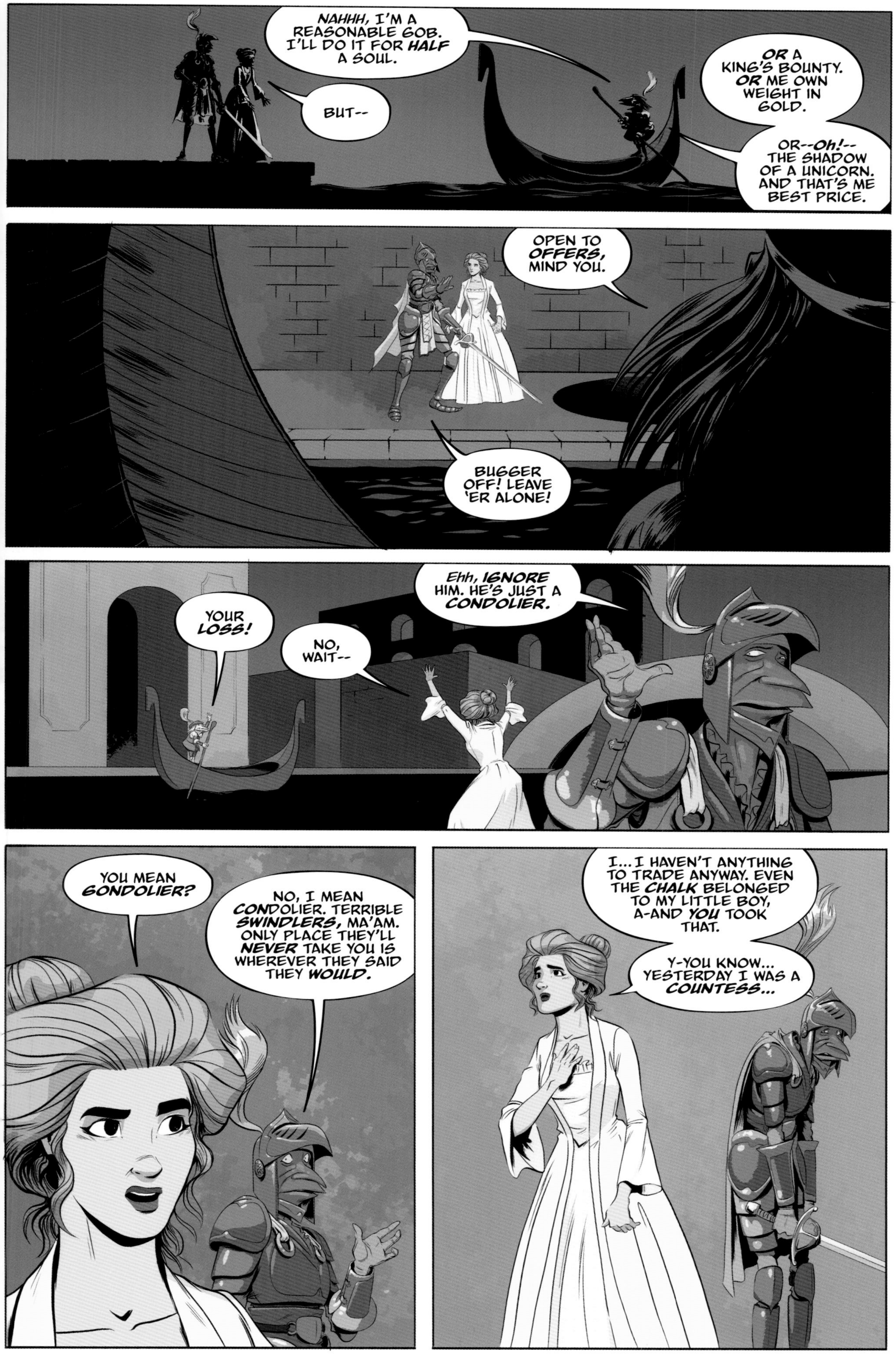
NAHHH, I'M A REASONABLE GOB. I'LL DO IT FOR HALF A SOUL.
BUT--
OR A KING'S BOUNTY. OR ME OWN WEIGHT IN GOLD.
OR--Oh!-- THE SHADOW OF A UNICORN. AND THAT'S ME BEST PRICE.
OPEN TO OFFERS, MIND YOU.
BUGGER OFF! LEAVE 'ER ALONE!
Ehh, IGNORE HIM. HE'S JUST A CONDOLIER.
YOUR LOSS!
NO, WAIT--
YOU MEAN GONDOLIER?
NO, I MEAN CONDOLIER. TERRIBLE SWINDLERS, MA'AM. ONLY PLACE THEY'LL NEVER TAKE YOU IS WHEREVER THEY SAID THEY WOULD.
I... I HAVEN'T ANYTHING TO TRADE ANYWAY. EVEN THE CHALK BELONGED TO MY LITTLE BOY, A-AND YOU TOOK THAT.
Y-YOU KNOW... YESTERDAY I WAS A COUNTESS...

T-TODAY, I HAVE LITERALLY **NOTHING.**

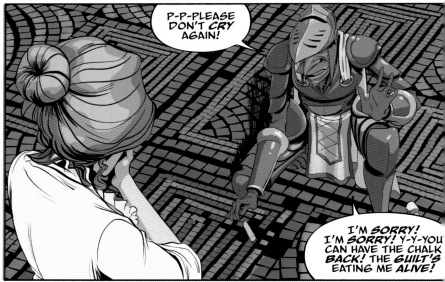

P-P-PLEASE DON'T *CRY* AGAIN!

I'M *SORRY!* I'M *SORRY!* Y-Y-YOU CAN HAVE THE CHALK *BACK!* THE GUILT'S EATING ME *ALIVE!*

GRRRRRRr I AM THE *WORST* VILLAIN *THE WORST* AND EVEN IF I *DID* KNOW THE STUPID WAY *OUT,* THE BANDIT HORDES WOULD JUST *LAUGH* AT ME *oh ohhhh...*

SKUBBIN.

KEEP IT. I-IT'S JUST *CHALK.* IT ONLY *SEEMS* IMPORTANT BECAUSE...IT WAS *HIS.*

BUT WE NEED TO THINK WITH OUR *HEADS* INSTEAD OF OUR *HEARTS*-- REMEMBER?

FLNK

I HAVE AN *IDEA.*

YOU'RE QUITE, *uhm--SHINY,* AREN'T YOU? I BET YOU HAVE SOME *VALUABLE* THINGS?

S-SO...?

SO YOU COULD JUST... *GIVE ME* SOMETHING...

B-BUT...BUT WOULDN'T THAT MEAN I'D REALLY JUST *BOUGHT* THIS CHALK?

BOUGHT? *Oh HEAVENS* NO! YOU *STOLE* THAT FAIR AND SQUARE. THAT'S LEGITIMATE *BANDITRY LOOT,* THAT IS.

NO, WHAT I'M SUGGESTING'S MORE LIKE A--A *GIFT.* A TOKEN OF *ESTEEM.*

YOU'RE STILL A FEARSOME ROBBER AND *I'M* STILL YOUR *VICTIM*--BUT WE'D PART AS *FRIENDS.* YOU WOULDN'T NEED TO FEEL *GUILTY.*

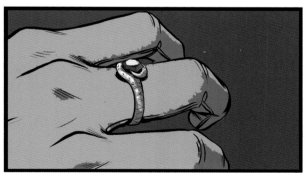

A-AFTER ALL, I WON'T NEED IT. NOT WHERE I'M GOING.

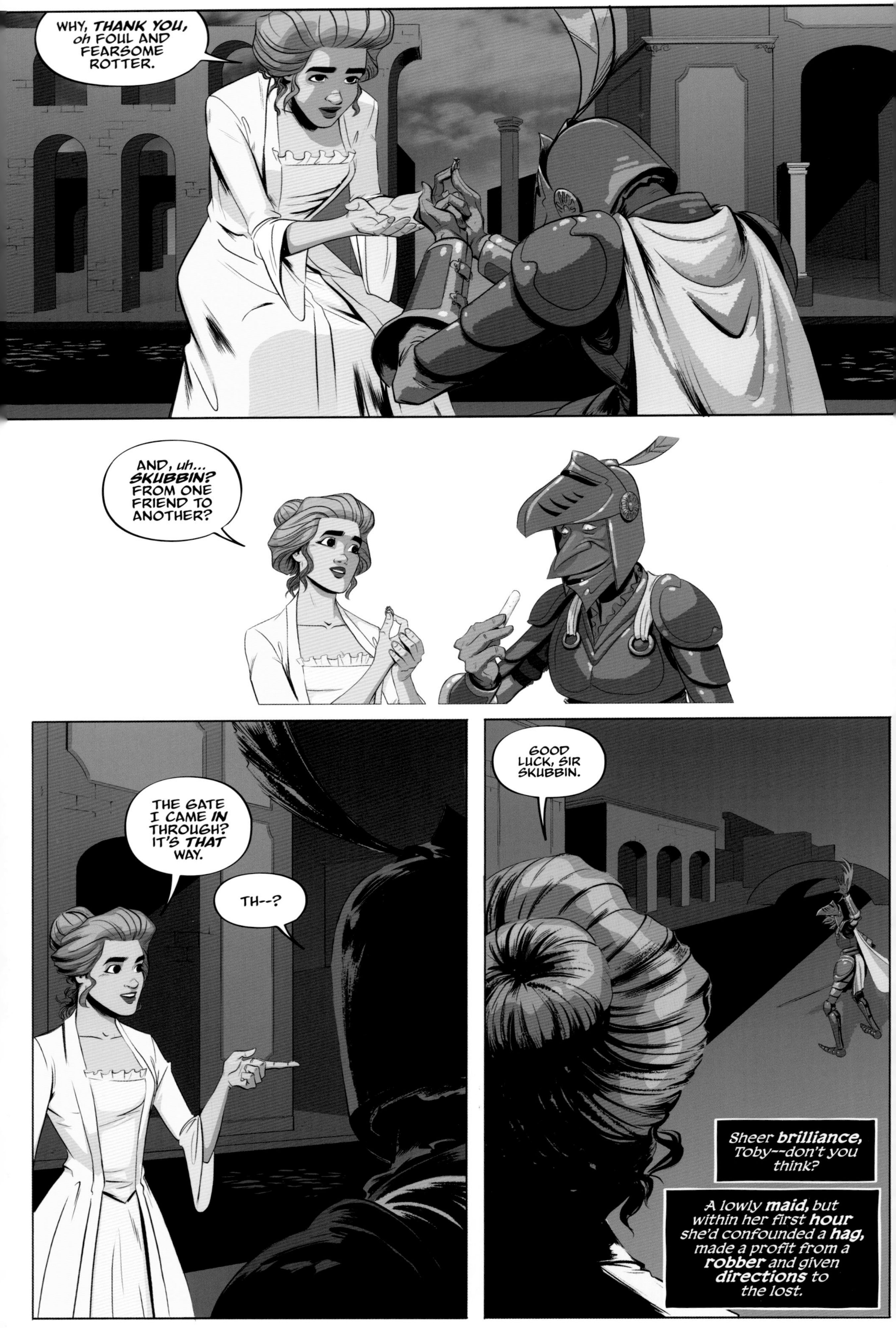
WHY, THANK YOU, oh FOUL AND FEARSOME ROTTER.
AND, uh... SKUBBIN? FROM ONE FRIEND TO ANOTHER?
THE GATE I CAME IN THROUGH? IT'S THAT WAY.
TH--?
GOOD LUCK, SIR SKUBBIN.
Sheer brilliance, Toby--don't you think?
A lowly maid, but within her first hour she'd confounded a hag, made a profit from a robber and given directions to the lost.

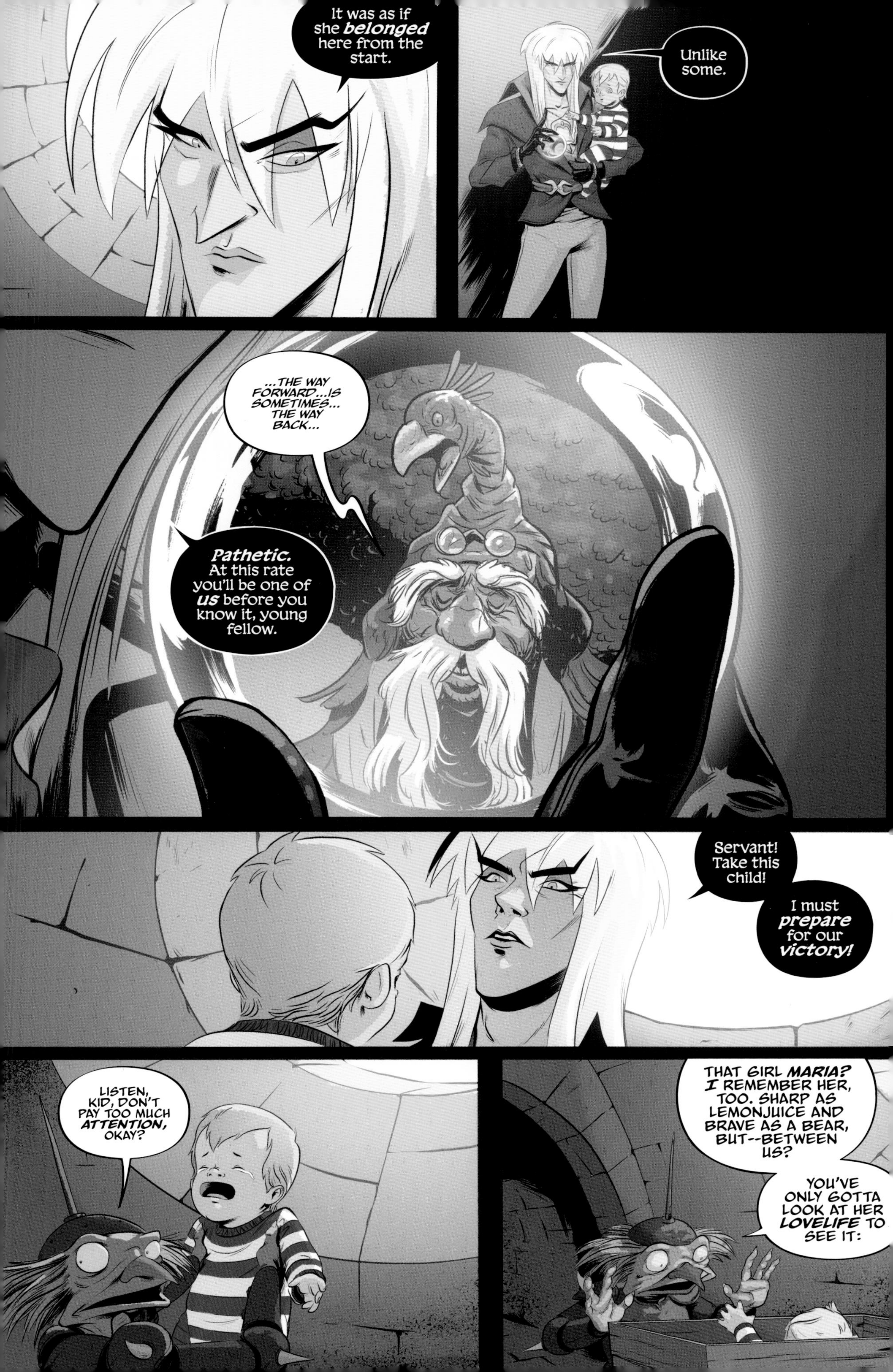
It was as if she ***belonged*** here from the start.
Unlike some.
...THE WAY FORWARD...IS SOMETIMES... THE WAY BACK...
Pathetic. At this rate you'll be one of ***us*** before you know it, young fellow.
Servant! Take this child!
I must ***prepare*** for our ***victory!***
LISTEN, KID, DON'T PAY TOO MUCH ***ATTENTION,*** OKAY?
THAT GIRL ***MARIA? I*** REMEMBER HER, TOO. SHARP AS LEMONJUICE AND BRAVE AS A BEAR, BUT--BETWEEN US?
YOU'VE ONLY GOTTA LOOK AT HER ***LOVELIFE*** TO SEE IT:

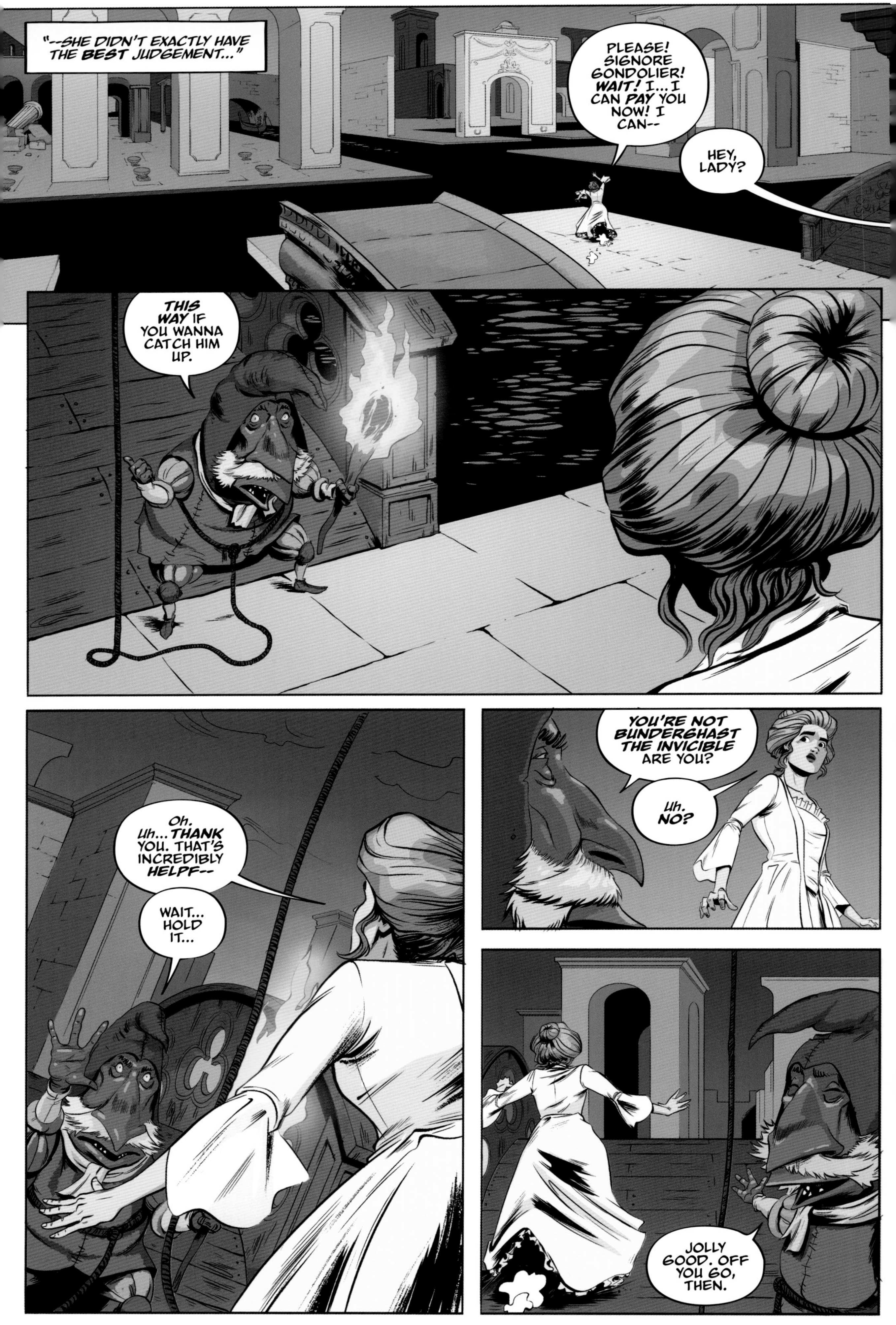
"--SHE DIDN'T EXACTLY HAVE THE BEST JUDGEMENT..."
PLEASE! SIGNORE GONDOLIER! WAIT! I... I CAN PAY YOU NOW! I CAN--
HEY, LADY?
THIS WAY IF YOU WANNA CATCH HIM UP.
Oh. Uh... THANK YOU. THAT'S INCREDIBLY HELPF--
WAIT... HOLD IT...
YOU'RE NOT BUNDERGHAST THE INVICIBLE ARE YOU?
Uh. NO?
JOLLY GOOD. OFF YOU GO, THEN.

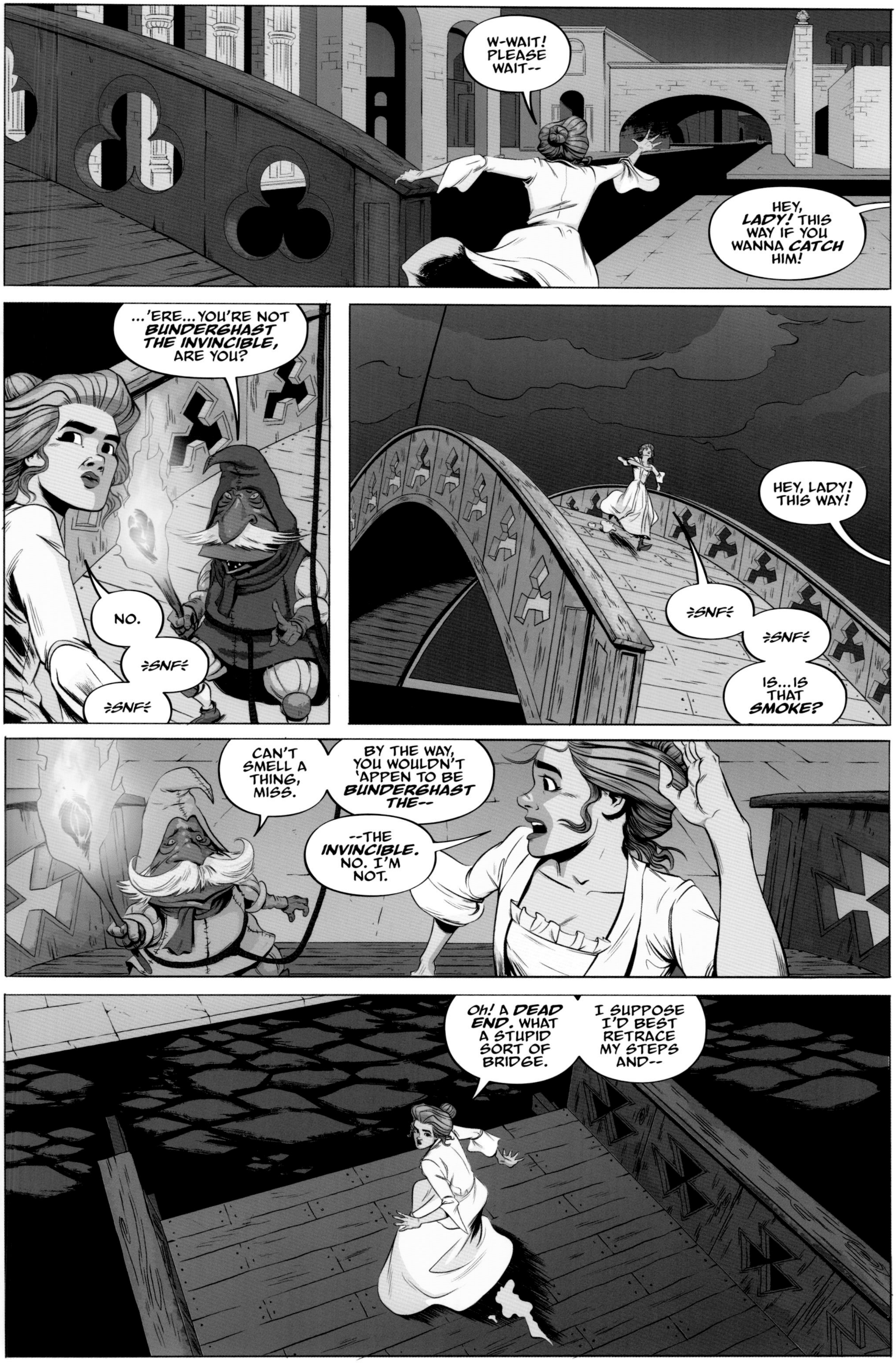
W-WAIT! PLEASE WAIT--
HEY, LADY! THIS WAY IF YOU WANNA CATCH HIM!
...'ERE...YOU'RE NOT BUNDERGHAST THE INVINCIBLE, ARE YOU?
NO.
≈SNF≈
≈SNF≈
HEY, LADY! THIS WAY!
≈SNF≈
≈SNF≈
IS...IS THAT SMOKE?
CAN'T SMELL A THING, MISS.
BY THE WAY, YOU WOULDN'T 'APPEN TO BE BUNDERGHAST THE--
--THE INVINCIBLE. NO. I'M NOT.
Oh! A DEAD END. WHAT A STUPID SORT OF BRIDGE.
I SUPPOSE I'D BEST RETRACE MY STEPS AND--

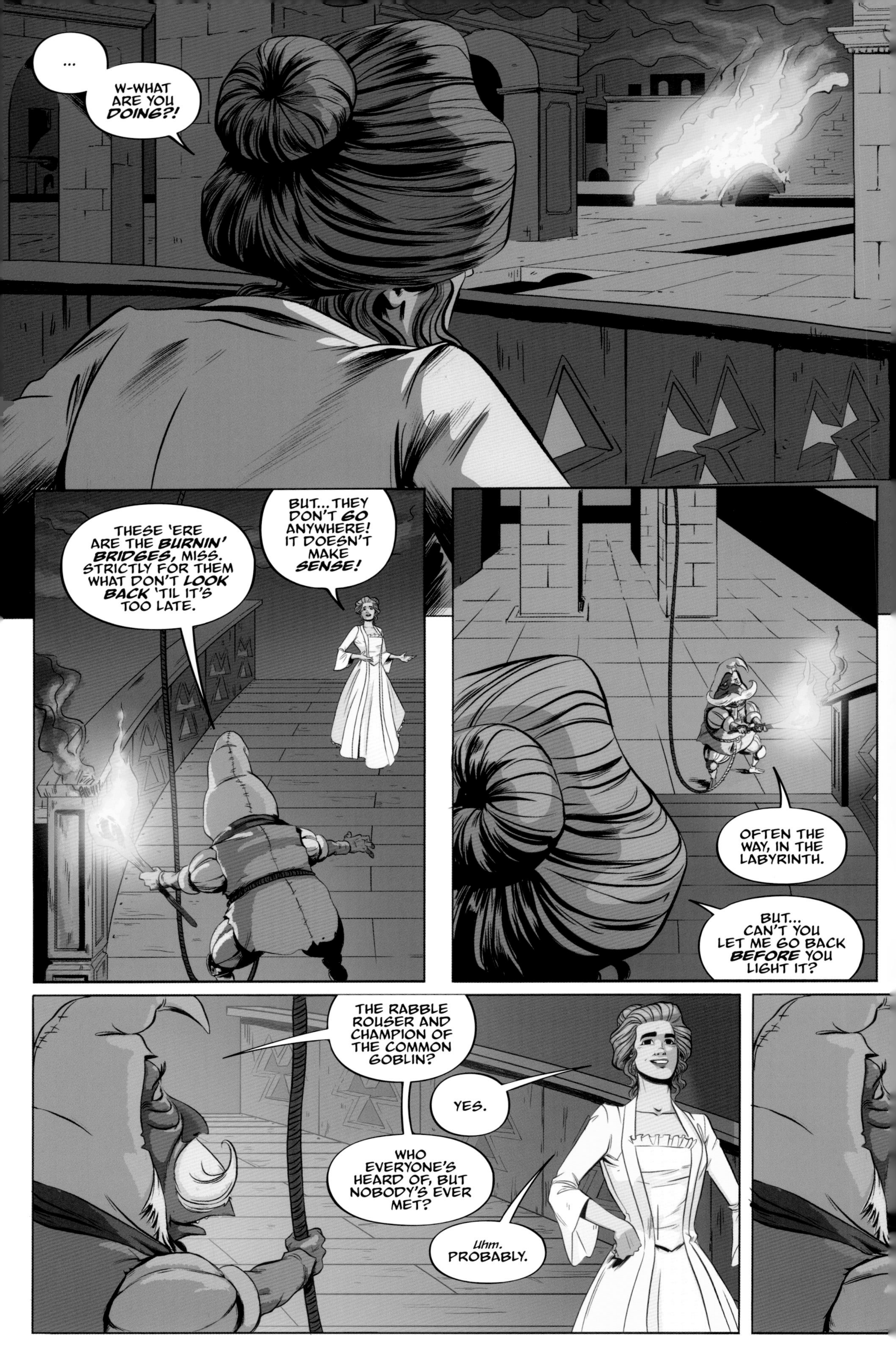
...
W-WHAT ARE YOU *DOING?!*
THESE 'ERE ARE THE *BURNIN' BRIDGES*, MISS. STRICTLY FOR THEM WHAT DON'T *LOOK BACK* 'TIL IT'S TOO LATE.
BUT... THEY DON'T *GO* ANYWHERE! IT DOESN'T MAKE *SENSE!*
OFTEN THE WAY, IN THE LABYRINTH.
BUT... CAN'T YOU LET ME GO BACK *BEFORE* YOU LIGHT IT?
THE RABBLE ROUSER AND CHAMPION OF THE COMMON GOBLIN?
YES.
WHO EVERYONE'S HEARD OF, BUT NOBODY'S EVER MET?
Uhm. PROBABLY.

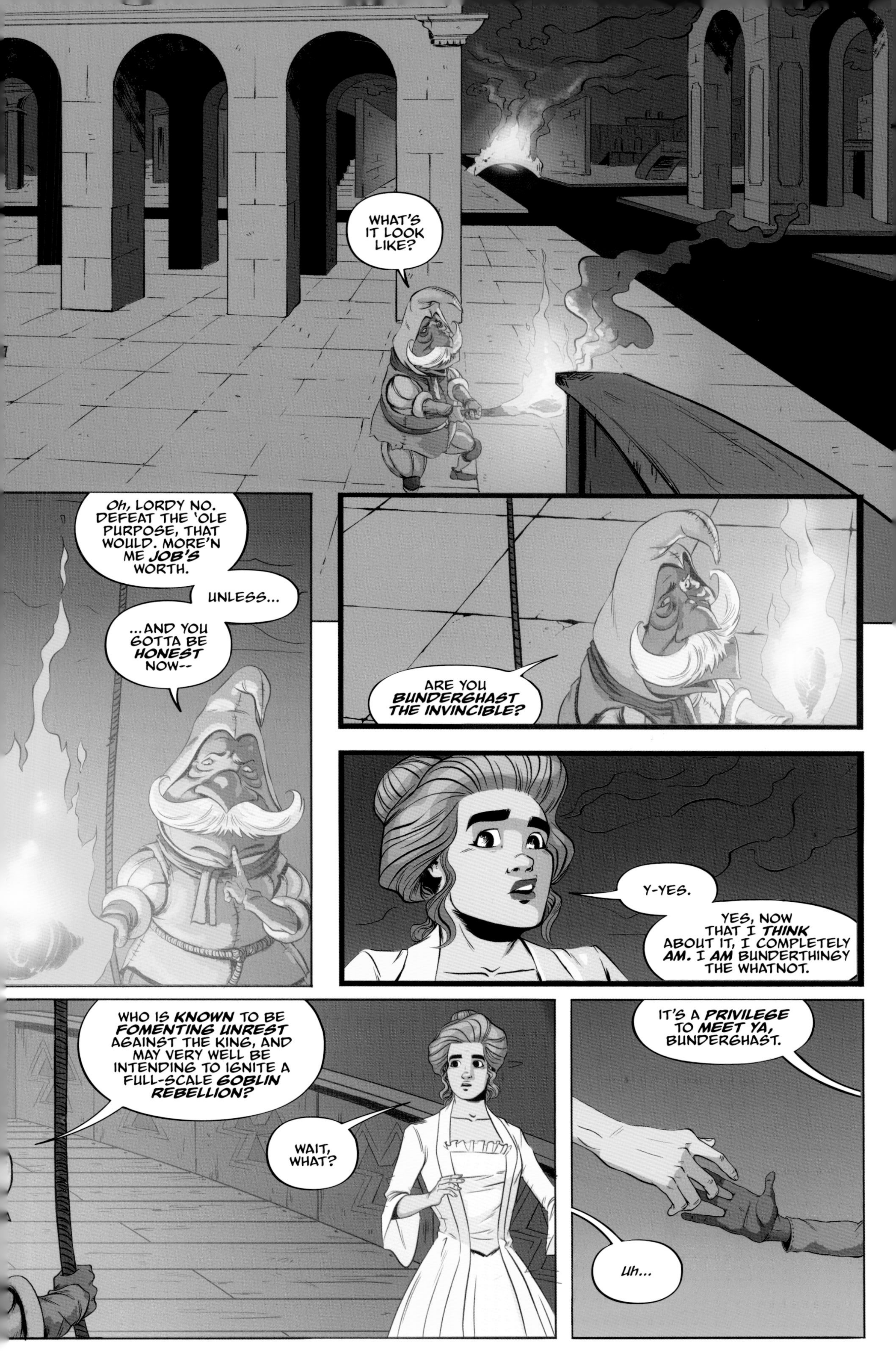
WHAT'S IT LOOK LIKE?
Oh, LORDY NO. DEFEAT THE 'OLE PURPOSE, THAT WOULD. MORE'N ME JOB'S WORTH.
UNLESS...
...AND YOU GOTTA BE HONEST NOW--
ARE YOU BUNDERGHAST THE INVINCIBLE?
Y-YES.
YES, NOW THAT I THINK ABOUT IT, I COMPLETELY AM. I AM BUNDERTHINGY THE WHATNOT.
WHO IS KNOWN TO BE FOMENTING UNREST AGAINST THE KING, AND MAY VERY WELL BE INTENDING TO IGNITE A FULL-SCALE GOBLIN REBELLION?
WAIT, WHAT?
IT'S A PRIVILEGE TO MEET YA, BUNDERGHAST.
Uh...

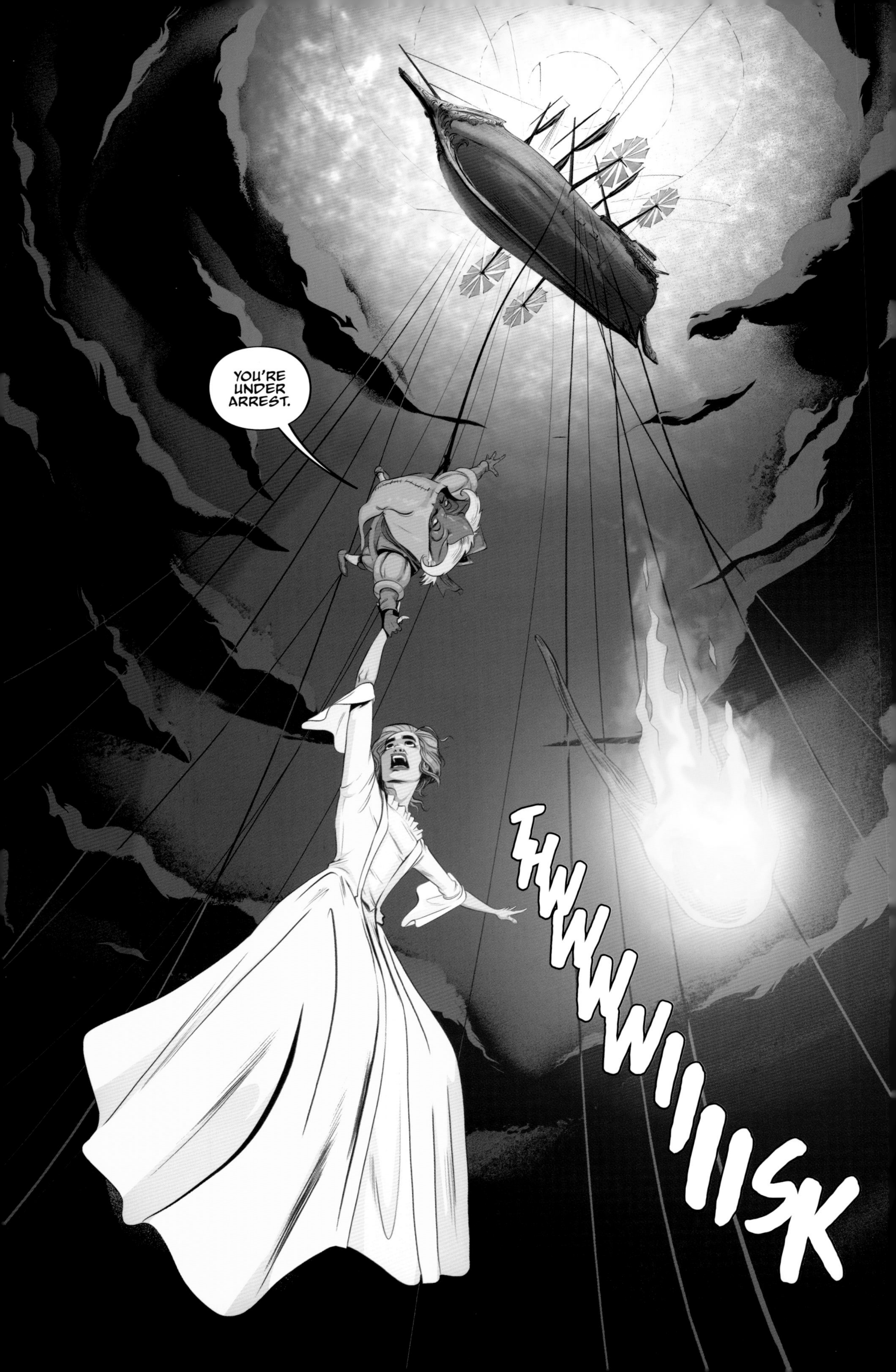
YOU'RE UNDER ARREST.
THWWWIIIISK

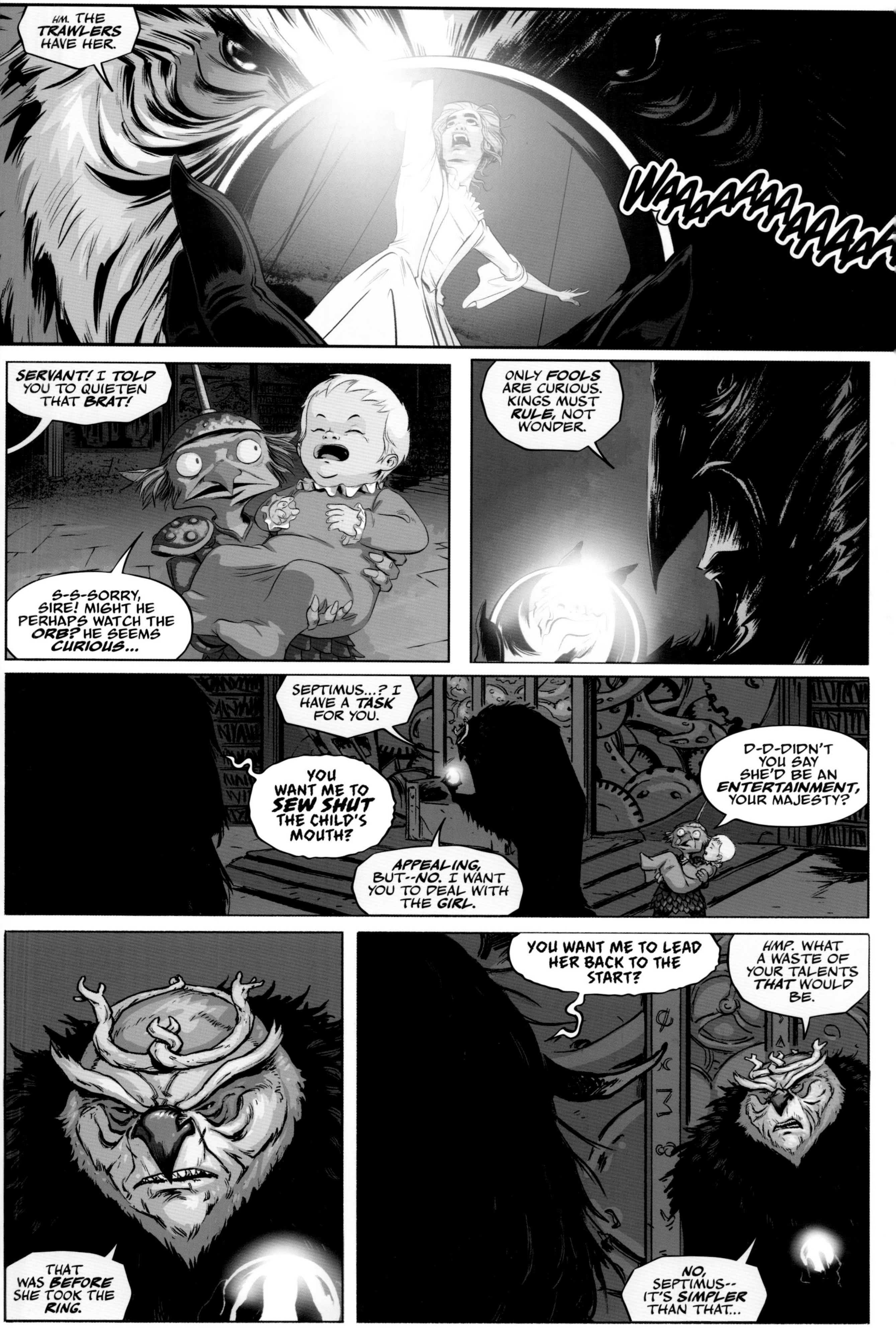
HM. THE TRAWLERS HAVE HER.
WAAAAAAAAAAAA
SERVANT! I TOLD YOU TO QUIETEN THAT BRAT!
S-S-SORRY, SIRE! MIGHT HE PERHAPS WATCH THE ORB? HE SEEMS CURIOUS...
ONLY FOOLS ARE CURIOUS. KINGS MUST RULE, NOT WONDER.
SEPTIMUS...? I HAVE A TASK FOR YOU.
YOU WANT ME TO SEW SHUT THE CHILD'S MOUTH?
APPEALING, BUT--NO. I WANT YOU TO DEAL WITH THE GIRL.
D-D-DIDN'T YOU SAY SHE'D BE AN ENTERTAINMENT, YOUR MAJESTY?
THAT WAS BEFORE SHE TOOK THE RING.
YOU WANT ME TO LEAD HER BACK TO THE START?
HMP. WHAT A WASTE OF YOUR TALENTS THAT WOULD BE.
NO, SEPTIMUS-- IT'S SIMPLER THAN THAT...

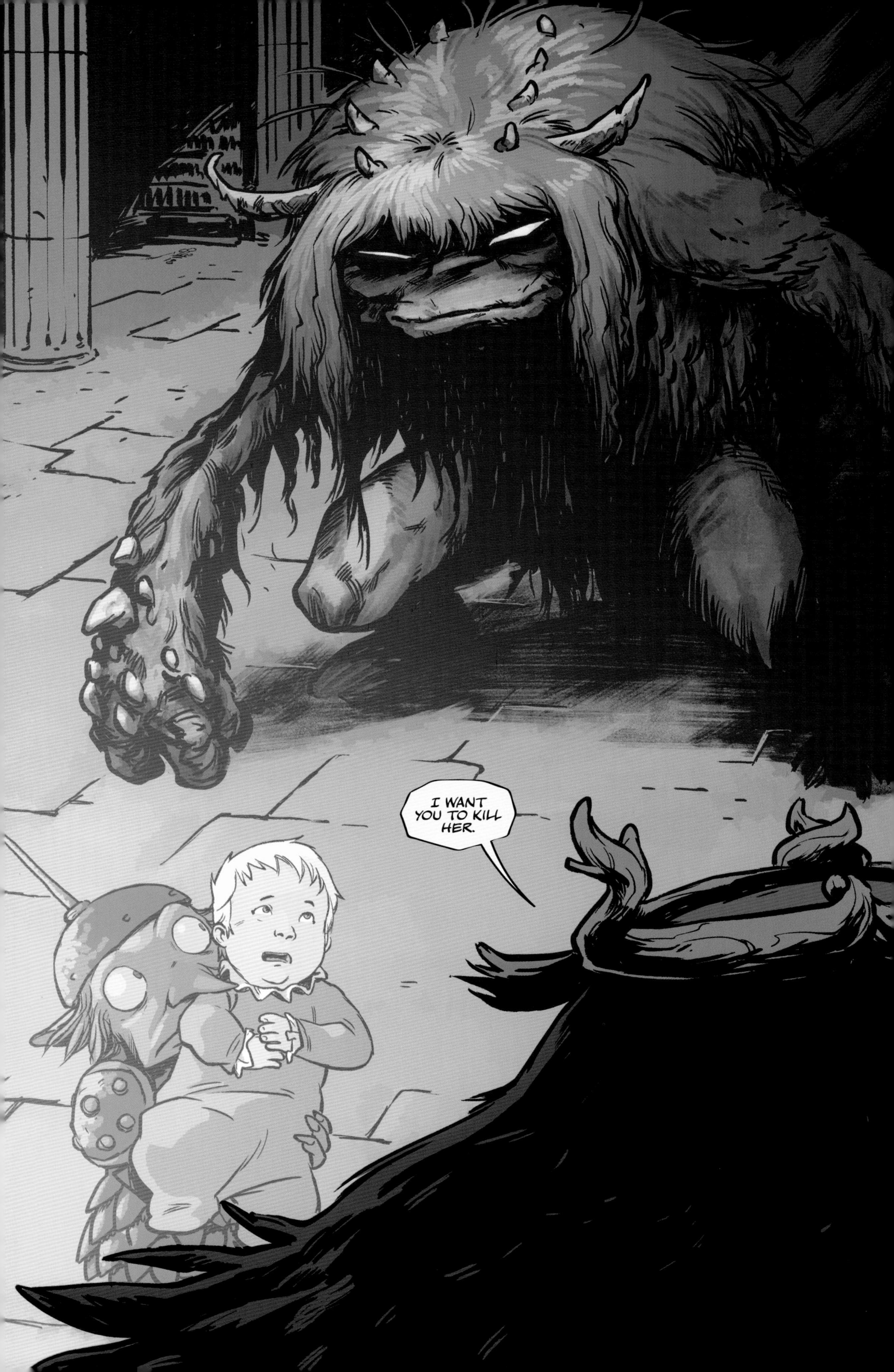
I WANT YOU TO KILL HER.

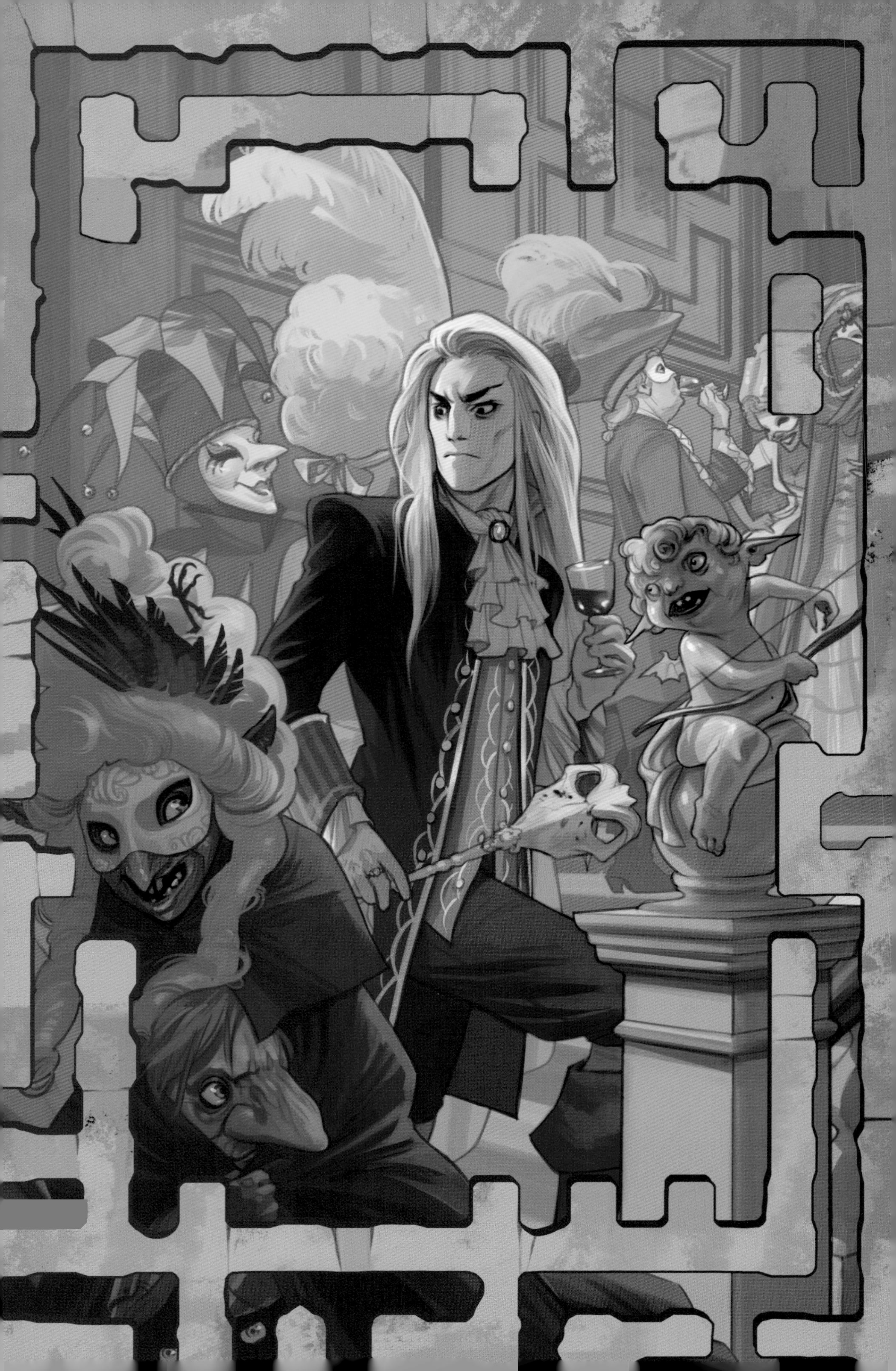

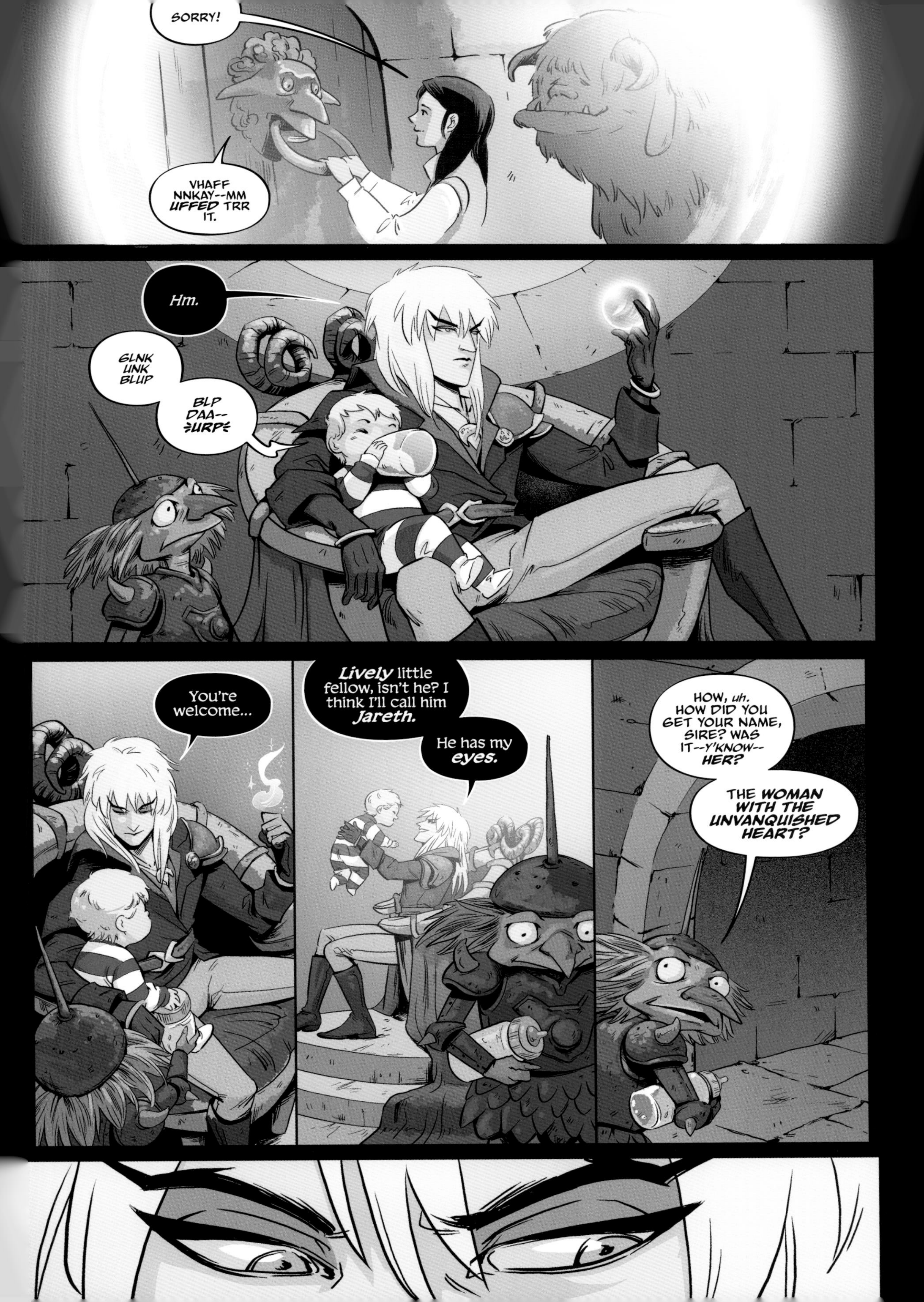
SORRY!
VHAFF NNKAY--MM UFFED TRR IT.
Hm.
GLNK UNK BLUP
BLP DAA-- URP
You're welcome...
Lively little fellow, isn't he? I think I'll call him Jareth.
He has my eyes.
HOW, uh. HOW DID YOU GET YOUR NAME, SIRE? WAS IT--Y'KNOW-- HER?
THE WOMAN WITH THE UNVANQUISHED HEART?

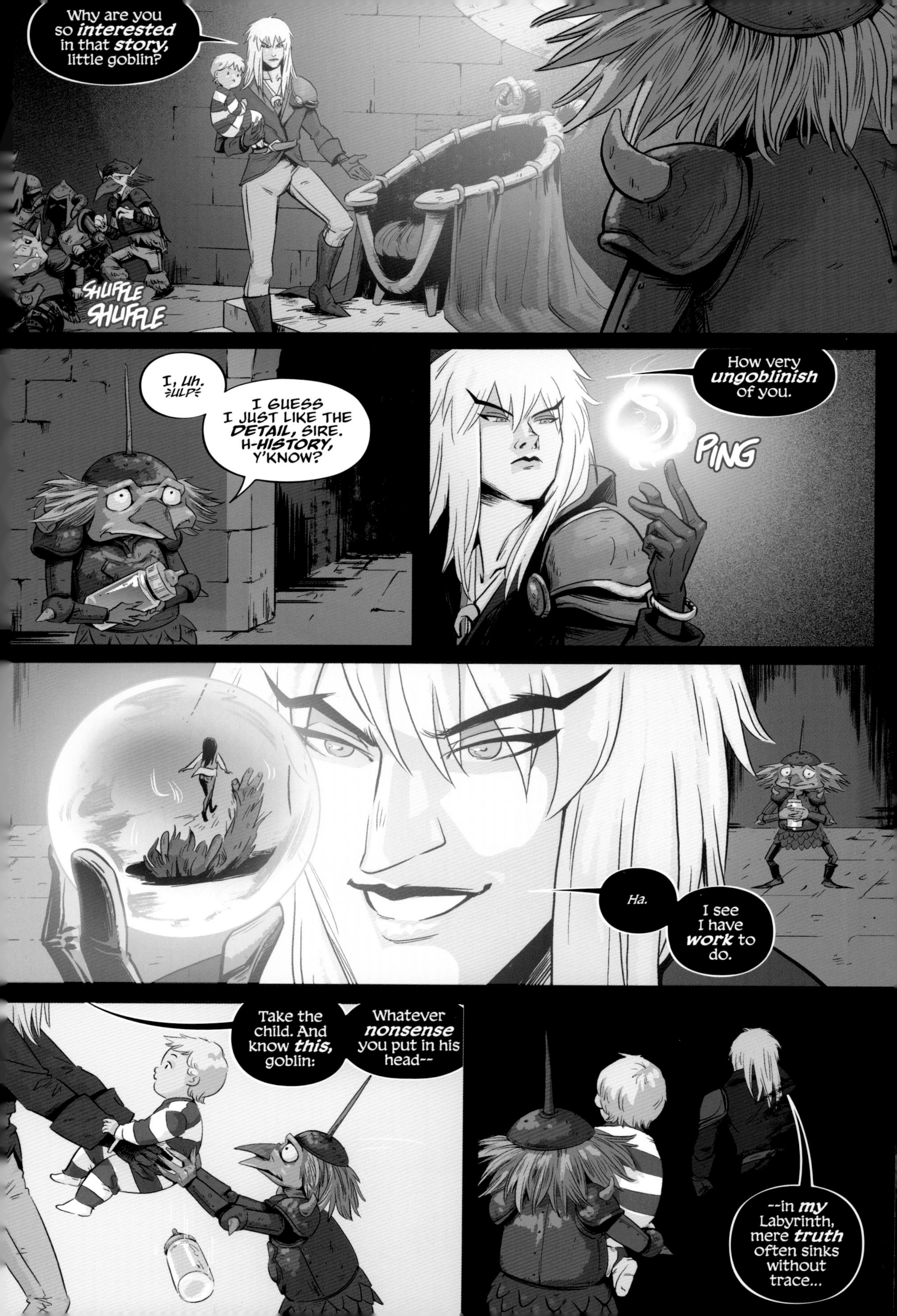
Why are you so *interested* in that *story,* little goblin?
SHUFFLE SHUFFLE
I, uh. ≠ULP≠
I GUESS I JUST LIKE THE *DETAIL,* SIRE. H-*HISTORY,* Y'KNOW?
How very *ungoblinish* of you.
PING
Ha.
I see I have *work* to do.
Take the child. And know *this,* goblin:
Whatever *nonsense* you put in his head--
--in *my* Labyrinth, mere *truth* often sinks without trace...

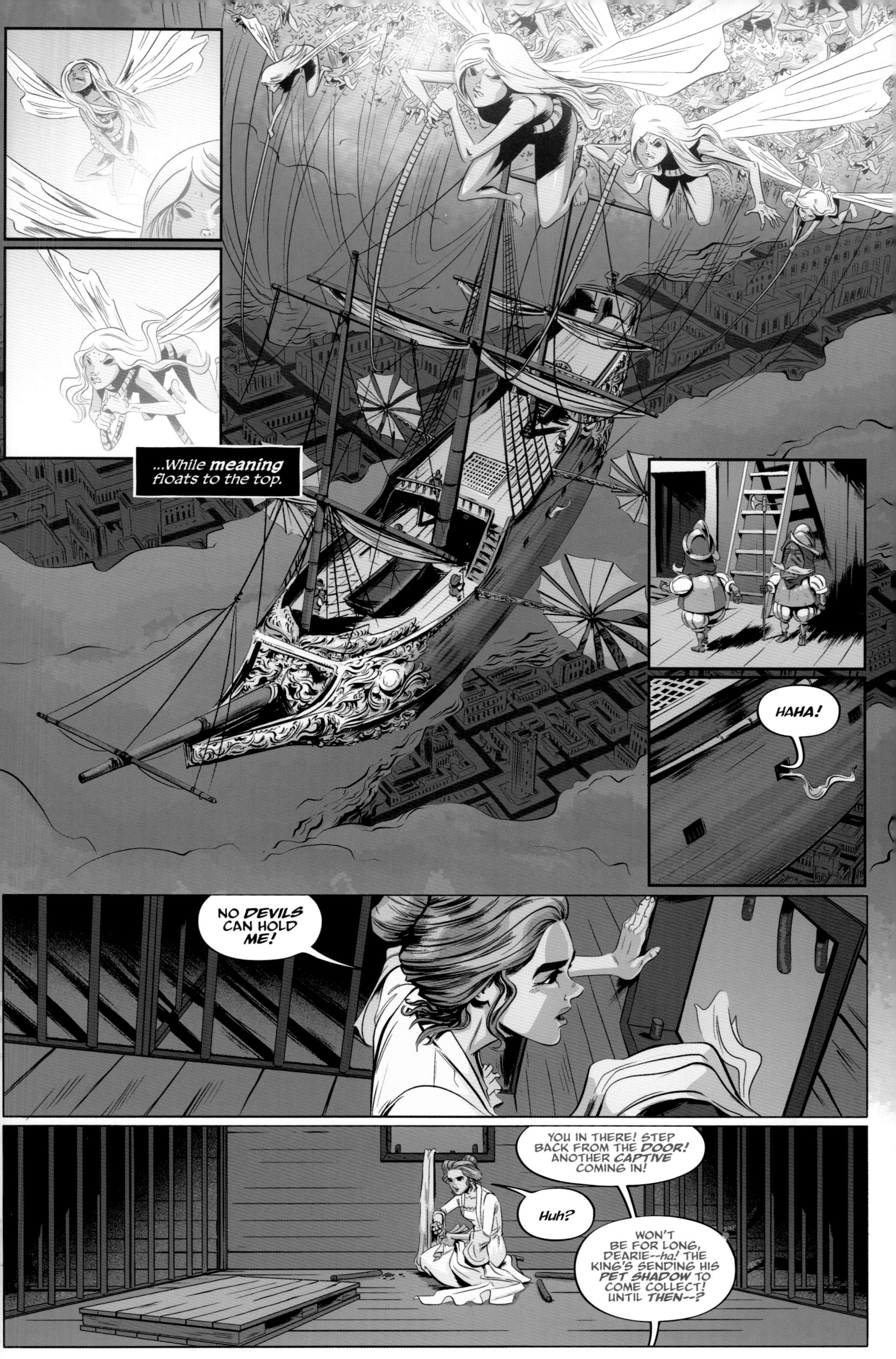

...While meaning floats to the top.
HAHA!
NO DEVILS CAN HOLD ME!
YOU IN THERE! STEP BACK FROM THE DOOR! ANOTHER CAPTIVE COMING IN!
Huh?
WON'T BE FOR LONG, DEARIE--ha! THE KING'S SENDING HIS PET SHADOW TO COME COLLECT! UNTIL THEN--?

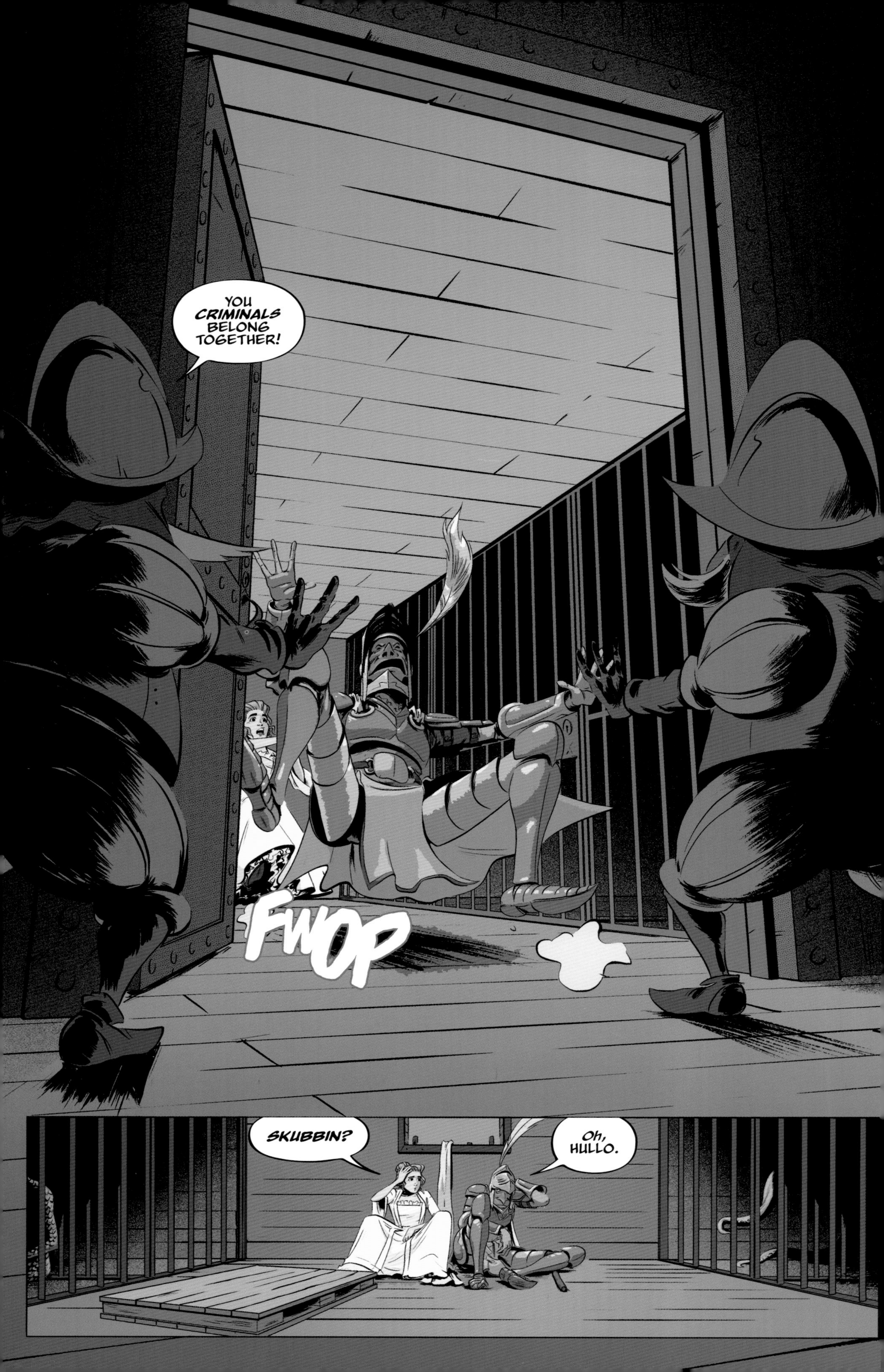
YOU *CRIMINALS* BELONG TOGETHER!
FWOP
SKUBBIN?
OH, HULLO.

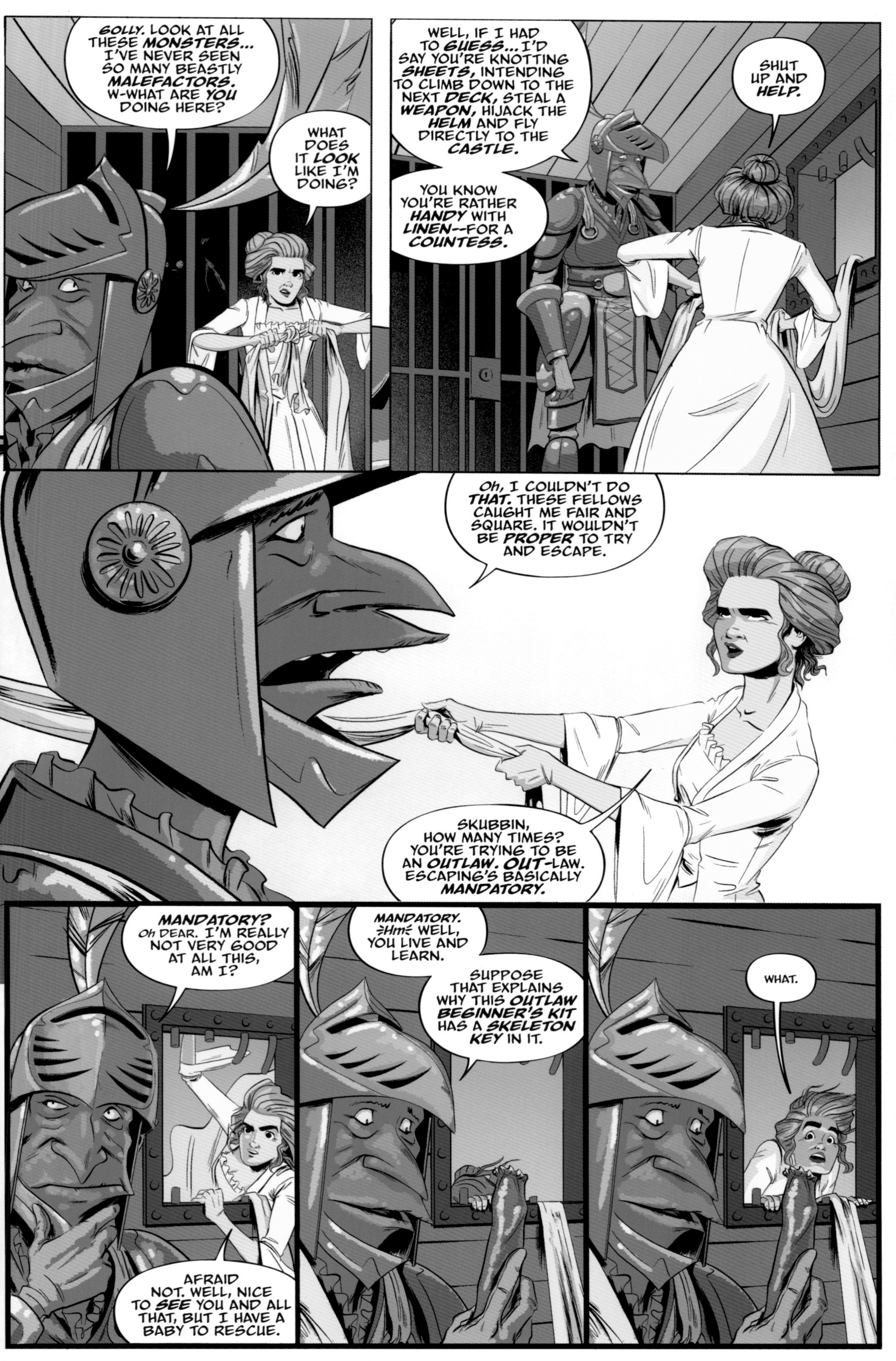
GOLLY. LOOK AT ALL THESE MONSTERS... I'VE NEVER SEEN SO MANY BEASTLY MALEFACTORS. W-WHAT ARE YOU DOING HERE?
WHAT DOES IT LOOK LIKE I'M DOING?
WELL, IF I HAD TO GUESS... I'D SAY YOU'RE KNOTTING SHEETS, INTENDING TO CLIMB DOWN TO THE NEXT DECK, STEAL A WEAPON, HIJACK THE HELM AND FLY DIRECTLY TO THE CASTLE.
YOU KNOW YOU'RE RATHER HANDY WITH LINEN--FOR A COUNTESS.
SHUT UP AND HELP.
Oh, I COULDN'T DO THAT. THESE FELLOWS CAUGHT ME FAIR AND SQUARE. IT WOULDN'T BE PROPER TO TRY AND ESCAPE.
SKUBBIN, HOW MANY TIMES? YOU'RE TRYING TO BE AN OUTLAW. OUT-LAW. ESCAPING'S BASICALLY MANDATORY.
MANDATORY? Oh DEAR. I'M REALLY NOT VERY GOOD AT ALL THIS, AM I?
AFRAID NOT. WELL, NICE TO SEE YOU AND ALL THAT, BUT I HAVE A BABY TO RESCUE.
MANDATORY. Hm WELL, YOU LIVE AND LEARN.
SUPPOSE THAT EXPLAINS WHY THIS OUTLAW BEGINNER'S KIT HAS A SKELETON KEY IN IT.
WHAT.

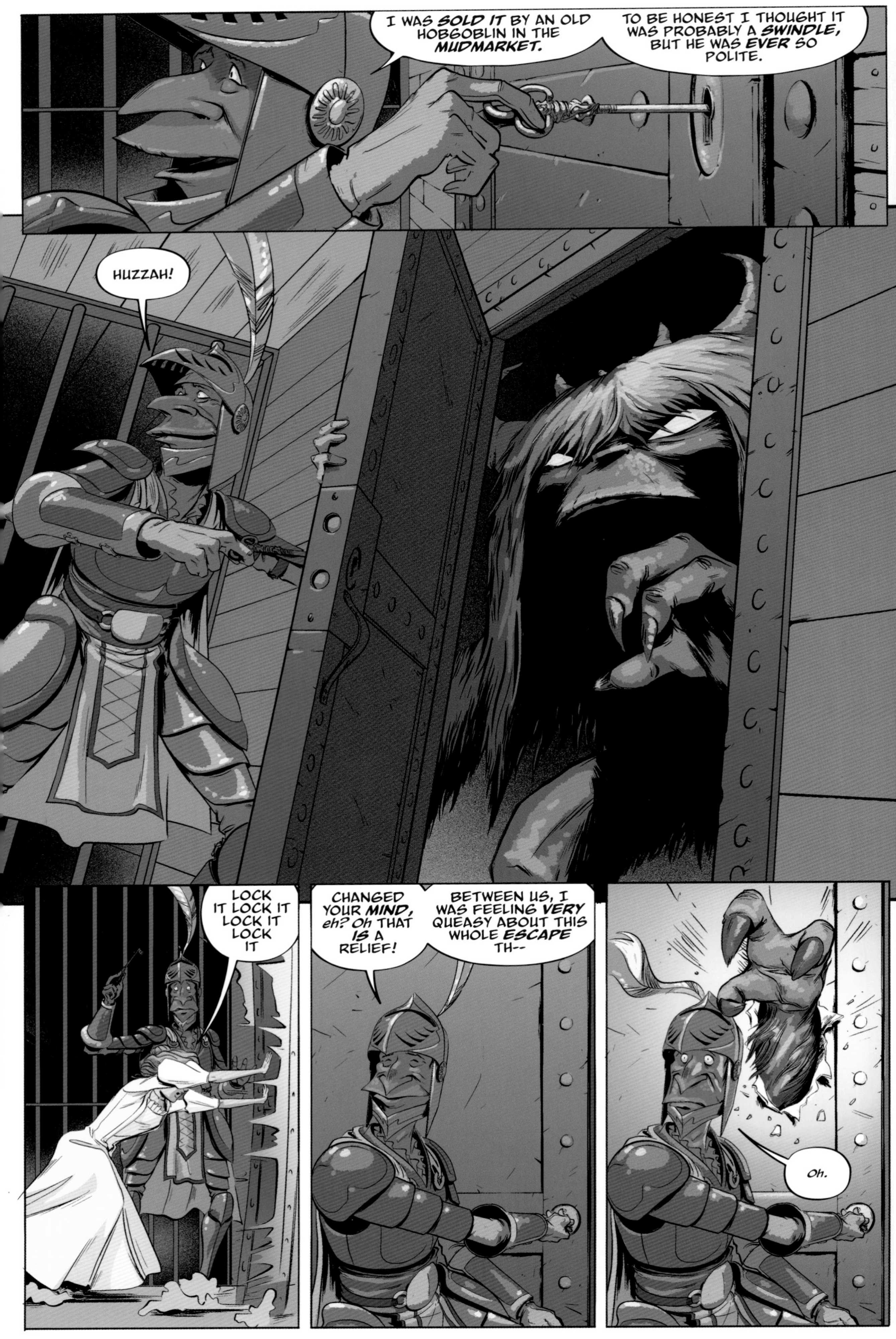
I WAS SOLD IT BY AN OLD HOBGOBLIN IN THE MUDMARKET.
TO BE HONEST I THOUGHT IT WAS PROBABLY A SWINDLE, BUT HE WAS EVER SO POLITE.
HUZZAH!
LOCK IT LOCK IT LOCK IT LOCK IT
CHANGED YOUR MIND, eh? Oh THAT IS A RELIEF!
BETWEEN US, I WAS FEELING VERY QUEASY ABOUT THIS WHOLE ESCAPE TH--
Oh.

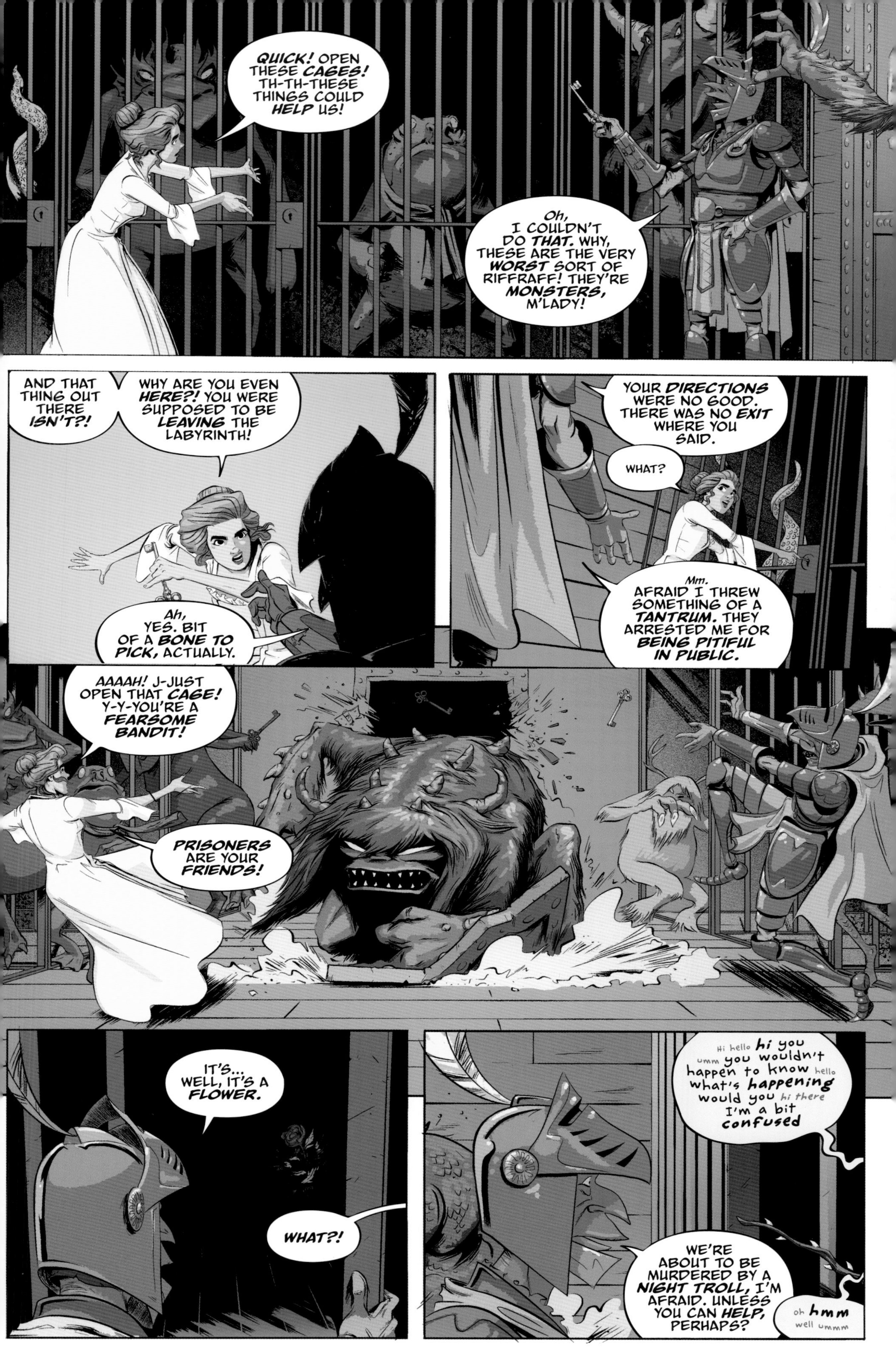
QUICK! OPEN THESE CAGES! TH-TH-THESE THINGS COULD HELP US!
Oh, I COULDN'T DO THAT. WHY, THESE ARE THE VERY WORST SORT OF RIFFRAFF! THEY'RE MONSTERS, M'LADY!
AND THAT THING OUT THERE ISN'T?!
WHY ARE YOU EVEN HERE?! YOU WERE SUPPOSED TO BE LEAVING THE LABYRINTH!
Ah, YES. BIT OF A BONE TO PICK, ACTUALLY.
YOUR DIRECTIONS WERE NO GOOD. THERE WAS NO EXIT WHERE YOU SAID.
WHAT?
Mm. AFRAID I THREW SOMETHING OF A TANTRUM. THEY ARRESTED ME FOR BEING PITIFUL IN PUBLIC.
AAAAH! J-JUST OPEN THAT CAGE! Y-Y-YOU'RE A FEARSOME BANDIT!
PRISONERS ARE YOUR FRIENDS!
IT'S... WELL, IT'S A FLOWER.
WHAT?!
Hi hello hi you umm you wouldn't happen to know hello what's happening would you hi there I'm a bit confused
WE'RE ABOUT TO BE MURDERED BY A NIGHT TROLL, I'M AFRAID. UNLESS YOU CAN HELP, PERHAPS?
oh hmm well ummm

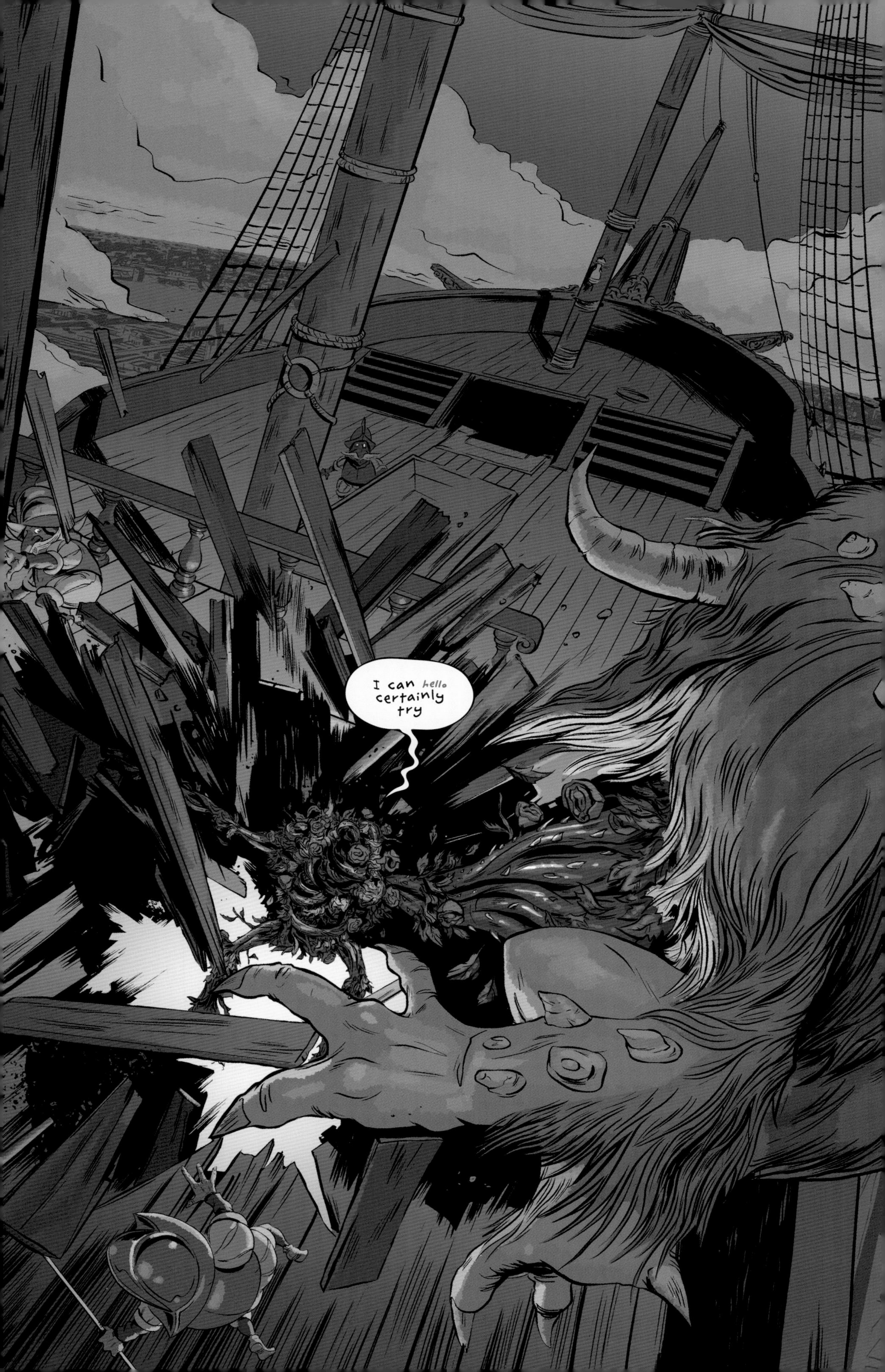
I can hello certainly try

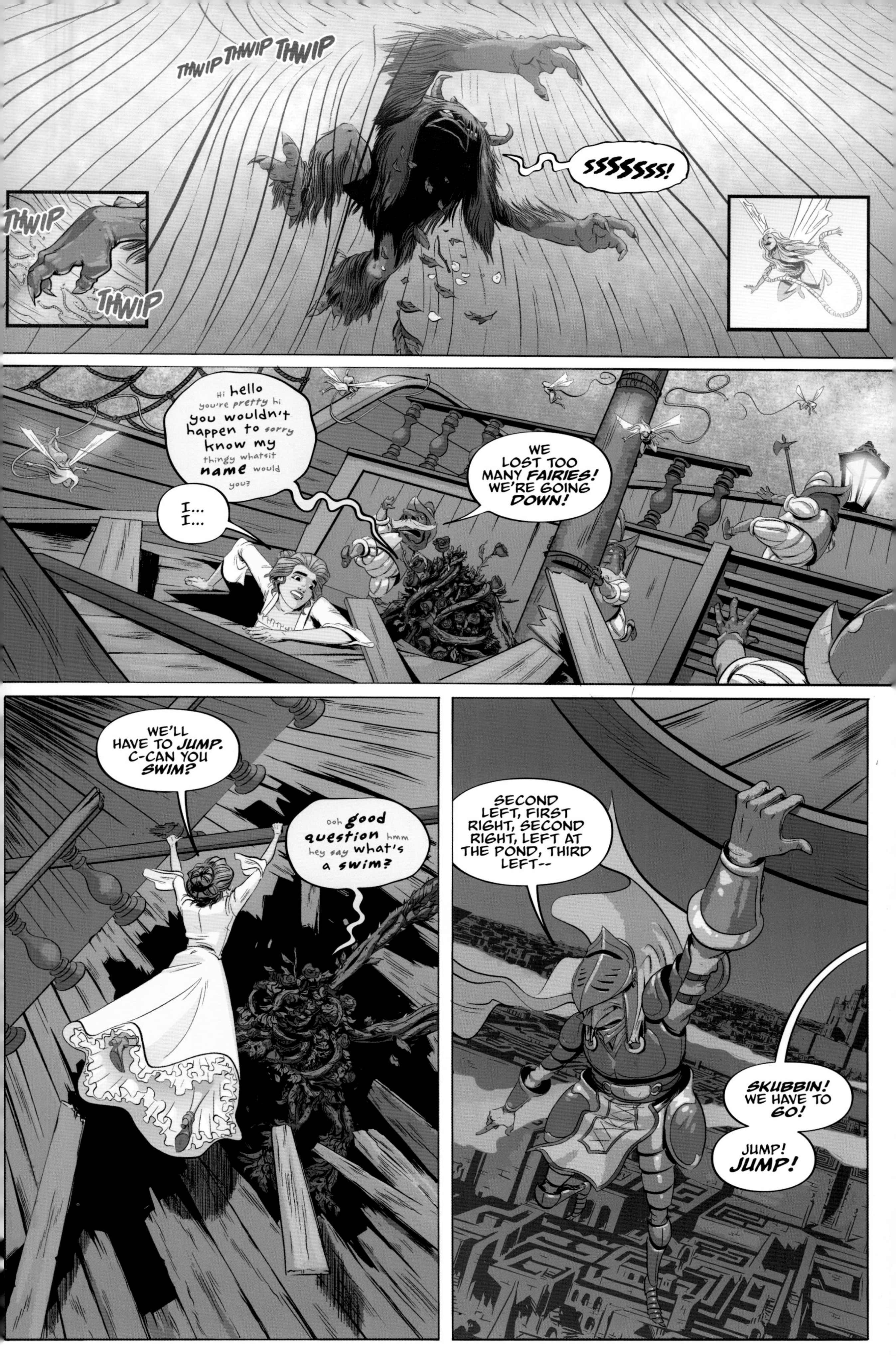
THWIP THWIP THWIP
SSSSSSS!
THWIP
THWIP
Hi hello you're pretty hi you wouldn't happen to sorry know my thingy whatsit name would you?
I... I...
WE LOST TOO MANY FAIRIES! WE'RE GOING DOWN!
WE'LL HAVE TO JUMP. C-CAN YOU SWIM?
ooh good question hmm hey say what's a swim?
SECOND LEFT, FIRST RIGHT, SECOND RIGHT, LEFT AT THE POND, THIRD LEFT--
SKUBBIN! WE HAVE TO GO!
JUMP! JUMP!

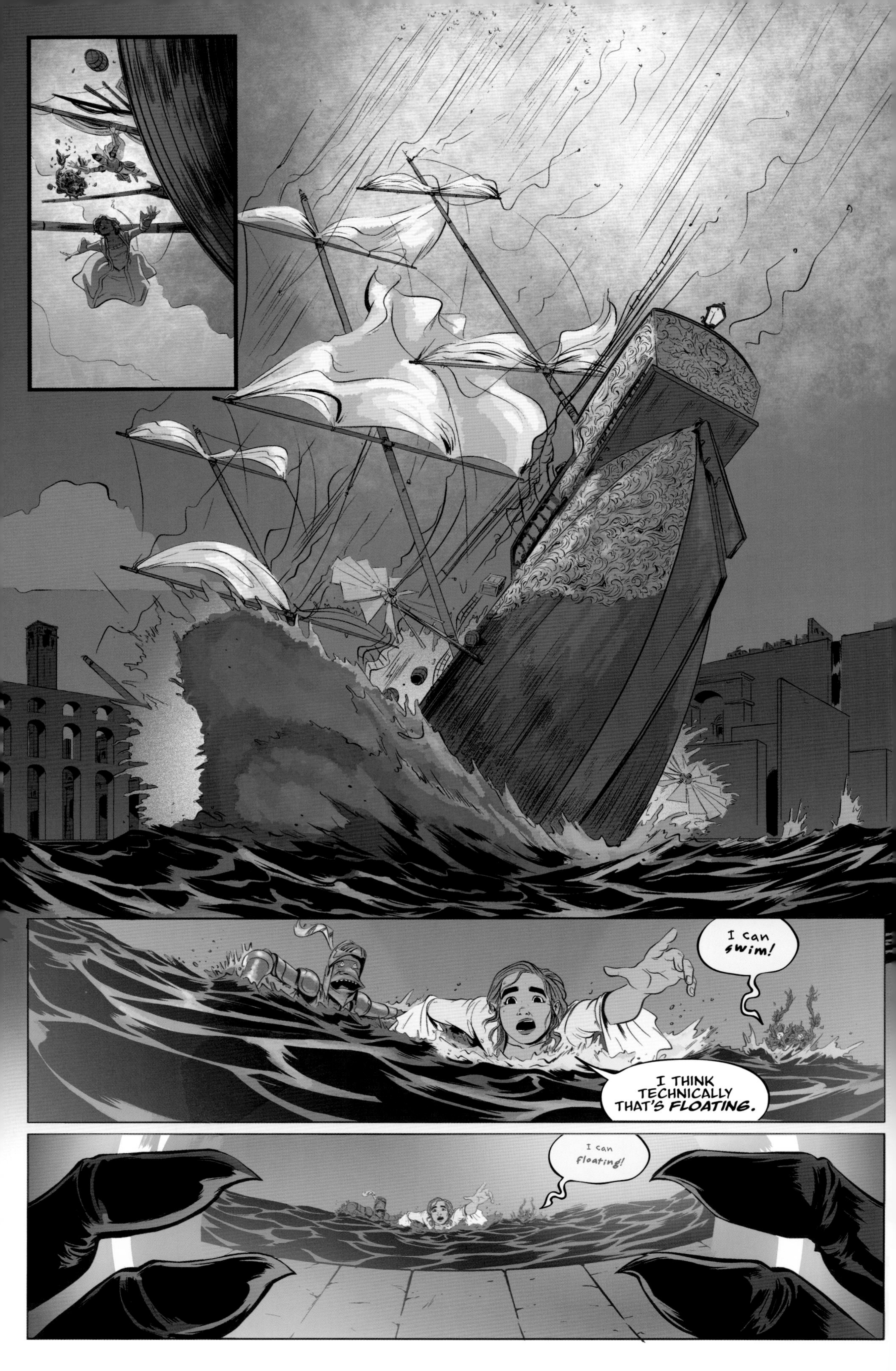
I can swim!
I THINK TECHNICALLY THAT'S FLOATING.
I can floating!

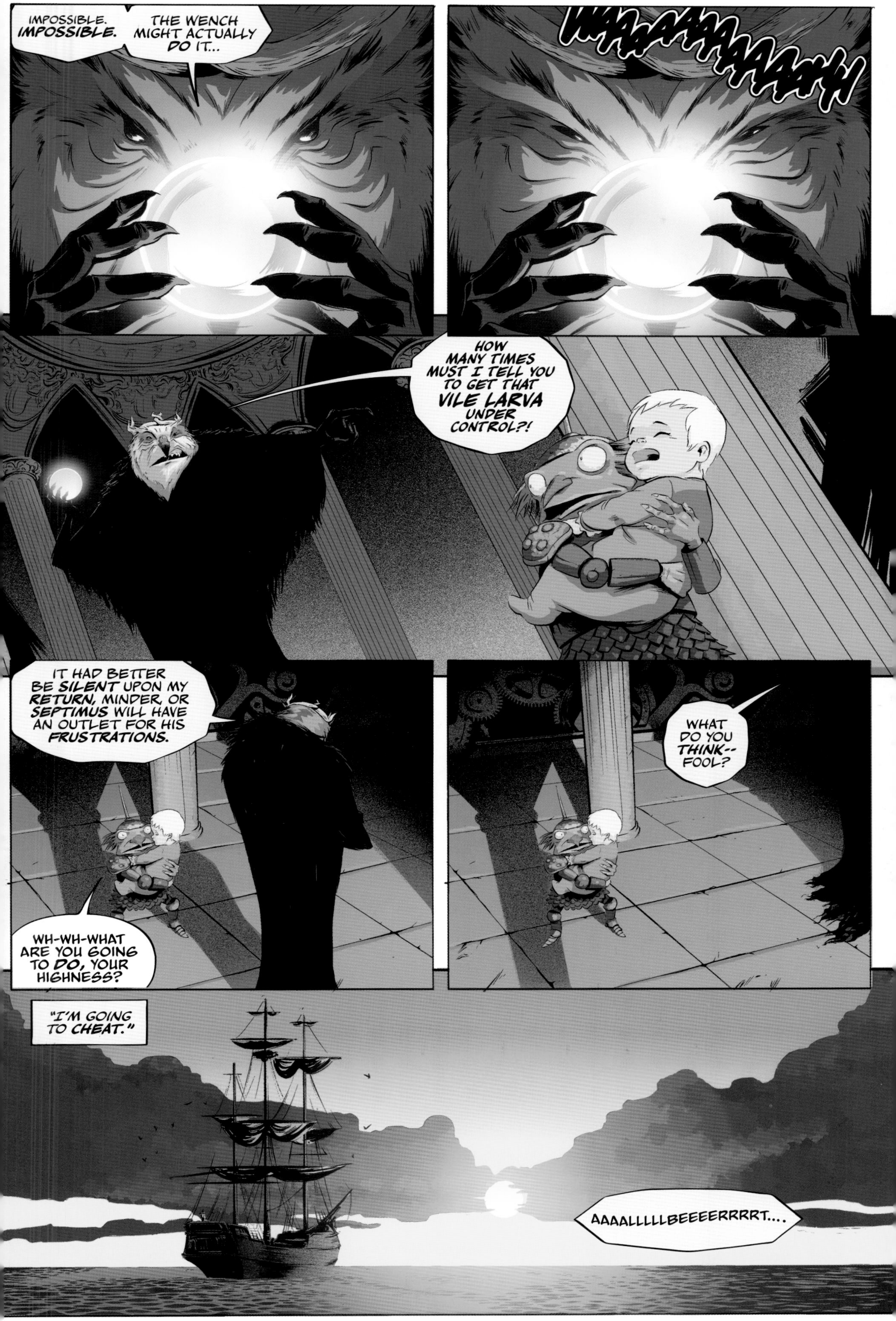
IMPOSSIBLE. IMPOSSIBLE.
THE WENCH MIGHT ACTUALLY DO IT...
WAAAAAAAAAAAAAAH
HOW MANY TIMES MUST I TELL YOU TO GET THAT VILE LARVA UNDER CONTROL?!
IT HAD BETTER BE SILENT UPON MY RETURN, MINDER, OR SEPTIMUS WILL HAVE AN OUTLET FOR HIS FRUSTRATIONS.
WH-WH-WHAT ARE YOU GOING TO DO, YOUR HIGHNESS?
WHAT DO YOU THINK--FOOL?
"I'M GOING TO CHEAT."
AAAALLLLLLBEEEERRRRT....

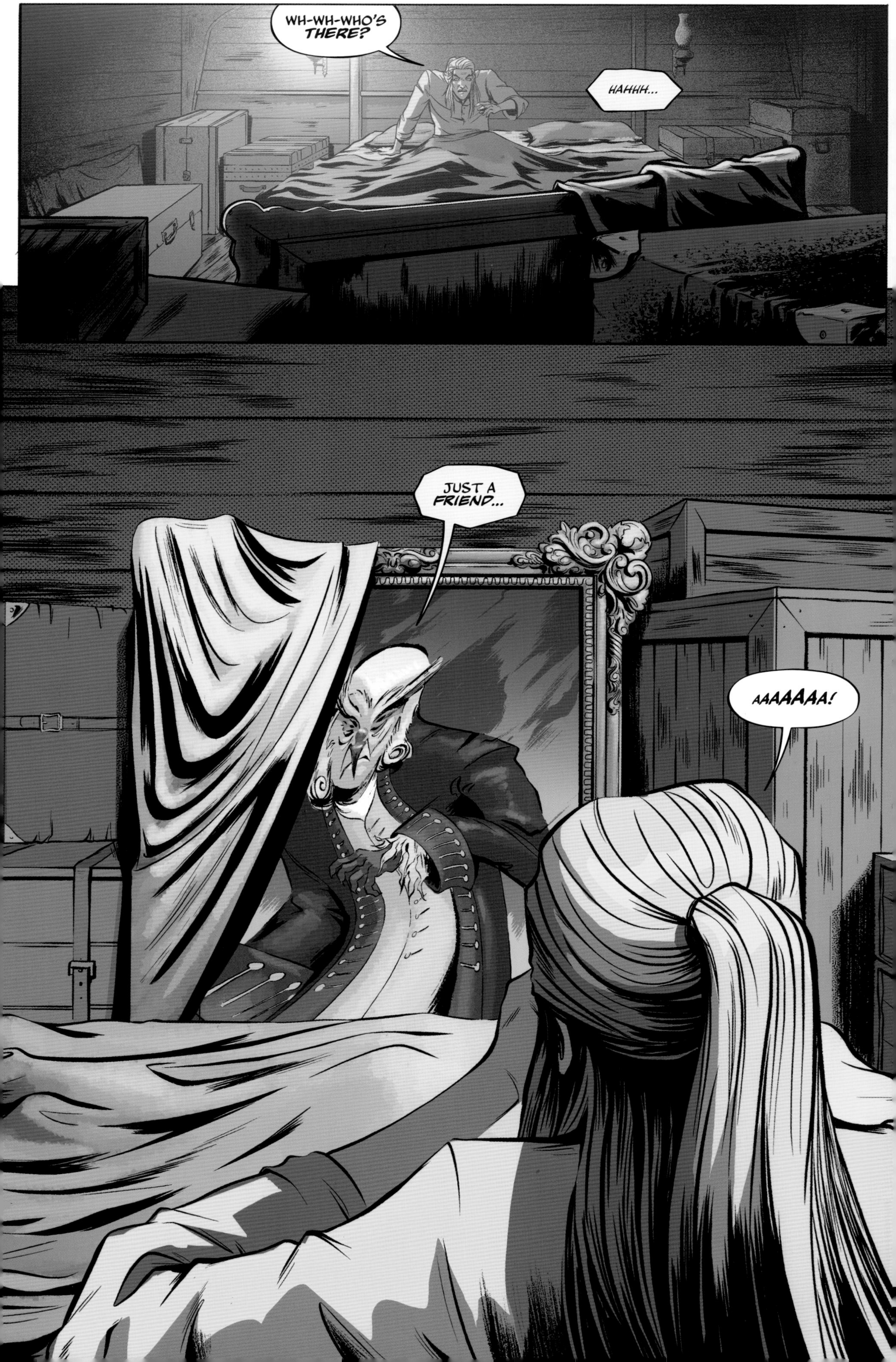
WH-WH-WHO'S THERE?
HAHHH...
JUST A FRIEND...
AAAAAAA!

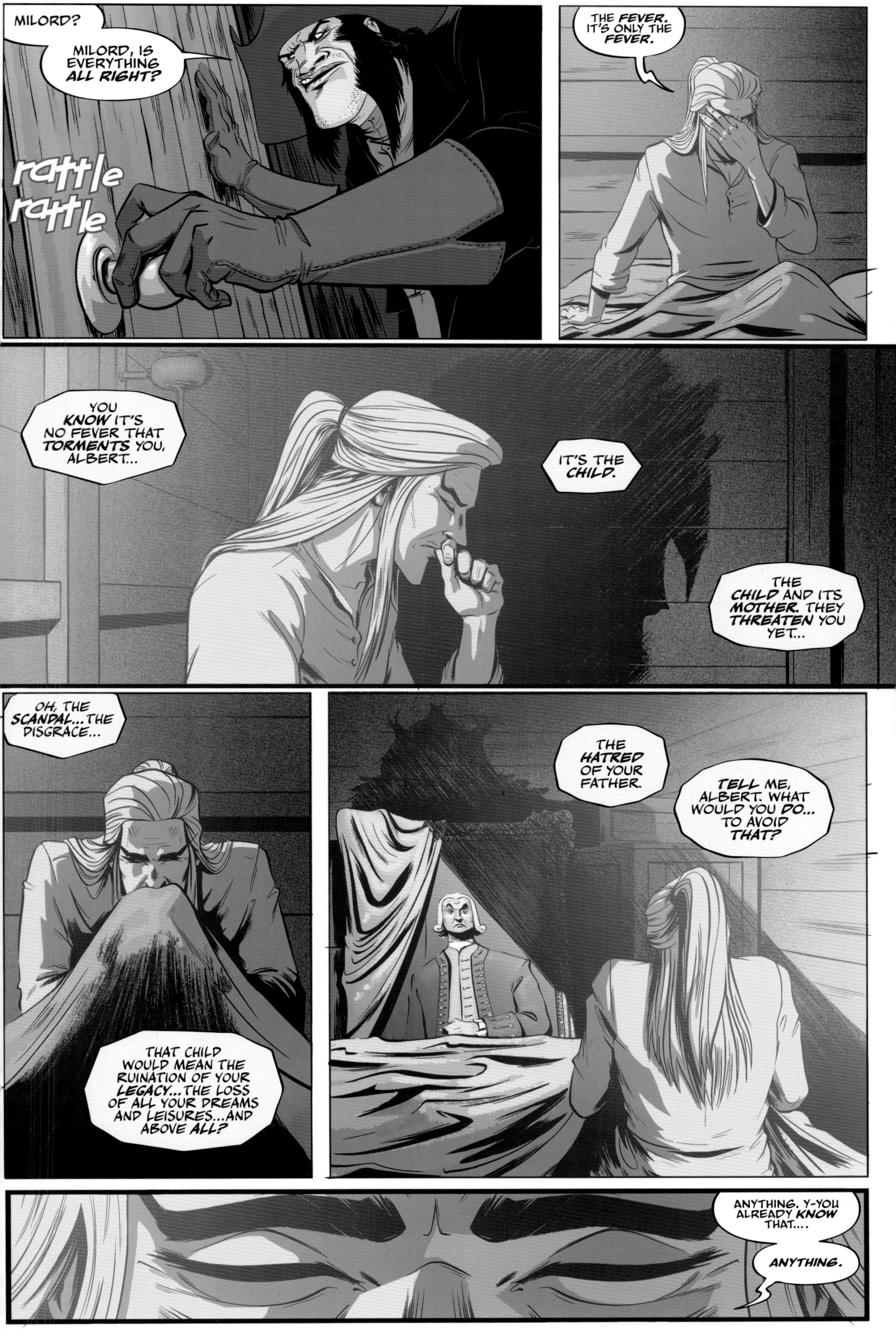
MILORD?
MILORD, IS EVERYTHING ALL RIGHT?
rattle rattle
THE FEVER. IT'S ONLY THE FEVER.
YOU KNOW IT'S NO FEVER THAT TORMENTS YOU, ALBERT...
IT'S THE CHILD.
THE CHILD AND ITS MOTHER. THEY THREATEN YOU YET...
OH, THE SCANDAL...THE DISGRACE...
THAT CHILD WOULD MEAN THE RUINATION OF YOUR LEGACY...THE LOSS OF ALL YOUR DREAMS AND LEISURES...AND ABOVE ALL?
THE HATRED OF YOUR FATHER.
TELL ME, ALBERT. WHAT WOULD YOU DO... TO AVOID THAT?
ANYTHING. Y-YOU ALREADY KNOW THAT....
ANYTHING.

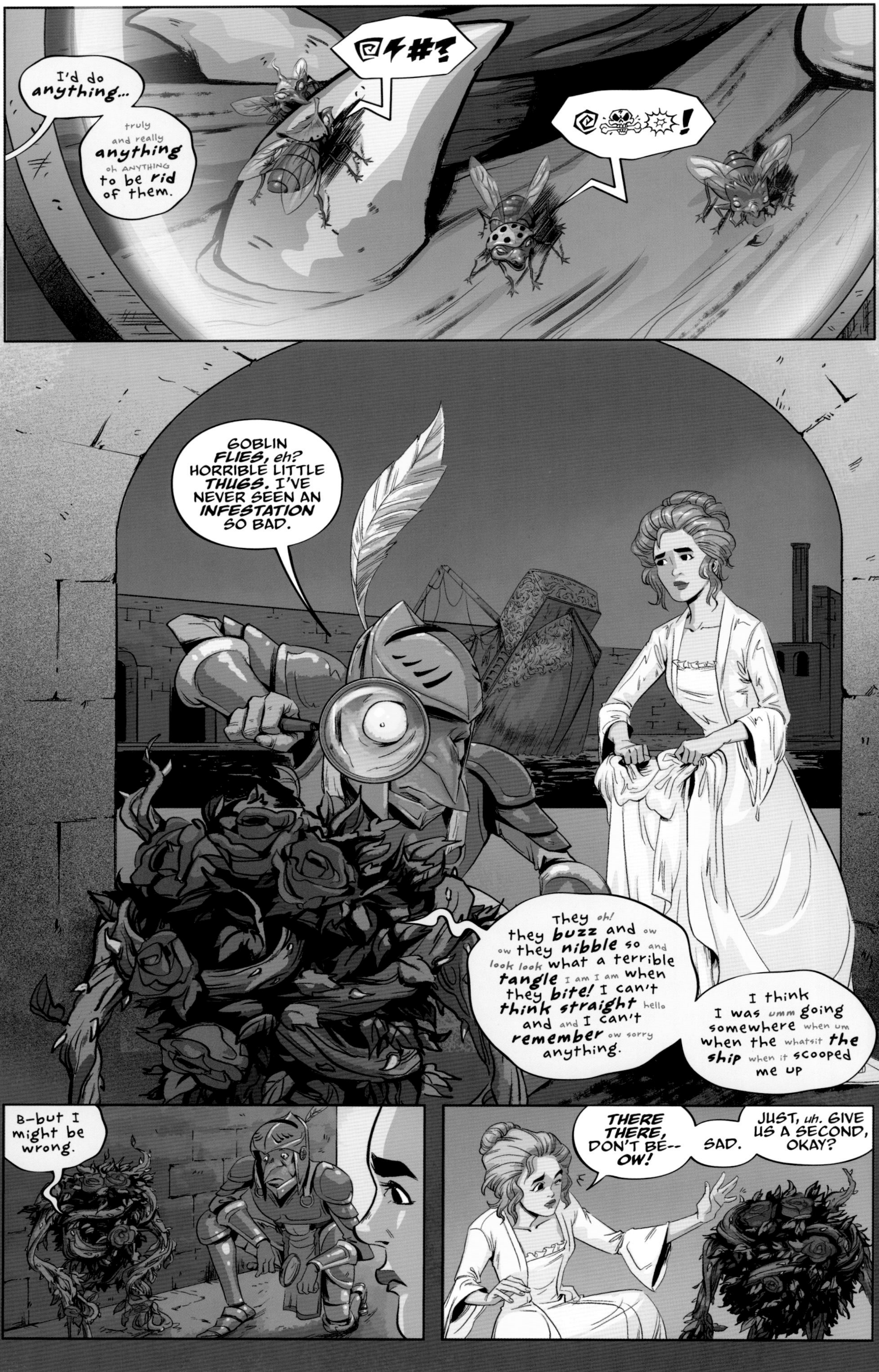

I'd do anything...
truly and really anything oh ANYTHING to be rid of them.
GOBLIN FLIES, eh? HORRIBLE LITTLE THUGS. I'VE NEVER SEEN AN INFESTATION SO BAD.
They oh! they buzz and ow ow they nibble so and look look what a terrible tangle I am I am when they bite! I can't think straight hello and and I can't remember ow sorry anything.
I think I was umm going somewhere when um when the whatsit the ship when it scooped me up
B-but I might be wrong.
THERE THERE, DON'T BE-- OW!
SAD.
JUST, uh. GIVE US A SECOND, OKAY?

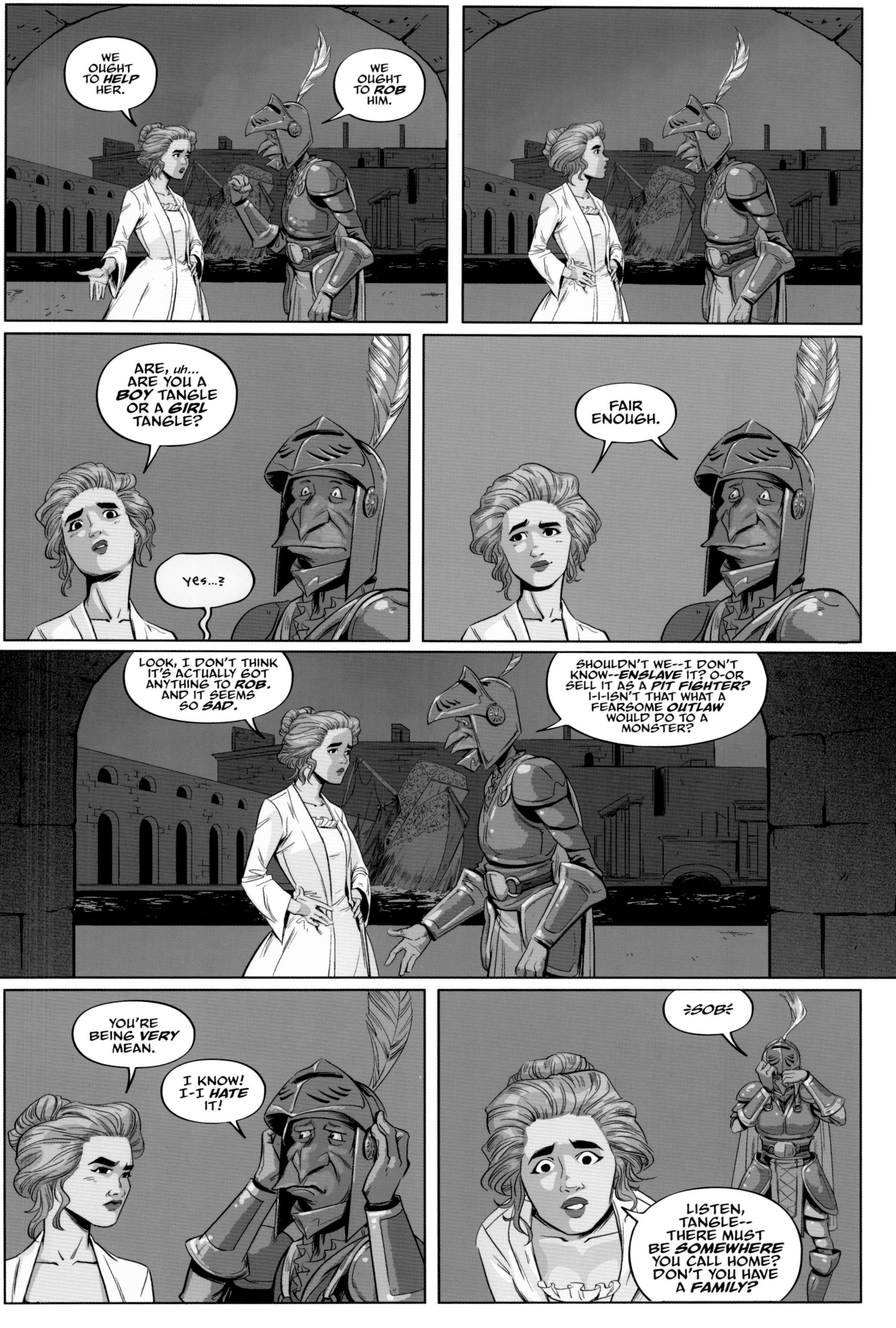
WE OUGHT TO HELP HER.
WE OUGHT TO ROB HIM.
ARE, uh... ARE YOU A BOY TANGLE OR A GIRL TANGLE?
yes...?
FAIR ENOUGH.
LOOK, I DON'T THINK IT'S ACTUALLY GOT ANYTHING TO ROB. AND IT SEEMS SO SAD.
SHOULDN'T WE--I DON'T KNOW--ENSLAVE IT? O-OR SELL IT AS A PIT FIGHTER? I-I-ISN'T THAT WHAT A FEARSOME OUTLAW WOULD DO TO A MONSTER?
YOU'RE BEING VERY MEAN.
I KNOW! I-I HATE IT!
SOB
LISTEN, TANGLE-- THERE MUST BE SOMEWHERE YOU CALL HOME? DON'T YOU HAVE A FAMILY?

WAAAAAHuhHUH!

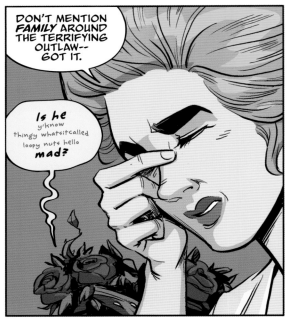

DON'T MENTION *FAMILY* AROUND THE TERRIFYING OUTLAW-- GOT IT.

Is he y'know thingy whatsitcalled loopy nuts hello *mad*?

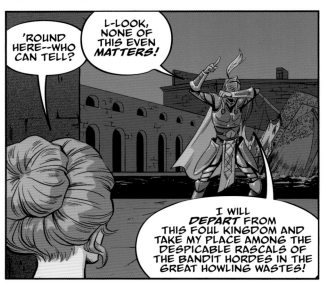

'ROUND HERE--WHO CAN TELL?

L-LOOK, NONE OF THIS EVEN *MATTERS*!

I WILL *DEPART* FROM THIS FOUL KINGDOM AND TAKE MY PLACE AMONG THE DESPICABLE RASCALS OF THE BANDIT HORDES IN THE GREAT HOWLING WASTES!

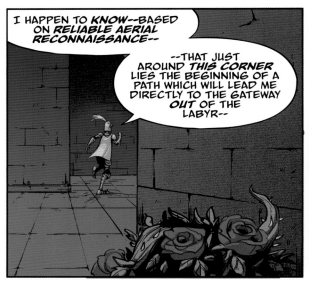

I HAPPEN TO *KNOW*--BASED ON *RELIABLE AERIAL RECONNAISSANCE*--

--THAT JUST AROUND *THIS CORNER* LIES THE BEGINNING OF A PATH WHICH WILL LEAD ME DIRECTLY TO THE GATEWAY *OUT* OF THE LABYR--

...

WHAT *YOU* LOOKIN' AT?

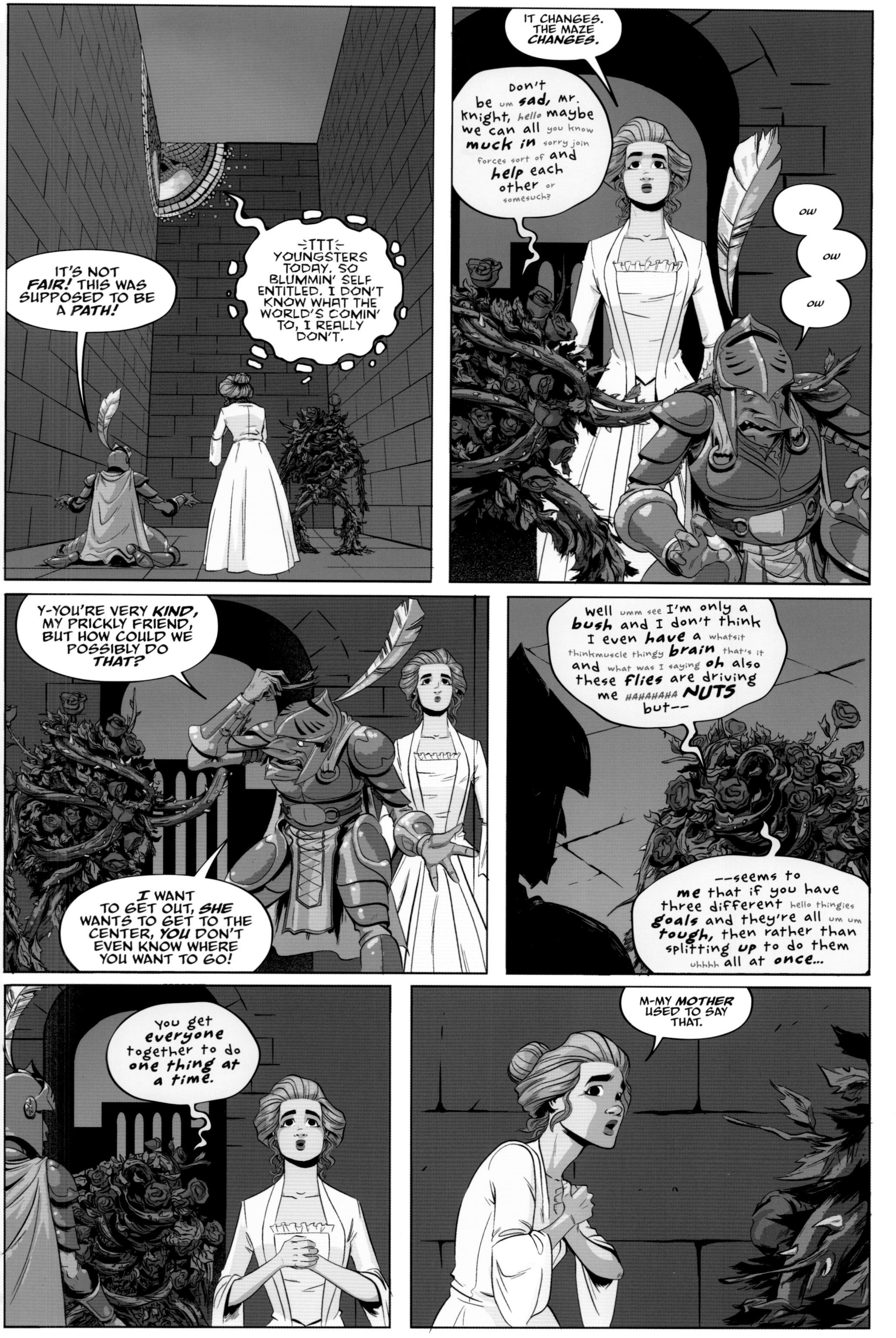
IT'S NOT FAIR! THIS WAS SUPPOSED TO BE A PATH!
-TTT- YOUNGSTERS TODAY. SO BLUMMIN' SELF ENTITLED. I DON'T KNOW WHAT THE WORLD'S COMIN' TO, I REALLY DON'T.
IT CHANGES. THE MAZE CHANGES.
Don't be um sad, mr. knight, hello maybe we can all you know muck in sorry join forces sort of and help each other or somesuch?
ow
ow
ow
Y-YOU'RE VERY KIND, MY PRICKLY FRIEND, BUT HOW COULD WE POSSIBLY DO THAT?
I WANT TO GET OUT, SHE WANTS TO GET TO THE CENTER, YOU DON'T EVEN KNOW WHERE YOU WANT TO GO!
well umm see I'm only a bush and I don't think I even have a whatsit thinkmuscle thingy brain that's it and what was I saying oh also these flies are driving me HAHAHAHA NUTS but--
--seems to me that if you have three different hello thingies goals and they're all um um tough, then rather than splitting up to do them uhhhh all at once...
You get everyone together to do one thing at a time.
M-MY MOTHER USED TO SAY THAT.

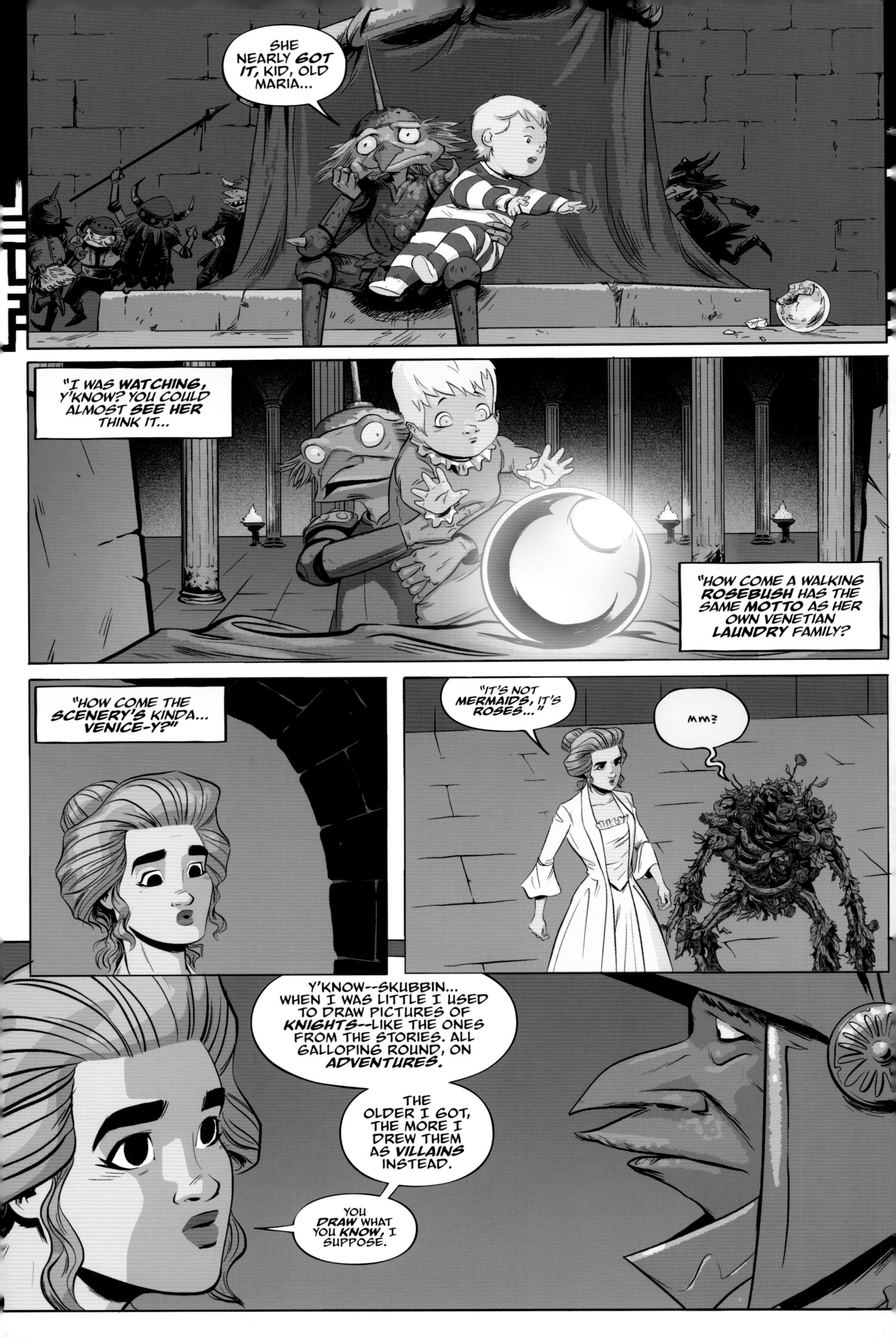

SHE NEARLY GOT IT, KID, OLD MARIA...
"I WAS WATCHING, Y'KNOW? YOU COULD ALMOST SEE HER THINK IT...
"HOW COME A WALKING ROSEBUSH HAS THE SAME MOTTO AS HER OWN VENETIAN LAUNDRY FAMILY?
"HOW COME THE SCENERY'S KINDA... VENICE-Y?"
"IT'S NOT MERMAIDS, IT'S ROSES..."
MM?
Y'KNOW--SKUBBIN... WHEN I WAS LITTLE I USED TO DRAW PICTURES OF KNIGHTS--LIKE THE ONES FROM THE STORIES. ALL GALLOPING ROUND, ON ADVENTURES.
THE OLDER I GOT, THE MORE I DREW THEM AS VILLAINS INSTEAD.
YOU DRAW WHAT YOU KNOW, I SUPPOSE.

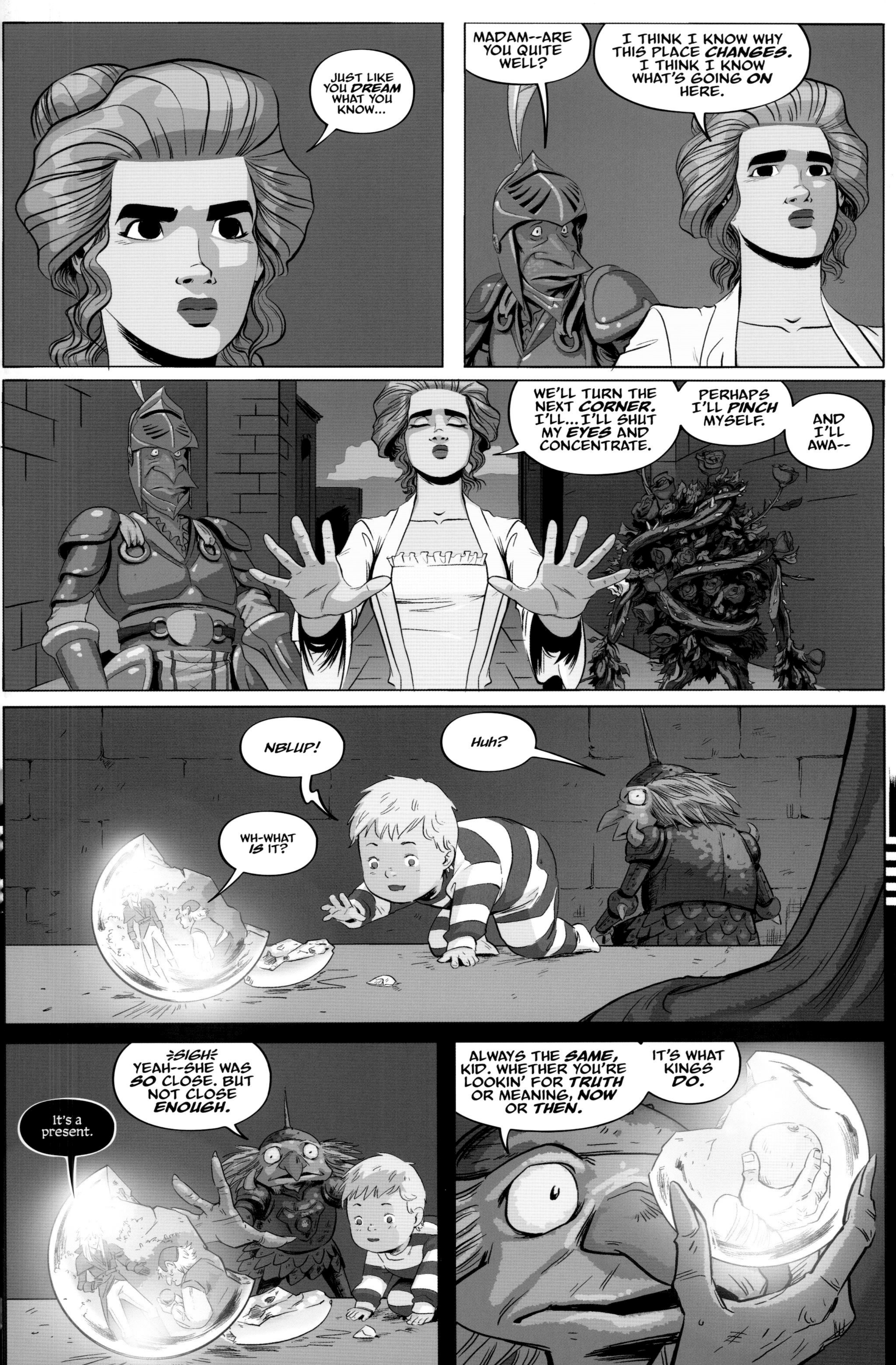
JUST LIKE YOU DREAM WHAT YOU KNOW...
MADAM--ARE YOU QUITE WELL?
I THINK I KNOW WHY THIS PLACE CHANGES. I THINK I KNOW WHAT'S GOING ON HERE.
WE'LL TURN THE NEXT CORNER. I'LL... I'LL SHUT MY EYES AND CONCENTRATE.
PERHAPS I'LL PINCH MYSELF.
AND I'LL AWA--
NBLUP!
Huh?
WH-WHAT IS IT?
It's a present.
SIGH
YEAH--SHE WAS SO CLOSE. BUT NOT CLOSE ENOUGH.
ALWAYS THE SAME, KID. WHETHER YOU'RE LOOKIN' FOR TRUTH OR MEANING, NOW OR THEN.
IT'S WHAT KINGS DO.

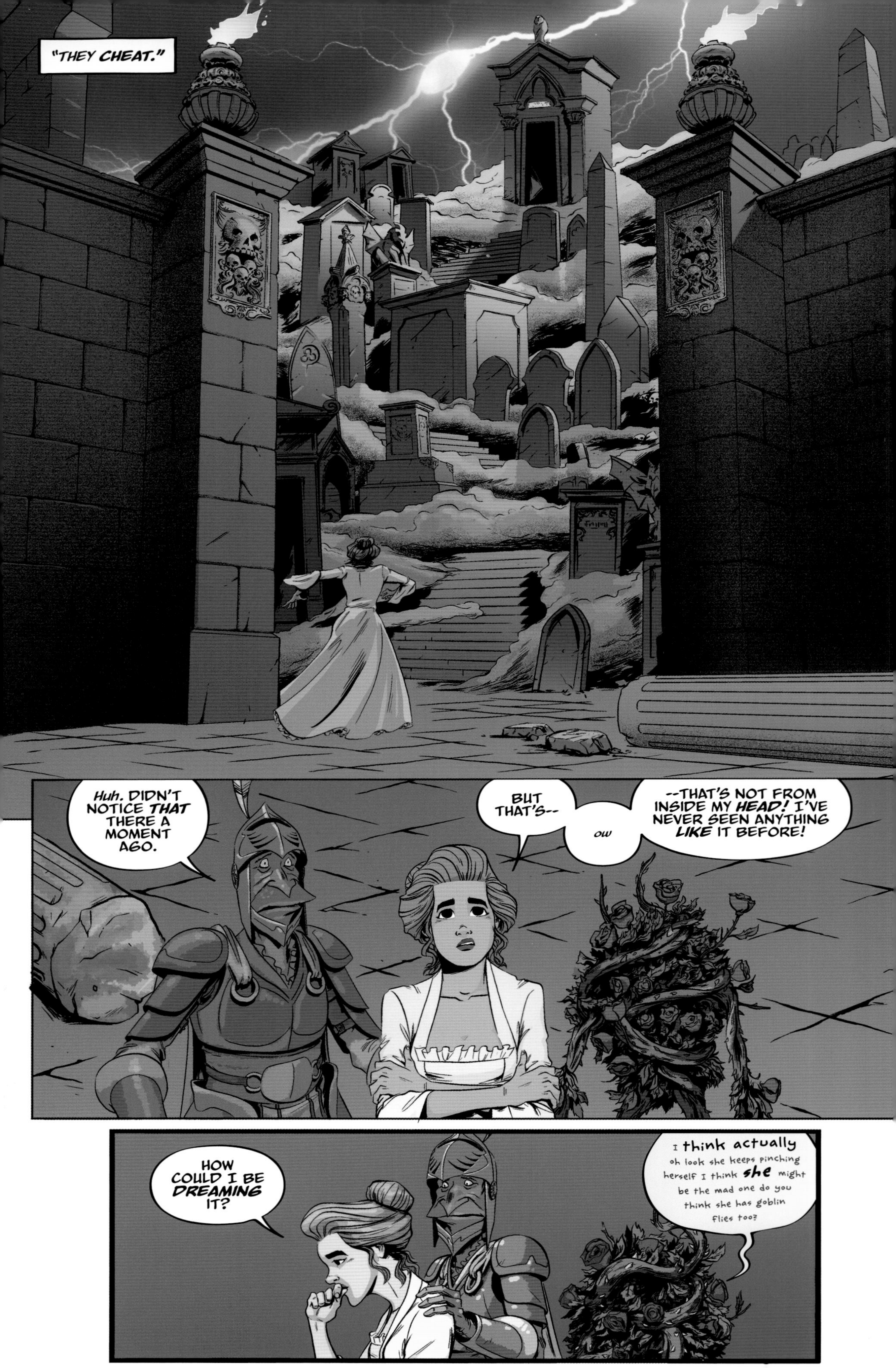

"THEY CHEAT."
Huh. DIDN'T NOTICE THAT THERE A MOMENT AGO.
BUT THAT'S--
ow
--THAT'S NOT FROM INSIDE MY HEAD! I'VE NEVER SEEN ANYTHING LIKE IT BEFORE!
HOW COULD I BE DREAMING IT?
I think actually oh look she keeps pinching herself I think she might be the mad one do you think she has goblin flies too?

POOR THING. I DON'T SUPPOSE IT'S *TOO* UN-BANDITLIKE TO *ESCORT* HER. JUST A *SHORT* WAY.

does that mean oh I hope so that you'll *help* us find where we're *going*, mr. knight?

≶SIGH≶ WELL. YOU KNOW WHAT THEY SAY, TANGLE:

"...EVERYONE TOGETHER, DOING ONE THING AT A TIME."

TYTON

"...HE...HE MADE ME VISIT FOR THE FIRST TIME WHEN I WAS ONLY *SIX*..."

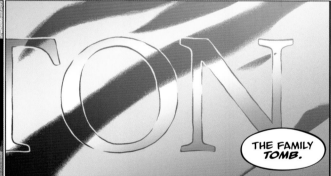

THE FAMILY *TOMB*.

W-WANTED TO SHOW ME H-HOW *FAR* THE LINE GOES BACK...B-B-BUT ALL I REMEMBER ARE THE BONES. MY GRANDFATHER'S SKULL STILL HAD HAIR.

I...I DON'T THINK I'VE BEEN SO *TERRIFIED* IN ALL MY LIFE.

SIR ALEXANDER TYTÓN

MMM. GOOD. "TERRIFIED" IS GOOD.

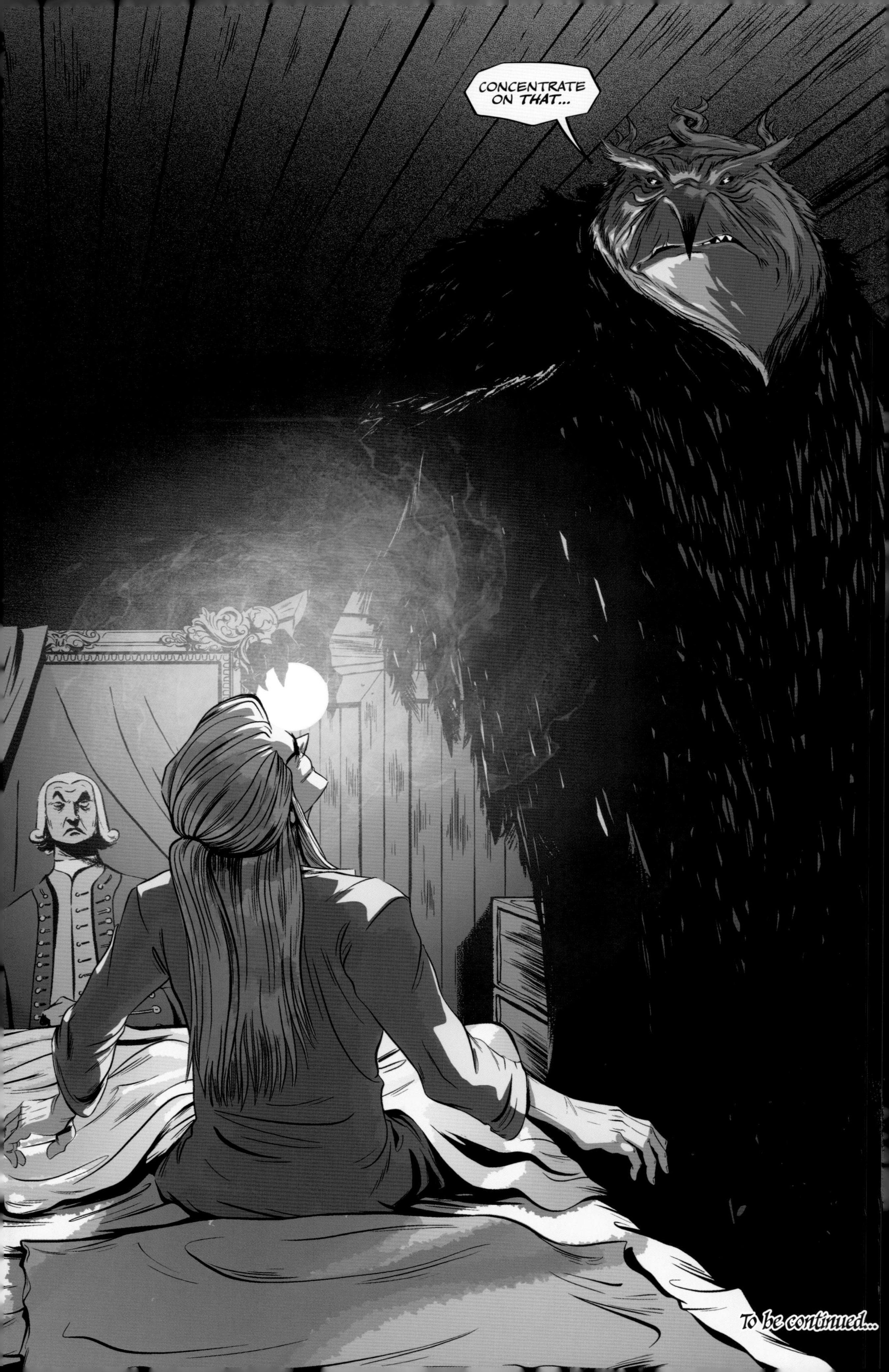
CONCENTRATE ON *THAT*...
To be continued...

COVER
GALLERY

Facing Page:
Issue #1 Subscription Cover by
Rebekah Isaacs

Following Pages:
Issues #2-4 Subscription Covers by
Rebekah Isaacs

Issue #1 Incentive Cover by
Laurent Durieux

Issue #1 ComicsPro Exclusive Cover by
David Petersen

Issue #1 Emerald City Comicon Exclusive Cover by
Benjamin Dewey

Issue #1 WonderCon Exclusive Cover by
Ramón K. Pérez

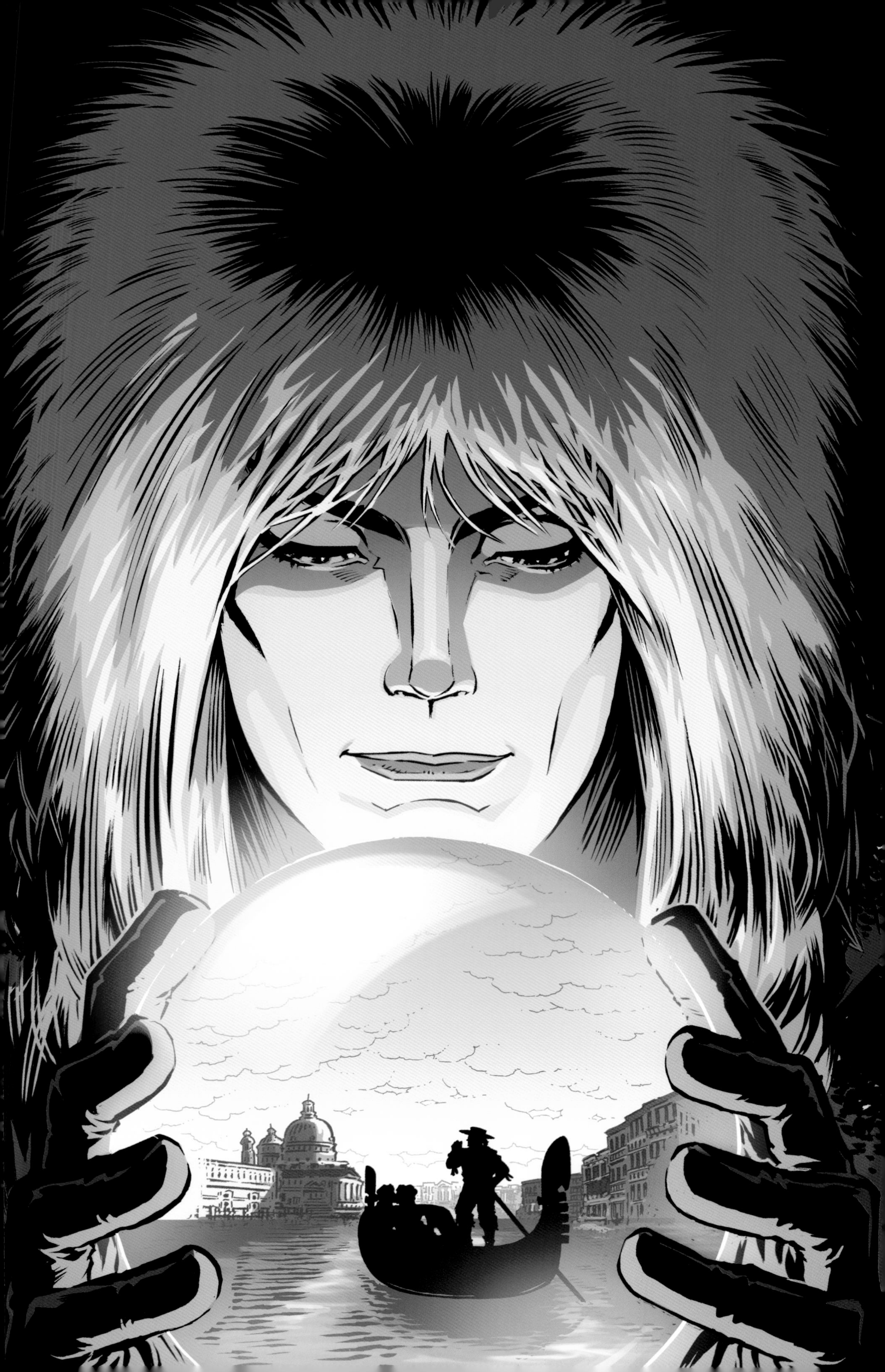

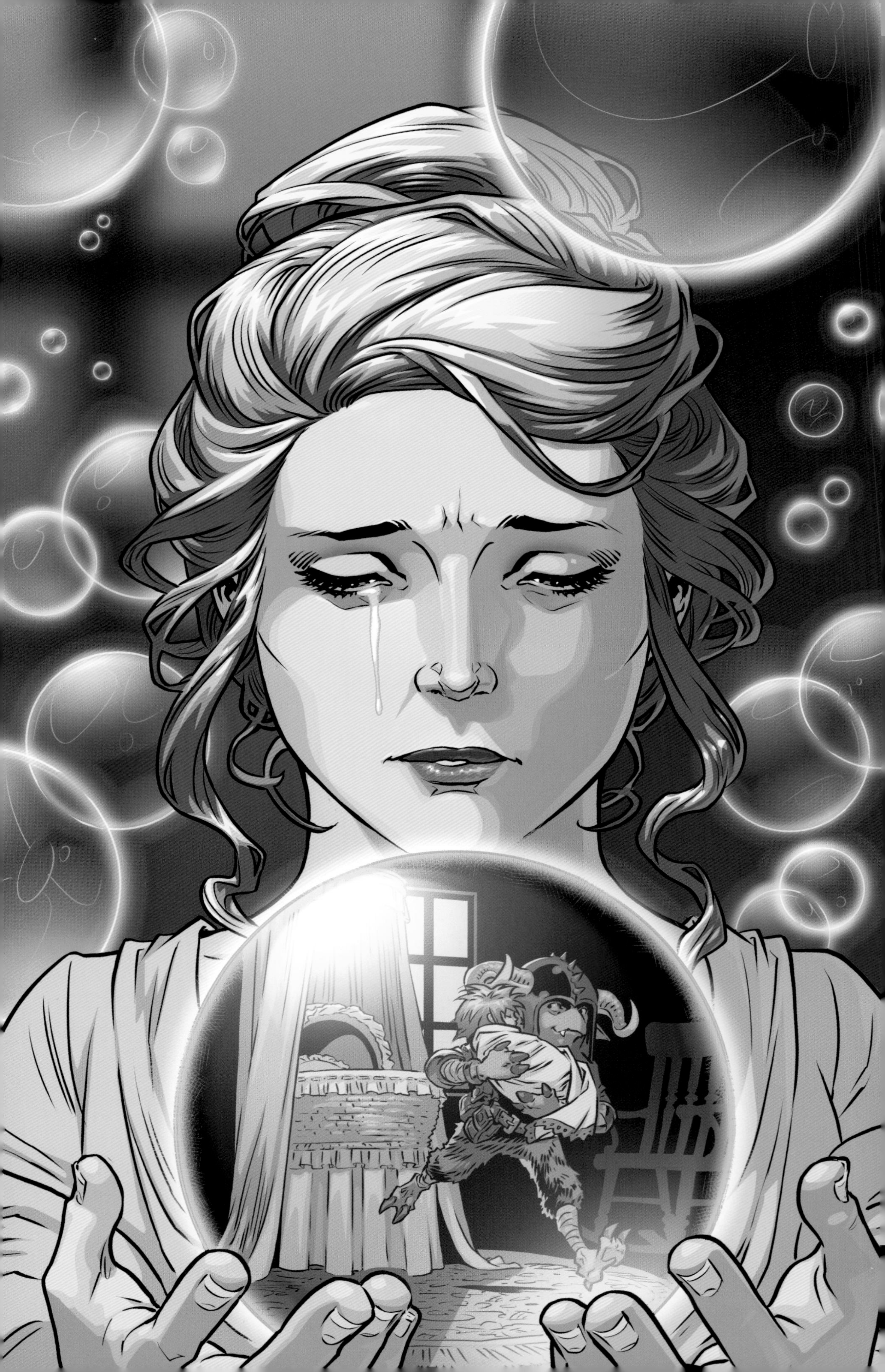

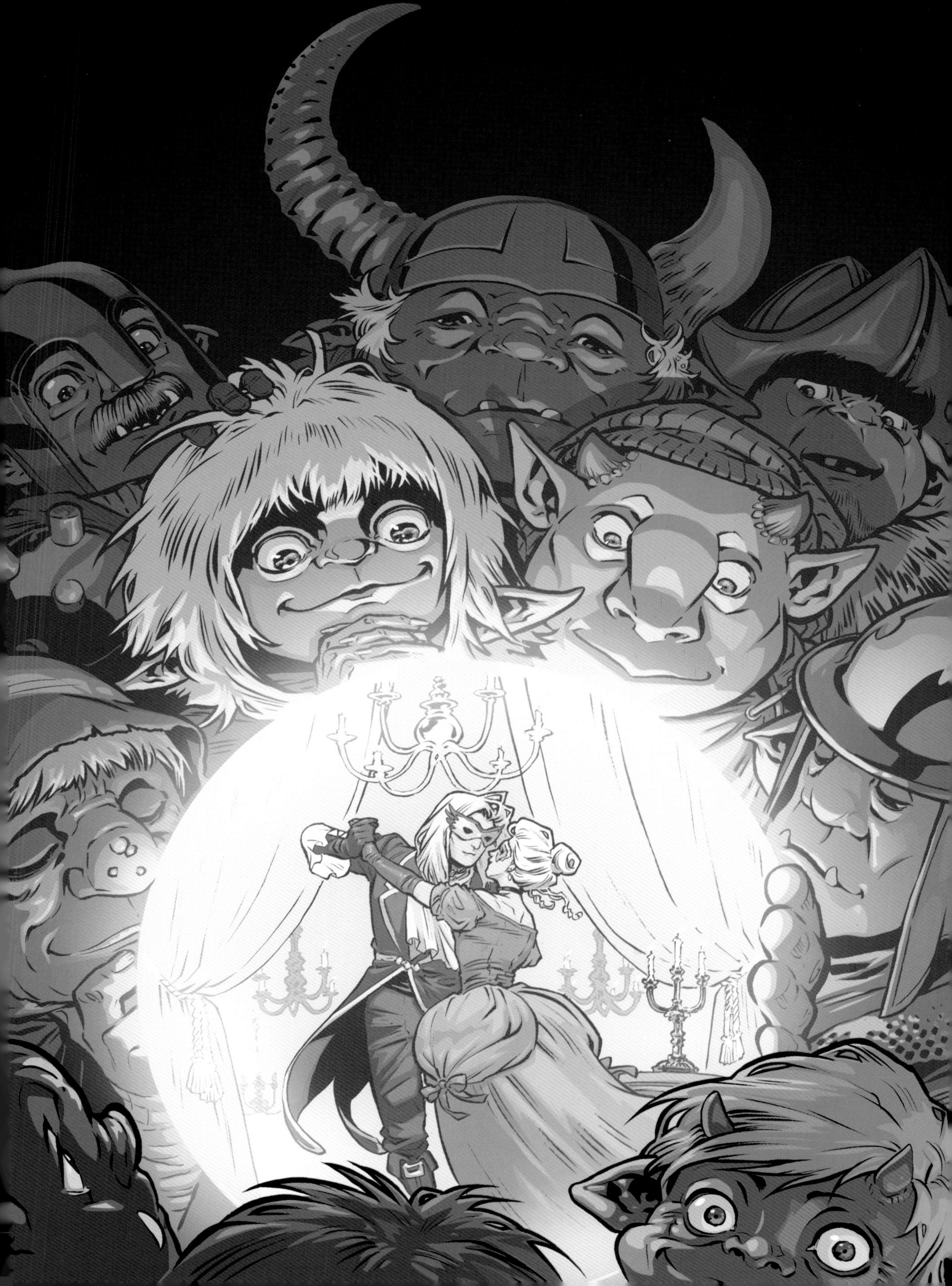

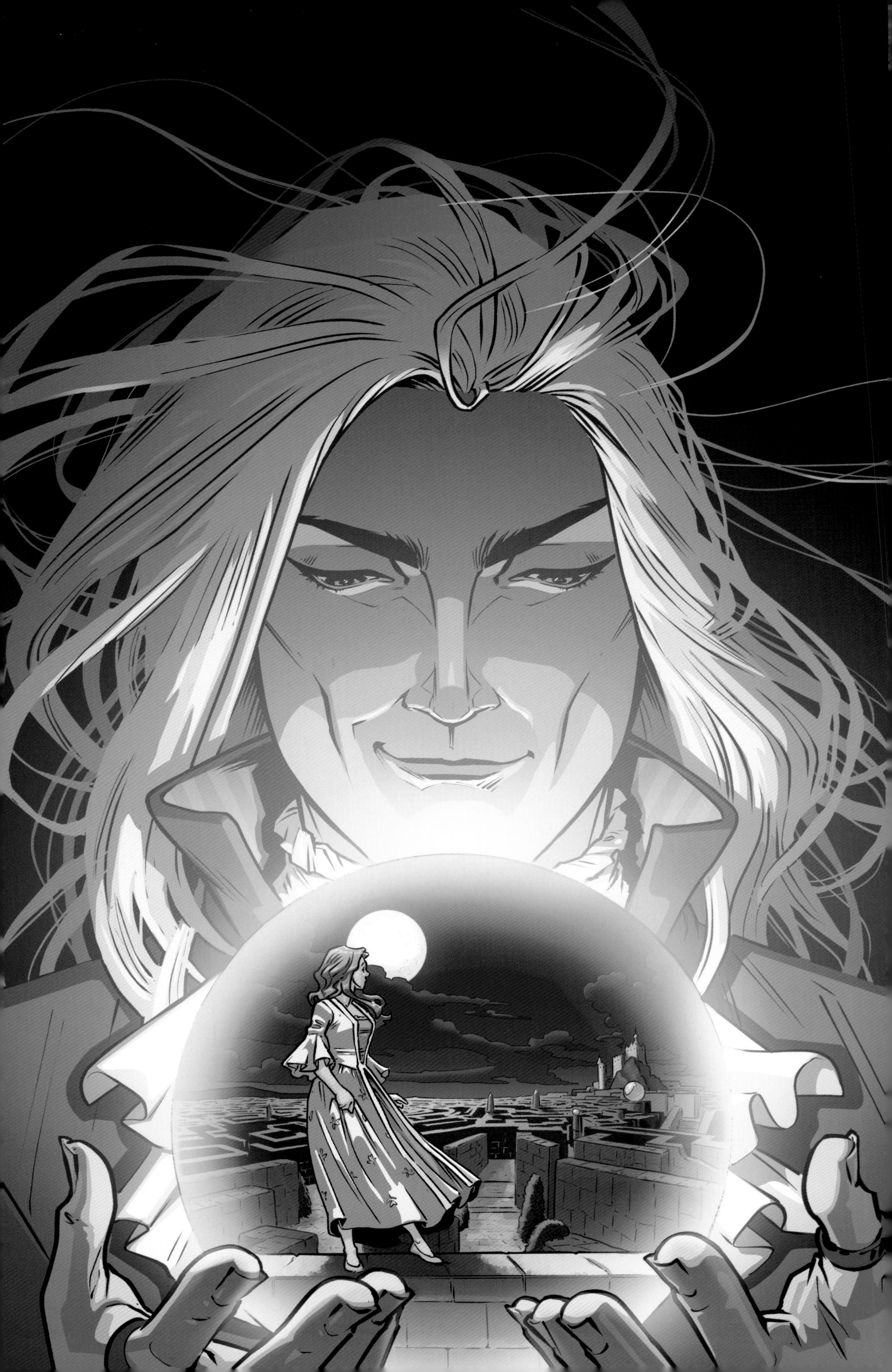

DAVID BOWIE
JENNIFER CONNELLY
L. FRANK BAUM
GRIMM'S FAIRY TALES
M.C. ESCHER
Jim Henson's
LABYRINTH
HENSON ASSOCIATES, INC. AND LUCASFILM LTD. PRESENT A JIM HENSON FILM
EXECUTIVE PRODUCER GEORGE LUCAS DIRECTED BY JIM HENSON CONCEPTUAL DESIGNS BY BRIAN FROUD STORY BY DENNIS LEE AND JIM HENSON
SCREENPLAY BY TERRY JONES SCORE COMPOSED BY TREVOR JONES EDITED BY JOHN GROVER SPECIAL EFFECTS BY GEORGE GIBBS EXECUTIVE PRODUCER DAVID LAZER
PRODUCED BY ERIC RATTRAY DIRECTOR OF PHOTOGRAPHY ALEX THOMSON, B.S.C. PRODUCTION DESIGNER ELLIOT SCOTT WITH CREATURES ANIMATED BY DAVID GOELZ,
STEVE WHITMIRE, KAREN PRELL, RON MUECK, SHARI WEISER, ANTHONY ASBURY, BRIAN HENSON AND FRANK OZ
LAURENT DURIEUX
MONDO

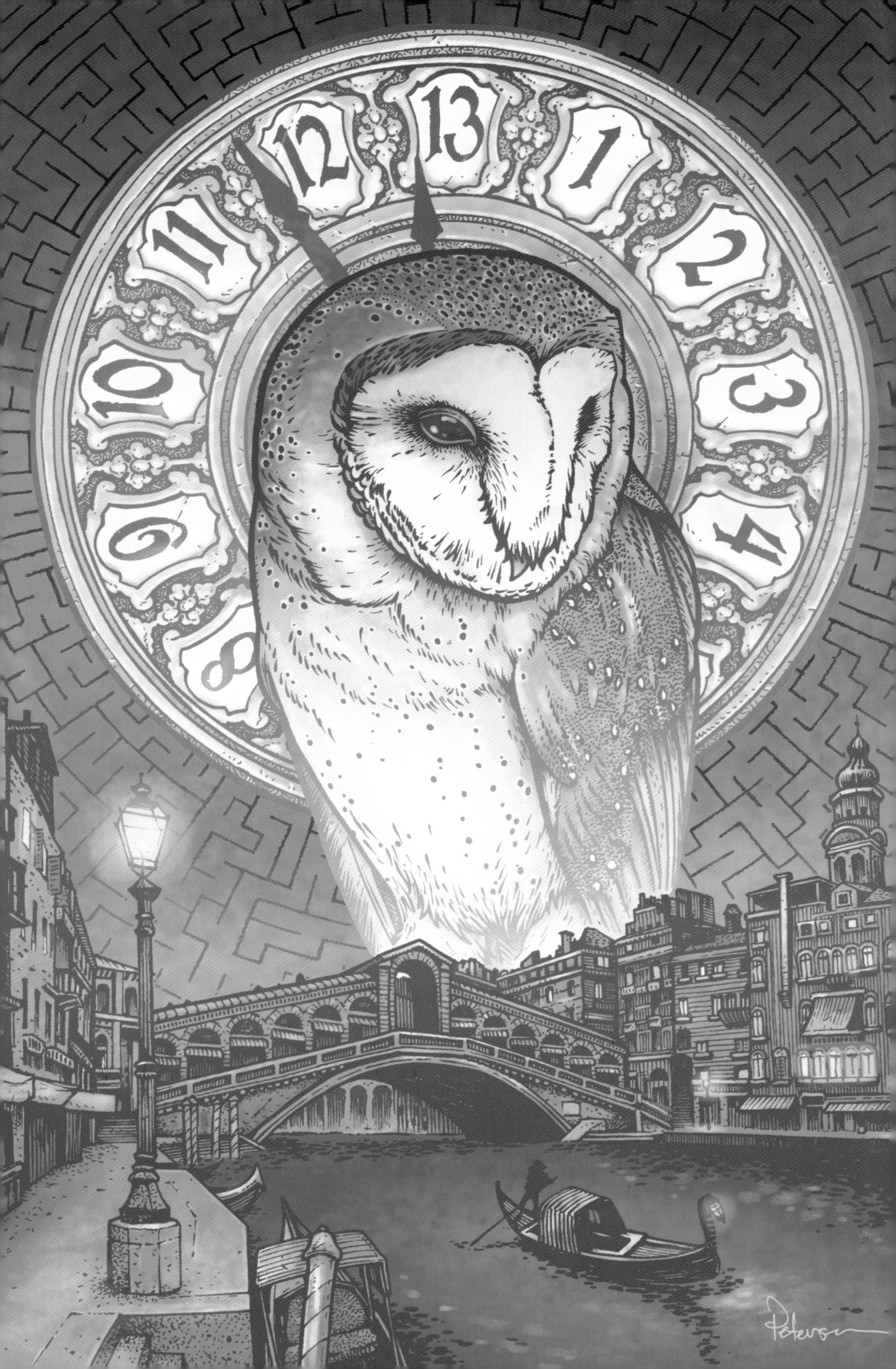
8
9
10
11
12
13
1
2
3
4

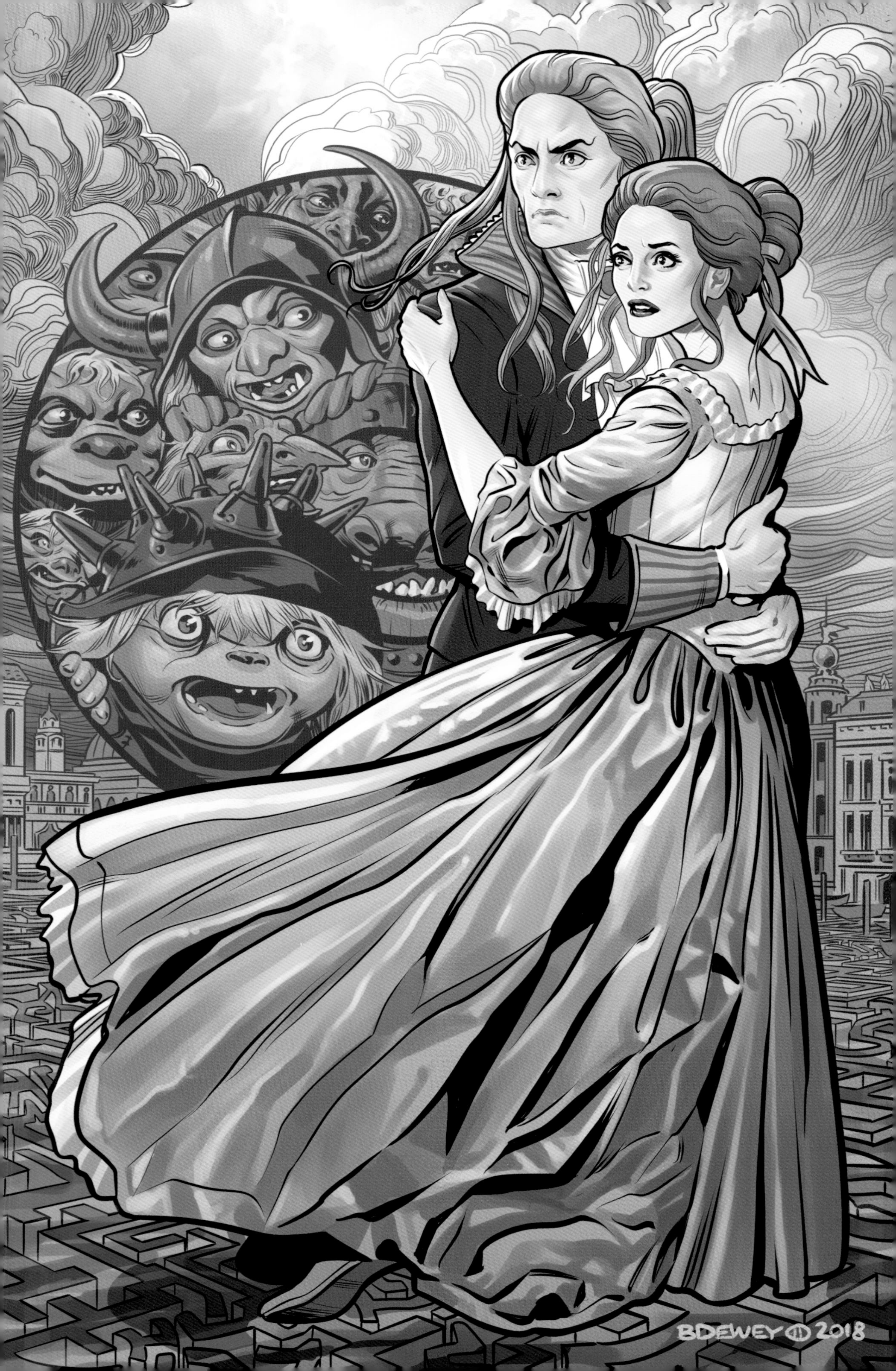
BDEWEY 2018

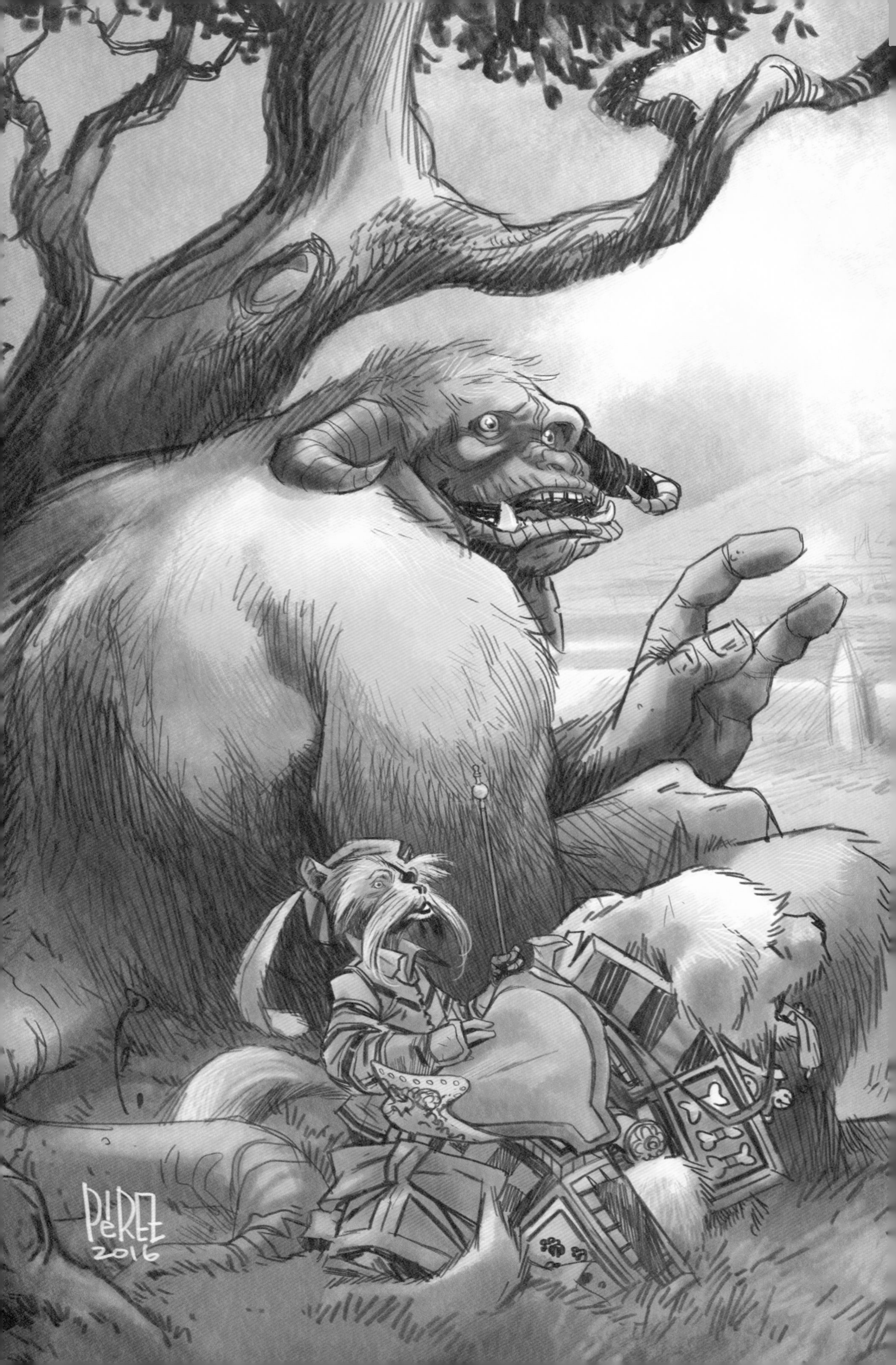
PEREZ
2016

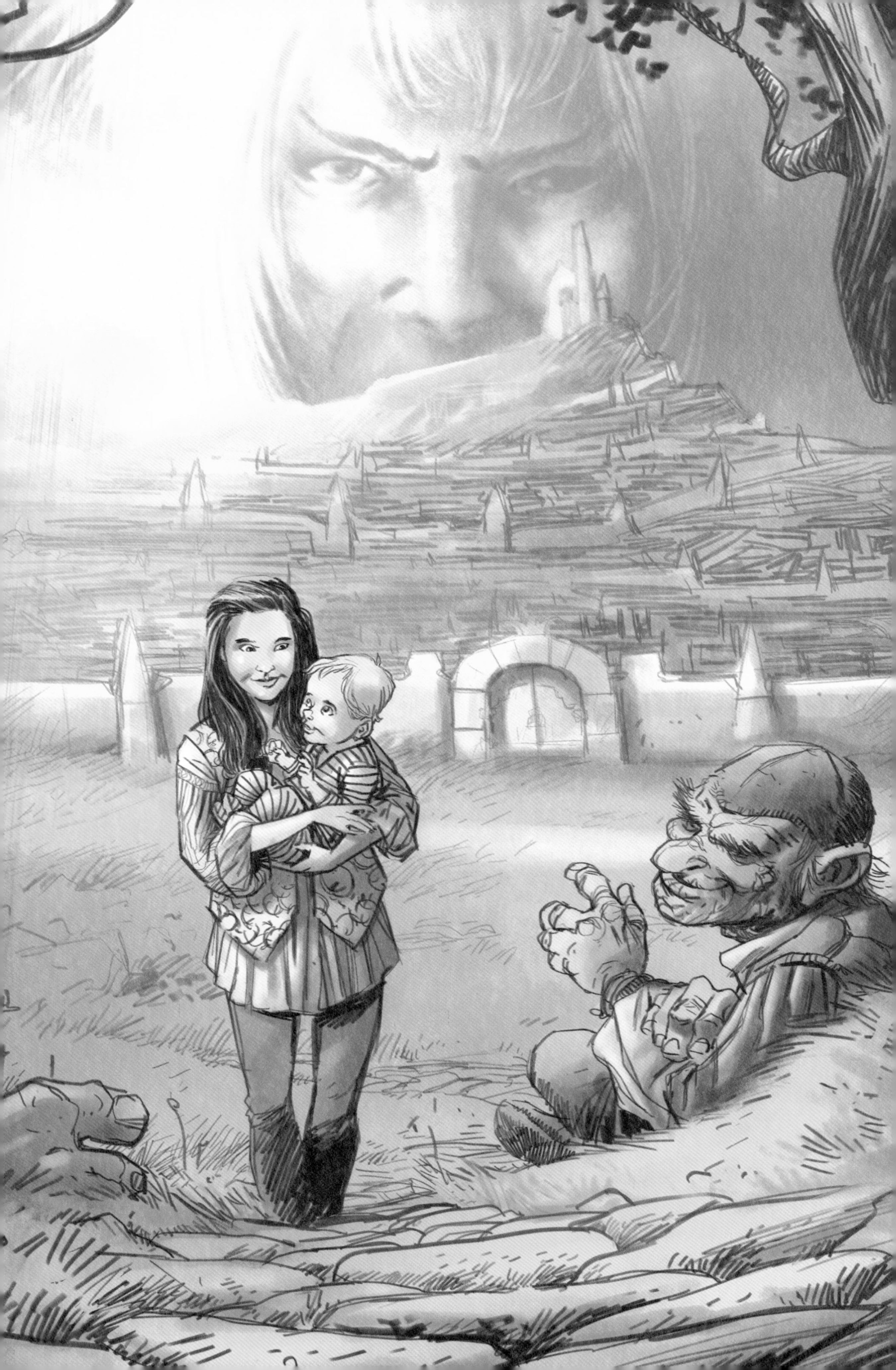

DISCOVER
THE WORLD OF JIM HENSON

Jim Henson's
TALE OF SAND
The lost screenplay by JIM HENSON and JERRY JUHL
As realized by RAMÓN K. PÉREZ

Jim Henson's
LABYRINTH
ARTIST TRIBUTE

Jim Henson's
THE POWER OF THE
DARK CRYSTAL
Simon Spurrier
Kelly Matthews
Nichole Matthews

Jim Henson's
THE
STORYTELLER
Dragons

Jim Henson's
The Dark Crystal
TALES

Jim Henson's
LABYRINTH
ADULT COLORING BOOK

ARCHAIA™

AVAILABLE AT YOUR LOCAL COMICS SHOP AND BOOKSTORE

To find a comics shop in your area, visit www.comicshoplocator.com

WWW.**BOOM-STUDIOS**.COM

Jim Henson's Tale of Sand
Jim Henson, Jerry Juhl, Ramón K. Pérez
ISBN: 978-1-93639-309-1 | $29.95 US

Jim Henson's The Dark Crystal: Creation Myths
Brian Froud, Alex Sheikman, Joshua Dysart, and others
Volume 1
ISBN: 978-1-60886-704-2 | $14.99 US
Volume 2
ISBN: 978-1-60886-887-2 | $14.99 US
Volume 3
ISBN: 978-1-60886-906-0 | $14.99 US

Jim Henson's The Power of the Dark Crystal
Simon Spurrier, Kelly and Nichole Matthews
Volume 1
ISBN: 978-1-60886-992-3 | $24.99 US

Jim Henson's The Dark Crystal Tales
Cory Godbey
ISBN: 978-1-60886-845-2 | $16.99 US

Jim Henson's Labyrinth Artist Tribute
Michael Allred, Dave McKean, Faith Erin Hicks, and others
ISBN: 978-1-60886-897-1 | $24.99 US

Jim Henson's Labyrinth Adult Coloring Book
Jorge Corona, Jay Fosgitt, Phil Murphy
ISBN: 978-1-68415-111-0 | $16.99 US

Jim's Henson's The Musical Monsters of Turkey Hollow
Jim Henson, Jerry Juhl, Roger Langridge
ISBN: 978-1-60886-434-8 | $24.99 US

Jim Henson's The Storyteller: Witches
S.M. Vidaurri, Kyla Vanderklugt, Matthew Dow Smith, Jeff Stokely
ISBN: 978-1-60886-747-9 | $24.99 US

Jim Henson's The Storyteller: Dragons
Daniel Bayliss, Jorge Corona, Hannah Christensen, Nathan Pride
ISBN: 978-1-60886-874-2 | $24.99 US

Jim Henson
THE JIM HENSON COMPANY

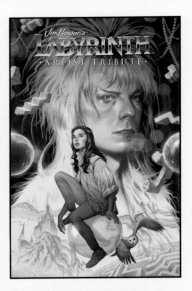

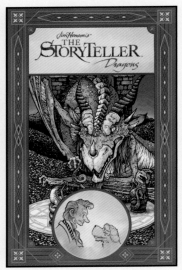